[LIFE in the SPIRIT]

YOUTH EDITION

ROBERTSON MCQUILKIN

LifeWay Press
Nashville, Tennessee

Dewey Decimal Classification: 231.3

Subject Heading: SPIRITUAL LIFE \ HOLY SPIRIT

This book is the text for course CG-0379 in the subject area "Personal Life" of

the Christian Growth Study Plan.

Unless otherwise noted, Scripture quotations are from the Holy Bible, *New International Version*

Copyright © 1973, 1978, 1984 by International Bible Society.

Other versions used: *New King James Version* (NKJV), © 1982, Thomas Nelson Inc., Publishers. Used by permission.

The Living Bible (TLB), © 1971 Tyndale House Publishers, Wheaton, Illinois. Used by permission.

Good New Bible, the Bible in Today's English Version (GNB), Old Testament © American Bible Society 1976;

New Testament: © American Bible Society 1966, 1971, 1976. Used by permission.

New American Standard Bible (NASB), © The Lockman Foundation, 1960, 1962, 1963, 1968, 1971,

1972, 1973, 1975, 1977. Used by permission.

Revised Standard Version of the Bible (RSV), © 1946, 1952, 1971, 1973.

Reprinted with permission of Macmillan Publishing Co., Inc. from J. B. Phillips: *The New Testament in Modern English,*

Revised Edition. © J. B. Phillips 1958, 1960, 1972.

King James Version (KJV).

Printed in the United States of America

LifeWay Press

127 Ninth Avenue, North

Nashville, Tennessee 37234-0151

ACTIVITIES OF THE SPIRIT

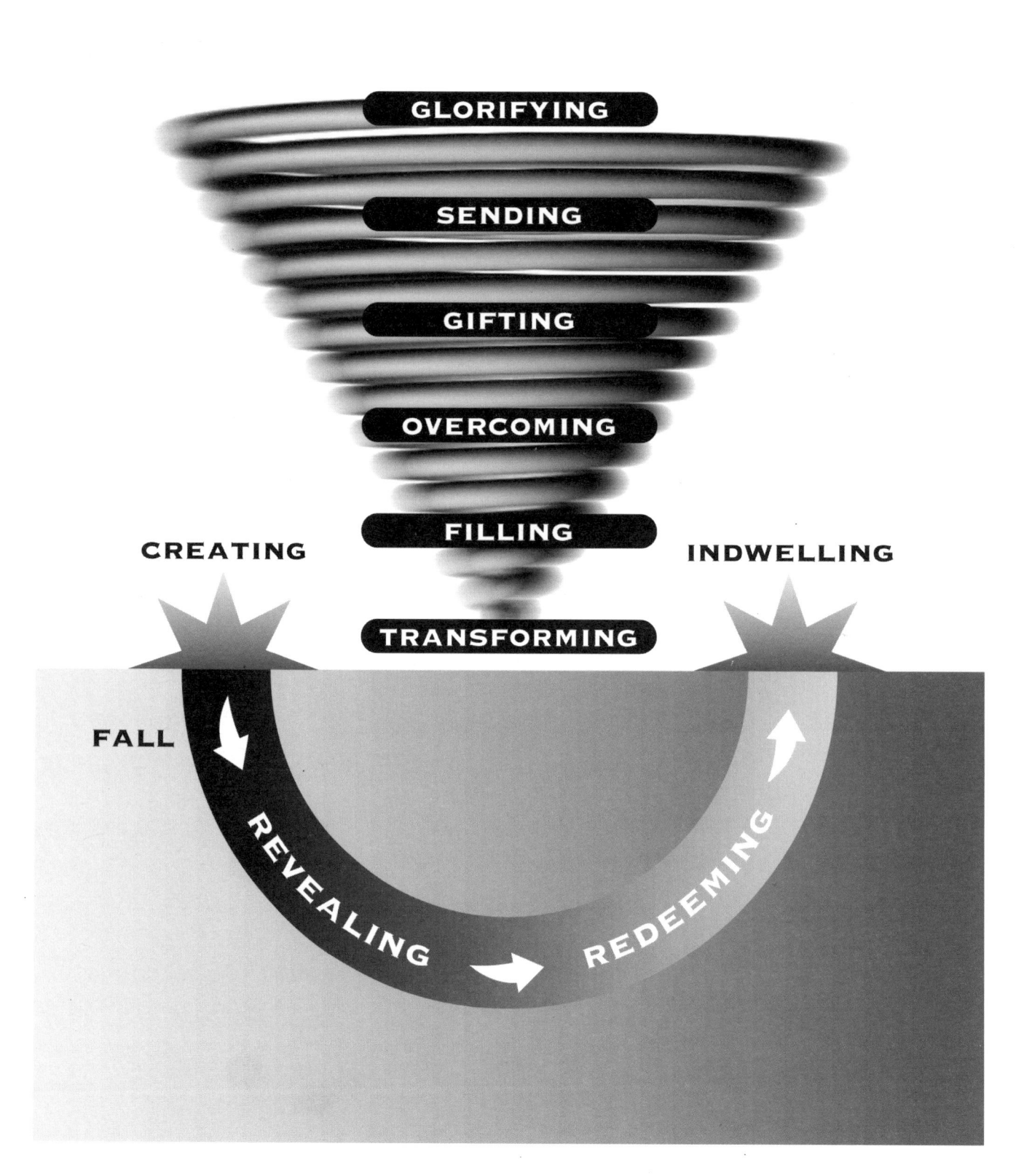

[CONTENTS]

[THE AUTHOR]

Robertson McQuilkin

Robertson McQuilkin is a homemaker, conference speaker, and writer.

Robertson served as president of Columbia International University, Columbia, South Carolina, for 22 years. In 1990 he stepped down to care full time for his wife Muriel, who had reached the stage of Alzheimer's disease in which she needed the care of her husband 24 hours a day. To his surprise, that decision which he considered easy and unremarkable continues to echo throughout the evangelical world. Two articles about Muriel, "Living Vows" and "Muriel's Blessing," have been published in dozens of magazines and books in many languages.

Robertson and Muriel served in full partnership as missionaries in Japan for 12 years prior to his presidency at Columbia. In Columbia, Muriel started many ministries: a TV puppet show for children, a morning radio talk show, ministries among students' wives, along with constant counseling, entertaining, and various art projects.

The McQuilkins have six children. Mardi is an artist, living with her husband in Myrtle Beach, South Carolina; Bob is in heaven, having died in a diving accident in 1988; David is an executive with Xerox in Japan and the father of two; Jan is a pastor's wife in Wisconsin and mother of three; Amy serves with her husband as missionaries to Japan and has three children; Kent ministers among the slum dwellers of Calcutta, India.

Robertson has written scores of articles for journals or as chapters in books and has published several books, three of which continue to have wide influence: *An Introduction to Biblical Ethics, The Great Omission,* and *Understanding and Applying the Bible.*

[FOREWORD]

Dorothy Sayers tells of a Japanese convert struggling to grasp Christian theology. "Honorable Father, very good," he said to his missionary teacher. Honorable Son, very good. But Honorable Bird, I do not understand at all." Misunderstanding swirls around the third member of the Trinity, which is a great irony, for the Holy Spirit is the most personally intimate of the three. The Spirit lives inside us and prays on our behalf when we know not what to pray.

I readily admit to my own problems in understanding the Holy Spirit. I grew up in churches that used—and misused—the Spirit like some kind of magic genie. "The Spirit told me…" the pastor would say to justify some of his bizarre schemes. Members of the congregation would talk about being "filled with the Spirit" and living the "victorious Christian life" even as they manifested glaring faults. In a denomination down the street, other churchgoers would fall down in a trance after being "slain in the Spirit." As an adolescent, I developed a hard-shell resistance to talk about the Holy Spirit.

To break through this resistance, I needed a very wise guide: one who was down-to-earth practical and who lived out the Spirit-filled life in a consistent, attractive way. I found such a guide in Robertson McQuilkin.

Robertson McQuilkin was reared in a home that hosted many of the leaders of the Victorious Christian Life movement. Growing into a mature faith, he always managed to keep his feet on the ground and his head in the clouds. He never lowered the lofty standards of the Christian life as described in the New Testament, yet neither did he deny his very real struggles with temptation and doubt. Twelve years in Japan, as a missionary in one of the cultures most resistant to Christianity, increased that sense of realism and forced a daily dependence on the Holy Spirit.

I got to know Robertson McQuilkin after he returned from Japan and became president of Columbia Bible College, which I was attending. There, I had the opportunity to observe his life at close range. As a teacher, he genuinely listened to students and their point of view. He never acted as if he were dispensing propaganda from on high; rather he gently and persuasively presented his own beliefs and perspectives. From that example I learned that the Holy Spirit is a gentleman: He does not coerce, but rather coaxes and prompts.

Serving as president for more than two decades, McQuilkin led the school to a new plateau. For the first time the school attained fully credentialed status from regional associations. New buildings got under way, board members squabbled, faculty members came and went. I watched McQuilkin manage each of these challenges with a rare combination of humility and strength.

More important than these accomplishments, though—and I'm sure he would agree—I also observed McQuilkin in the role of father and husband. His oldest son, Bob, was my close friend until he died tragically while scuba diving at the age of 36. Through Bob's eyes, I saw a long-suffering father who would let his children choose their own paths while praying earnestly for their spiritual warfare. Then in 1990, at the peak of his career, Robertson McQuilkin shocked the Bible College community by announcing his resignation. His beloved wife Muriel had developed an advanced case of Alzheimer's disease, and he resigned in order to become a homemaker and care for her.

McQuilkin has written two articles about his experience caring for Muriel, which have been reprinted around the world. "Life in the Spirit" is put to the ultimate test when a man feels called by God to leave a position of prestige and influence in order to clean, change diapers, and care for the shell of a person who has been his partner and lover for forty years. To students at Columbia Bible College, McQuilkin's decision offered a profound close-up example of sacrificial love. "Husbands love your wives just as Christ loved the Church and gave himself up for her," Paul urges. I know of no more poignant illustration of Christ's love for us His church than the daily ministrations of Robertson McQuilkin for a wife whose mind is nearly vacant, who is in need of his constant attention.

McQuilkin himself seems genuinely shocked that anyone would view his actions as exceptional. "I took marriage vows, didn't I?" he protests. In his own mind, he is merely living out in quiet faithfulness the promises he made nearly half a century ago. In the end, it is that kind of faithfulness that defines life in the Spirit—and you will learn from a master as you work through this course of intense practicality.

Philip Yancey

[INTRODUCTION]

You'll notice that this book is not designed for you to sit down and read from cover to cover. It is designed for you to carefully study, understand, and apply biblical principles to your life. It's about living life in the Spirit, day-by-day, moment-by-moment.

To get the most out of this course, you must take your time by studying only one day's lesson at a time. Do not try to study through several lessons in one day. You need time to let the new information and ideas "sink in." You can experience a wonderful new relationship with a dear, personal friend—the Spirit of God. Time and prayer are necessary to allow the Holy Spirit to be more than a friendly stranger to you.

 The learning activities will begin (like this paragraph) with a symbol pointing you to indented type. Follow the instructions given to complete the activity. After you have completed the activity you will continue reading.

Normally, you will be given answers following the activity, so you can check your work. Write your own answer before reading mine. Sometimes your response to the activity will be your personal response or opinion, and no right or wrong answer can be given. If you have difficulty with an activity, write a note in the margin. Discuss the answer with your leader or small group.

Do not skip any of the learning activities. Each one is designed to help you learn and apply to life the truths presented in the content. Each day you will need to review the lesson and pray. As you review and pray, do the following:
- Ask God to identify a statement or Scripture from the lesson that He wants you to understand, learn, or practice.
- Anticipate a change in your life, a powerful transformation as you study God's Word and pray. Thank God for what He is teaching you through this study.
- Keep a journal as you go through this study. You will be asked to write your innermost thoughts and prayers in a private journal. Keep your journal for reference when you have finished the study.

Once each week you should attend a small group session that is designed to help you discuss the ideas and concepts you studied the previous week, share insights and testimonies, encourage one another, and pray together. The group covenant below is for use in your "Life in the Spirit" group. If you are not involved in a small group, enlist a few friends to study through this course with you. You'll discover that other members of the body of Christ can help you more fully know and understand and be transformed to live life in the Spirit.

LIFE IN THE SPIRIT GROUP COVENANT

I,_____covenant with my Life in the Spirit group to do the following.

1. Complete the study of Life in the Spirit workbook each week before the group session.
2. Pray regularly for the other group members.
3. Participate in all group sessions. (If unable to attend due to circumstance beyond my control, I'll make up the session at the earliest possible time.)
4. Participate openly and honestly in the group sessions.
5. Keep confidential any personal matters shared by others in the group.
6. Be patient with my Christian brothers and sisters and my church as God works to make us what He wants us to be. I'll trust God to convince others of His will. I will not try to manipulate or pressure others to do what I think is best.
7. Others:

Signed:_____Date:_____

Life in the Spirit Group Members:

_____   _____

_____   _____

_____   _____

[the SPIRIT
the SPIRAL]

Something happened to me in preparing this study, something I never expected. When asked to write I was excited—hadn't I spent my whole life teaching about life in the Spirit? And yet...to my surprise, I found myself developing an even closer relationship with Him—something I call "spiraling up."

The good news is, wherever you are today, you can have a wonderful new relationship with the Spirit of God. And as a result you can anticipate a powerful change in your life, becoming more and more like Jesus.

So to begin this "spiraling up" journey, the first question we must settle is to determine that our objective is to live our life in the Spirit: If we experience life in the Spirit, what will we be like—what is our goal, our destination? The second question is, who says so? And how can we be sure they know what they're talking about?

A great theologian of the 20th century was visiting the United States where he lectured at a leading university. Scholars and excited students met for a question-and-answer session with him. Someone asked, "Professor, what is the most profound thought you ever had?" The audience waited in anticipation. They were shocked to hear him say, "The most profound truth I have ever encountered is this, 'Jesus loves me, this I know, for the Bible tells me so.' " And you know, it's true, the Bible tells us and Jesus shows us.

During this study I'll ask you to think about some very important issues. You may not have an answer to some of the questions and that's OK. We'll study the issues together. The point of the questions is to help you focus your thoughts as we begin this journey together.

As we conclude each lesson in our study, we want to talk with God about what we've studied. We aren't trying to just learn a bunch of information about the Spirit, but to get acquainted with Him personally. Sometimes I'll suggest a prayer. If you feel the same way, don't hesitate to pray that prayer along with me. Or you might use it as a suggestion on how you want to say your own prayer. At other times I'll just suggest something you may want to pray about. Be sure to close each lesson by talking with God about the truths we've been studying.

Do your best each week to memorize the verse given. Our memory verse for Life in the Spirit is also a kind of outline of the course. It's "my" verse, chosen early as a life theme, but it began to take on fresh meaning as I prepared this course.

[Unit Memory Verse]

We, who with unveiled faces all reflect the Lord's glory, are being transformed into his likeness with ever-increasing glory, which comes from the Lord, who is the Spirit.

—2 Corinthians 3:18, NIV

[DAY 1] ···························· GOD'S STANDARD

"Blessed are those who aim at nothing for they shall hit it every time!" states a popular proverb. We need to know what we're aiming at—in our schools, our homes, our responsibilities, and in our relationship with God.

➤ **Here's the first question: What are you aiming at? What is the big goal in life for you? Check all that apply.**

❑ just make it through today   ❑ be filled with the Spirit
❑ get along with my family   ❑ find a girlfriend/boyfriend
❑ get a good paying job one day   ❑ get a really cool car
❑ become like Jesus   ❑ stay healthy and happy

None of those objectives are bad, though some are more worthy than others. Since this course is called Life in the Spirit, you may have chosen "be filled with the Spirit." Whatever you checked, it's important to be honest about it. If we want our goals in life to fit together and not compete, we've got to set an ultimate goal that brings them all together. Paul gives us a good one: We…are being transformed into his [Jesus] likeness *(2 Cor. 3:18)*. To be just like Jesus! Now there's a worthy goal, and one that will purify and focus all the other goals. But why did God choose such a high goal for us?

God created us in His image *(Gen. 1:27)*. So that's where we will begin in this study, with the Spirit's activity of creating us.

Activity of the Spirit = Creating

➤ **Look at the course map for Life in the Spirit. The course map is the drawing on the inside front cover. It pictures 10 activities of the Spirit and our journey of living in the Spirit. The map begins with the first activity of the Spirit: creating.**

So God created man in his own image, in the image of God he created him; male and female he created them.
—Genesis 1:27

God created us, but we rebelled against His purpose. On the course map you see the word we use to describe that event. We call it the *fall*. We became a fallen or broken model of God. Because of the fall, we can't always act like Jesus. We fail to have His attitude about people or His kind of relationship with the Father. But God has a reconstruction plan to take us—broken models of Himself—and remake us into His likeness.

Before we come to know Jesus, we are all on the downward spiral away from God. His purpose is to turn us around and spiral us up toward ever greater likeness to Jesus: *We…are being transformed into his likeness.* But before God could transform us, He had to get our attention and reveal Himself to us.

Activity of the Spirit = Revealing

➤ **If you wanted to know what God expects of you or plans for you, how would you find out?**

❑ look at Jesus
❑ let your conscience be your guide
❑ watch other Christians carefully, especially the pastor/youth minister
❑ try out some options and see what works
❑ use the Bible as a road map
❑ make choices and, if it feels right, it probably is

Jesus is our model of what God is like. He is our standard. He is our goal. The Bible teaches us not only about Jesus but also about God and what He expects of us. The Bible is God's revelation of His will for us; it's our only sure road map for life.

We'll study God's road map for us later. We have to lay a solid foundation for all the other wonderful truths that follow.

We need to be sure of our foundation. How can we know this instruction manual is reliable? (See *2 Tim. 3:16-17; Matt. 5:17-18* in margin.) Some people say, "Try it and see for yourself." That's good common sense, but the "what works is true" test doesn't prove the instruction manual is accurate. What if our attempts to follow the Bible don't seem to work all that well?

We try to do what we think the Bible teaches and everything comes unglued. Or the pieces of life don't fit together in the first place. Does that mean the instruction manual is unreliable? Or does it mean we misread it and must study it more carefully? The bottom line is this: Jesus fully trusted the Scriptures. And we're not smarter than He is!

Mark the statements below with a _T_ (true) if they are completely true and an _F_ (false) if they are even partly in error.

____ 1. God's standard for Christian living is His own character.

____ 2. The example of Jesus is the only way we know for sure what God wants of us.

____ 3. Humankind was originally designed on God's own pattern.

____ 4. None of us can measure up fully to God's standard in this life.

____ 5. The Holy Spirit is in the business of remaking us into something we are not naturally at birth.

____ 6. The Holy Spirit gave us the Bible to show us the way to experience life in the Spirit.

____ 7. The Bible is true because Jesus said so.

____ 8. God's plan is not to change us instantaneously into Christ's likeness, but to gradually remake us.

____ 9. The greatest evidence of the truth of Scripture is that it works.

I marked all of them true except numbers 2 and 9. I don't think 2 is true because the Holy Spirit gave the entire Bible—not just the life of Jesus—to instruct us. As number 9 suggests, Scripture does work and that's reassuring. It strengthens our confidence, but the greatest evidence of the reliability of Scripture is that Jesus trusted it, not that it works. Scripture is true whether it seems to work for me or not. If you don't understand why I answered any question the way I did or if you don't agree with my answer, that might be a good topic to discuss at your next group meeting.

Heavenly Father, Thank You for creating me in Your image so that I can live with You as best friends. When I go against Your plan for me and sin against Your loving purposes for me, You still love me and provide a way for me to be restored to Your image. Thank You for showing me what I'll be like when I'm like You and, Holy Spirit, thank You for the Bible You gave to show me the way. I want to understand Your plan and, more importantly, to experience it fully. In Jesus' name I pray. Amen.

GOD'S PROVISION ·························· [DAY 2]

Many churches and Christians reject all miracles and do not emphasize the ministry of the Spirit at all. This attitude is a tragic loss since the Holy Spirit is the source of all spiritual blessing. We find it easier to take one side of biblical truth to

All Scripture is God-breathed and is useful for teaching, rebuking, correcting and training in righteousness, so that the man of God may be thoroughly equipped for every good work.

—2 Timothy 3:16-17

"Do not think that I have come to abolish the Law or the Prophets; I have not come to abolish them but to fulfill them. I tell you the truth, until heaven and earth disappear, not the smallest letter, not the least stroke of a pen, will by any means disappear from the Law until everything is accomplished."

—Matthew 5:17-18

The Holy Spirit is the source of all spiritual blessings.

one extreme or the other, neglecting the balancing truths of Scripture, rather than finding the center of biblical balance.

Many attitudes about the Holy Spirit can be found in the Christian community. Sincere believers differ about how we relate to the Holy Spirit. In this study we'll discover hard facts in the Bible about the person and activity of the Holy Spirit. We'll explore the truths on which we can all agree. Apart from Him there's no way you can experience a close friendship with God or become the person He intends you to be.

A NEW CREATION

Since the mid-eighties I've used a computer for my writing. I was happy with the way my computer worked—after all, it used to be state-of-the-art. But increasingly I experienced difficulties. Gradually my computer could "talk" with fewer and fewer other computers. It couldn't read what other people sent me. I began to use electronic mail, but the Internet was designed for speedy new models, not for my old clunker. I upgraded, but it wasn't enough. I needed a new model altogether. Dressing up the old one wasn't good enough.

The man without the Spirit does not accept the things that come from the Spirit of God, for they are foolishness to him, and he cannot understand them, because they are spiritually discerned.
—1 Corinthians 2:14

Our experience with the Spirit of God resembles my situation with the computer. We were originally created God-compatible—we could communicate with Him. At least our first ancestor, Adam, could. But a breakdown occurred. We could try self-improvement—reprogramming our minds to think more like God so we could understand what He was saying in His Word—but it won't work. We need to be an altogether new model, a new creation. Read *1 Corinthians 2:14* in the margin. That's exactly what the Holy Spirit provides—a new creation. He's in the process of redeeming fallen humanity. Our bodies and brains are the same, but when He re-creates us He puts a new spirit within us. In computer language, He puts state-of-the-art "processors" in our "computers." Now our new inner workings are different from the old inner workings—they are now God-compatible. Bible scholars call this change regeneration. It represents so radical a transformation, the Bible calls it "a new birth" *(1 Pet. 1:3).*

Activity of the Spirit = Redeeming

A NEW CREATION

 In the space below, write a definition for regeneration using your own words.

Regeneration—"Being born again with a brand new life. A fresh start with God."

If anyone is in Christ, he is a new creation; the old has gone, the new has come!
—2 Corinthians 5:17

We underestimate the potential in the new model. We don't tap into the resources the Holy Spirit has provided by making us new. Read *2 Corinthians 5:17* in the margin.

In the list below, circle the statements which sound like a person who has been re-created and cross through those that sound like a person who has not been re-created.
1. The Bible doesn't make much sense to me.
2. I can sin, but I don't have to continue on deliberately choosing to sin.
3. I can't help sinning, and I enjoy sinful things.
4. I pray sometimes, but I'm not sure God is listening.
5. I feel weird around Christians who live out their faith.
6. I like being around Christians who talk about what God is doing in them.
7. I am growing in my understanding of spiritual truths.
8. I like reading the Bible, praying, and being with Christian friends.

Numbers 2, 6, 7, and 8 are a few of the signs of someone who's been re-made by the Holy Spirit. What if you're feeling more like a 1, 3, 4, or 5 sort of person right now? Don't worry. If you've been born again the Spirit has already made you into something altogether new, so hang in there—we'll be studying all about how to experience the "new you."

INDWELLING: FAITH AND OBEDIENCE

Not only does the Holy Spirit re-make us into new models, He begins a new personal relationship with us. His name hints at the personal aspect of our relationship. He is called Comforter and Counselor. Descriptions of His activity, such as convicting of sin and teaching us all things also point to His personal ministry in our lives. The activity of the Spirit is indwelling.

Activity of the Spirit = Indwelling

 Which of the names or activities of the Spirit focus on your personal relationship with Him? Circle them below.

Helper   Healer   Being Filled with the Spirit
Walking with the Spirit   Constant Friend

All of them may tell you something about the Spirit. Actually the list could be very long. The Holy Spirit is God's provision for Christian living. The Spirit's goal is not merely to make us like Jesus in attitude and behavior, as wonderful as that is. The Spirit's goal in making us like Jesus in the way we think and behave has an even more astounding purpose. Being like Jesus enables us to have a love relationship with the Father—a relationship like the one Jesus has. The new relationship we enter into at the time of our salvation is only the beginning of an eternity of growing closeness in our companionship with God.

A NEW RELATIONSHIP

Activity of the Spirit = Transforming

SPIRALING UP

Notice the course map divides into two sections. The activities you have considered up till now appear on the lower half of the diagram. They are the activities of the Spirit in history and in bringing you into a love relationship with God. These activities take us from the moment of creation to our return to fellowship. The Spirit immediately begins to transform us as into likeness to Jesus. Spiraling up is about beginning the sanctification process, being made holy. The activity of the Spirit is transforming.

Sanctification—"To be set apart for God's work. A gradual and progressive changing into the likeness of Christ."

 On the course-map portion in the margin, fill in the first five activities of the Spirit. Check your work with the inside front cover.

FILLED FULL

There is so much disagreement about what being filled with the Spirit really means that I'm tempted to skip the subject altogether. But we can't do that! Stay with me on this one so you do not misunderstand me. The New Testament contains far too much about "fullness" to pretend it's not there. We'll examine the meaning of being filled with the Spirit in this study too. We don't want to skip the fullness theme for another reason—the truth about our potential relationship to the Spirit is so glorious. The only way to hint at its true meaning is to say, "full"!

 What does the word *full* bring to your mind? Underline the first two or three terms triggered in your thinking when you hear the word.

total   all-absorbing   comprehensive   dominant   unlimited
    unrestrained   extending to all parts (of life, for example)   complete
bountiful   abundant   I couldn't eat another bite

Imagine any of those words describing your relationship with God! That kind of relationship can be yours, not a one-time event, but a daily experience. Full!

When movies or fairy tales transform one creature into another, some secret formula or powerful potion works the magic. But God doesn't do it that way. When God reconstructs us in His likeness, He doesn't stay at a distance and send us a do-it-yourself kit. God's way of changing us is personal: He gives us Himself. The Holy Spirit comes and works the miracle. He makes new people out of us, and then comes inside as a constant companion. Better than that—He fills us up with Himself!

 Write *2 Corinthians 3:18* in the space below. Practice memorizing the verse.

[DAY 3] .... MY RESPONSIBILITY

We've seen how God Himself, by the Spirit, has made spiraling up possible for us into His likeness and into intimate companionship with Him. But maybe that isn't happening. Maybe you've leveled off in your Christian life. Perhaps you are starting to spiral away from God. What's wrong? Why doesn't the Spirit-filled life seem to work?

 In the following list, check the response that best describes you at this time.

❑ This is all new to me—I really don't know how to make it happen.
❑ It's too good to be true. It might happen for some people, but I can't see it working for me. Maybe I'm too difficult a case for God.
❑ I know exactly what sin I'm hiding. I don't want to let go of it.
❑ I'm not sure, but somehow I seem to be drifting out of reach. Things aren't like they used to be. Maybe I need to come back into that first relationship I had with God.

Possible reasons Christians fail to grow:
   1. ignorance of God's provision or of my responsibility;
   2. unbelief, lack of confidence in God; and
   3. disobedience.

If disobedience is the problem, it can occur in two different ways:
   •conscious decision to reject God's known will or
   •unconscious drift out of a close relationship.

 When we are prepared to obey God, no matter the cost, the power He promised will flow. The turn around for the sinner is called *repentance*. In the life of a Christian who has run from God, it's called *rededication* or *recommitment*. Name some other ways of describing this turn around in someone's life.

Repentance—"Turning from my sin to live God's way of life."

Throughout history, Christians have described this turning point in a number of ways. Like Jacob *(Gen. 32:22-32),* some say they wrestled with God. Some say the love of Jesus overwhelmed them. They realized that rebellion against God is like a slap in the face to Him. Others have seen their pride and been humbled by the example of Christ's suffering. Here are some words or ideas you might have included: *yield, surrender, commit, abandonment of self, under new management, getting out of God's way and letting Him lead my life,* or *letting Christ be the Lord of my life.* No matter how the Spirit breaks through to us, we must finally come to the place where we give Him our all. That's the turning point and the beginning of the joy-filled life.

 Have you had a turning point since your initial turning to God? If you have, write out your story in a paragraph, either in the margin or in your journal.

Here's a simple summary of how disobedience worked in my life. At first I knew I was saved and I thought that was enough. I didn't worry much about what salvation was supposed to produce in my life. Both the goal and the way to the goal were blurry in my thinking, but I sensed something was lacking. Surely Christianity was more than a fire-insurance policy! (You know, just get saved to stay out of hell.) The Holy Spirit convicted me of my sin. As a result I turned my life over to Him.

 Look in a hymnal or on a Christian CD or cassette tape cover and find a song about the Holy Spirit. In the space below, write some of the lyrics from the song that tells what the Holy Spirit can do for you.

Unfortunately, I was still being lazy in my walk: "God, You push me and I'll go." I wasn't trying to find out how to make Him happy. I wasn't trusting Him for any miraculous change in my life, but a longing for a more genuine Christian experience began to grow in me. Finally, I had an aha! moment—I realized that He has the power to do in me what I can't do on my own, and He will do it if I only trust Him.

I accepted that aha! as God speaking to me. I began to trust Him to keep the promises in His Word. I began to grow. I began to understand more about God's ways and experience the Spirit in my life. We know that in order to use a blow dryer, the thing has to be plugged in. The plug-in that got me moving had two prongs: *trust* and *surrender.* And that same connection has kept me moving, even years later.

TRUST AND OBEY

Trust is critical to our Christian lives. Trusting comes before surrender. We won't surrender to God until we trust Him. But trust follows commitment. In fact trust and surrender go hand-in-hand. We cannot have one without the other.

You may experience the "surrender" part of faith in a heartbeat, but the "trust" part is a different matter. Trust in people or trust in God must grow, so sometimes "just trust me" turns out not to be so simple! Since faith is a combina-

Faith—"Belief, surrender, trust, in God."

KNOW, SURRENDER, TRUST

tion of surrendering and trusting, we'll also consider what we can do to increase our faith.

Faith is the key to plug in with the Spirit. By faith His miraculous power flows to change you more and more into Christ's image. The word *faith* summarizes your responsibility in receiving God's power for the supernatural life. Of course faith assumes knowledge. To *have faith* you have to know the Holy Spirit and how to plug in. Ignorance can keep you disconnected. Genuine faith also involves surrendering. Knowing, surrendering, and trusting go together. They build on each other.

For each of the following spiritual illnesses diagnose by using the following key:

LK—those whose basic problem seems to be ignorance of what God wants or how to get there. Duh!

S—those whose problem seems to be a spirit of unwillingness to surrender.

LT—those who seem to have a lack of trust in God. Some may need both "S" and "LT"!

___ Tan has to lie and cheat to make it through his junior year.

___ Shelbi is amazed at the way some of her Christian friends seem to be so full of joy and strength. They remind her of Jesus and she'd like to be that way but doesn't know how.

___ Morgan keeps stumbling around in her Christian life, trying anything that comes along. She wants to please God, but the strength doesn't seem to be there.

___ Christy can't seem to quit drinking alcohol.

___ Mitch struggles with a bad temper and he can't overcome it.

___ Helen was only 7 when she was baptized. She was happy with her new friend, Jesus, and her hope of heaven. But the past few years she's been busy with school and work and can't seem to make it to church. On Sundays she feels a little weird, like something is missing.

___ Sondra finally gave in and admitted God wanted her to help with the little ones on Sunday nights. She hasn't committed to it yet hoping she can do it some day. Other things in her life seem to be going pretty bad.

___ Susan knows she shouldn't date a non-Christian, but this way she won't be alone and besides, she loves Harry. She's going to go out with him anyway.

Who is obviously in need of knowledge? Shelbi certainly is. Shelbi's problem is ignorance—she just never learned what the Christian life is all about. Helen's problem may be partly ignorance, too, but she definitely has a "surrender" problem. She needs to do at least what she knows to be right. If she went to church she just might discover there's more to the Christian life. Tan and Susan also have clear-cut surrender problems: they'll get nowhere until they decide to choose obedience to God over their selfish desires. Morgan and Mitch have a common need: to grow in trusting the Holy Spirit to do what they can't. Christy has one of the toughest problems. As with most people with addiction, she needs both a new surrender and a new level of confidence in the Spirit's power. Sondra needs to surrender and trust, too.

BATTLE PLAN

We tend to go to one of two unbiblical extremes regarding faith:

• We throw out faith completely and seek to live on our own power, or

• We get into a "kick back and watch" role and wait for God to work.

The Bible doesn't teach either extreme. We need to participate *with* the Spirit in His activity in our lives. Christian life is a battle. We need a battle plan that works.

When we're not obedient to the Holy Spirit it hurts our relationship with Him. Disobedience flaws our belief system. Unfortunately we often follow the pattern below.

1. We experience temptation.
2. Rather than follow God's Word and choose right, we give in to temptation.
3. We feel guilty because we have violated our value system.
4. We twist our beliefs and values to relieve our guilt.

When we live in disobedience, we automatically twist our understanding to justify our behavior. We blind ourselves to a true understanding of the Spirit and of the Christian life. Therefore, as you study *Life in the Spirit,* I will challenge you to be obedient. I will challenge you to trust and surrender yourself to God. Then I will challenge you to commit each area of your life to Him.

 Have you linked up with the Spirit by surrendering to His will and trusting in His power? The trust will grow, but the surrender part you can settle right now. Tell Him you're not able to live life as He intended on your own, but that you want to live a life of obedience. Commit yourself to God, through Jesus Christ, by the power of the Spirit. Ask Him to make you like Christ. Respond to the Spirit with a simple, straightforward, complete, "Yes!"

 Perhaps you have already surrendered completely to the Spirit of God. This would be a good time to reaffirm that and ask Him to increase your faith through these studies and spiral you up into even greater likeness to the Son. Thank Him, too, for the intimate relationship He offers.

 Fill in the blanks, then practice memorizing *2 Corinthians 3:18.*

We, who with _____ _____ all _____ the Lord's

glory, are being _____ into his _____ with ever-increas-

ing glory, which comes from the Lord, who is the _____.

RESULTS .... [DAY 4]

God is the standard for the Christian life, and God provides our way for reaching that standard. We have a responsibility to connect with that provision: faith, with its two parts—surrender and trust. When we surrender and trust what can we expect as a result? Again, sadly, we're tempted to go to one extreme or the other, either expecting too little of our lives in the Spirit, or having unbiblically high expectations.

 To see how our expectations influence life in the Spirit, mark the following examples with a (+) by those that seem to expect too much, (-) by those that expect too little, and a check (✓) by those that seem about right.

___ 1. Since I've been filled with the Spirit I'll never struggle with temptation.
___ 2. I sin often every day, knowing it's wrong but doing it anyway.

___ 3. Since I was baptized in the Spirit, I haven't sinned in thought, word, or deed.

___ 4. I've been growing more like Jesus; I'm not at all what I used to be.

___ 5. The same temptation gets me almost every day.

___ 6. The Holy Spirit is sort of like a friendly stranger to me.

___ 7. The Bible seems dry, reading it is like chewing chalk and it's so outdated.

___ 8. Prayer is just another routine even when I get around to serious praying.

___ 9. I know I'm far from perfect, but my friends and family say I've changed.

___10. I love our youth group and doing stuff for the Lord.

I marked + by 1 and 3, - by 2, 5, 6, 7, 8, and ✓ by 4, 9, 10.

One reason we tend to go to an extreme is that the Bible itself emphasizes both sides of the truth about our Christian experience. For example, John says some puzzling things:

If we claim to be without sin, we deceive ourselves and the truth is not in us (1 John 1:8).

He who does what is sinful is of the devil…No one who is born of God will continue to sin (1 John 3:8-9).

The two passages seem to cancel each other out, don't they? However, two truths, are clear:

If you think you can have an experience that will remove all chances of failure, and eliminate spiritual combat, you're badly deceived.

If you think you can live as you please, continue to deliberately sin and still be OK with God, you're even more deceived.

SPIRAL UP

Here's how it works. We all start out at a distance from God, some further away, less like Him than others.

As a starting point, mark with an (x) on the spiral above at some point you might have been when you were saved. You weren't as bad as you might have been. But you were apart, separated from God, so don't put that starting point too high, either! Now put an asterisk (*) at the stage you think you are now, indicating how much you've grown and how far you have to go. Finally mark an up arrow or a down arrow to indicate the direction your life has been going the past year.

When we make the big turnaround (repent), surrendering to God's will and trusting Him to work, the Holy Spirit begins to change us. We become more like Jesus in our attitudes, our thoughts, our goals and dreams, our responses, and actions. As a result, we get closer to Him in daily companionship. Read *2 Corinthians 3:18* in the margin. The more we know Him, the more we love Him; the more we love Him, the more we want to be with Him; the more we're with Him the more we want to be like Him; the more we change to be like Him, the better we know Him, the more we love Him—the spiral continues up and up toward likeness to Christ and we get a greater love relationship with God.

We, who with unveiled faces all reflect the Lord's glory, are being transformed into his likeness with ever increasing glory, which comes from the Lord, who is the Spirit.
–2 Corinthians 3:18, NIV

IN GOD' IMAGE AND UNITY WITH HIM

LOVE HIM MORE

KNOW HIM BETTER

BECOME MORE LIKE HIM

COMPANION WITH HIM

LOVE HIM

KNOW HIM

BEST FRIENDS

The ultimate goal God has in mind for you isn't just a change in character to resemble Jesus. God intends for you to be like Jesus in every way, especially in your love relationship with the Father.

 For starters, write here the name of one of your best (human) friends:

_____

How did you get to be such good friends? What helped the friendship grow? Name a few of the reasons that come to mind.

Here are some possibilities I thought of: spend time together; give/receive special gifts; make some sacrifice for each other, doing something your friend wants to do that you don't; go through tough times—cry together; do fun things—laugh together; focus on your friend's good points; accept differences.

 From the things you wrote and those I suggested, list the three most important factors which made you good friends.

1. _____
2. _____
3. _____

> God wants to be your very best friend. Go up to your list, and circle those factors that bond you to Him. Pause now and ask God to make this much more than a study; ask Him to bond you to Himself as you learn more about the wonderful Holy Spirit in the next 12 weeks.

> Write *2 Corinthians 3:18* in the margin then practice saying it from memory. Make it a habit to end every day's lesson with a time of Scripture memory.

DAY 5 ·································· 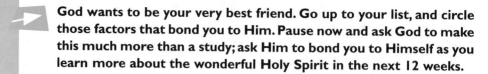 REACHING OUT

In studying the work of the Spirit in our lives, we could become very focused on self. We live in an age of radical "self-ism" and some people might see "spiraling up" as a selfish relationship just between God and ourselves. But the Holy Spirit won't let that happen! We were born in community and we were designed to live in community. And the more like God we become the more we'll be concerned about others, not with ourselves. And the amazing thing is this: God has chosen to do His work in the world through us!

DOING GOD'S WORK

"People reaching out," however, does not mean individuals doing God's work by themselves. God's method is called the church. Not the church building itself, but those who trust in God, the believers. The Spirit of God works primarily through the church.

> List all the things that are done or need to be done in your local church:

Did you write preaching, teaching, serving meals, counseling, ushering, singing, leading, managing the money, helping those with physical or material needs, playing a musical instrument, witnessing, starting new churches? Now go back to your list and mine and circle every activity that only the Spirit can make happen.

If we expect spiritual impact from any activity, the Spirit has to be involved! Unless you think the church activities have no spiritual result, you should have marked all of them! When the Spirit gives you an ability, it's called a *gift*. Spiritual gifts are not just natural abilities or talents. They are gifts from God to be used by Him to accomplish His purposes. Spiritual gifts point to something beyond natural abilities.

People:
1. listen
2. understand spiritual truth
3. begin to act on spiritual truth
4. are interested
5. learn
6. experience the Bible coming to life
7. experience changed lives
8. grow spiritually

> Think of two jobs in the church. How could we tell if the person doing them has the touch of the Spirit on his or her work? For example, what might result from a naturally gifted person's teaching in Sunday School and what might happen if the Spirit worked through the teacher?
> The phrases appearing in the margin describe what people do as the result of a teacher with either natural ability or spiritual giftedness. Below write each number under either natural or spiritual giftedness.

Natural gift of teaching   Spiritual gift of teaching

Under natural ability you may have put things like: people listen, it's interesting; people learn. Under the Spirit's gift you may have put things like: people understand spiritual truth and begin to act on it; the Bible seems to come alive; lives are changed—people grow spiritually.

SHARING YOUR FAITH

 Name several people you know, or you have heard about, who are evangelists.

Evangelist—"A Christian who shares the gospel to non-Christians and leads them to faith in Christ."

Not everyone is gifted in evangelism and even those who are more effective than others. Who can compare with Billy Graham, for example? But all of us are responsible to share our faith. Some call that witnessing. We witness by the way we live—drawing others to Jesus by the quality of our life or sending them away by living no differently. We witness by our talk—explaining how we got where we are. Every one of us is called to show and tell. If the church is witnessing, people will come to Christ.

GOD SO LOVED THE WORLD

 "God so loved the world…"—I'm glad He did, aren't you? But we tend to love people who are like us. Below write the names of people you believe need to know Jesus:

in your immediate family: _____

of another culture or race: _____

People you do not know personally, but know about, people missionaries work with or those mentioned in your youth group (this might be groups of people, rather than individuals):

_____

others for whom you are praying: _____

_____

Now go back and number from 1 to 4 those categories of lost people in order of how concerned you are for each group.

Let me see if I can guess your order: family, friends, friends of another culture, unknown people. That's natural and not necessarily wrong. But maybe you had few or none in the friends of another culture category or in the personally-unknown-but-prayer-request category. I think the more we have God's heart, the more we'll care about people at a distance, too, because God loves the whole world.

I hope you're getting excited about what is going to happen during this study! Identify which of the following seem true (T) and which false (F):

____ 1. The first activity of the Holy Spirit in our behalf was to create us in the image of God.

____ 2. The last activity of the Holy Spirit that we'll study is His role in uniting us in a completed love relationship with God.

____ 3. Everyone is gifted as an evangelist.

____ 4. It's not easy, but it's possible to reach sinless perfection in this life.

____ 5. All Christians live relatively at the same level of closeness with God.

____ 6. The "new me" is programmed by the Spirit with potential the "old me" never had.

____ 7. Biblical faith is a synonym for trust and doesn't always include surrendering to God's will.

____ 8. No one can be expected to love or try to work for the salvation of people they've never even seen.

____ 9. Thinking and behaving like Jesus are the goals of life in the Spirit.

____ 10. The Christian life isn't passive—there is a battle to be won against temptation and we are expected to fight to win.

____ 11. Christians are given a gift of the Spirit to serve God in the church.

____ 12. Without confidence in the truth and authority of the Bible, it's unlikely a person could live a Spirit-filled life.

My answers are True: 1, 2, 6, 10, 11, 12 and False: 3, 4, 5, 7, 8, 9. If you differ on any answers, do two things. First, go back to the lesson where the subject is covered and, if the issue is still fuzzy, bring it up for discussion in your group meeting.

My prayer for you is that the next few weeks will be a spark in your spiritual growth. That's what preparing this study has been for me. Perhaps you can identify with my prayer response:

> Holy Spirit, you are incredible! Thank You for making me with so much potential—to think and act like Jesus and to be one with You. When I blow it, You don't give up. Thank You for taking my mistakes and making me into a new person. Thank You for showing me what You want me to be and how I can become what you desire. Thank You for making me more like Jesus already and for all the growth to come. Thank You for being with me daily and for giving me prayer, the Bible, and the church. I want to be a true reflection of You. I want to be used by You. I want to walk with You every day of my life. I do trust and love You. Here's my life—all of it, past, present, and future to do with as You please. Amen.

DESIGNER MODEL

What do you think of when you hear the words Designer Model? Is it "original"? "one-of-a-kind"? "top-of-the-line"? "designer's best"? Did you know you're a designer model? You were created as a designer model—fashioned after God Himself!

The off-duty flight attendant sitting beside me on the plane liked to talk. As we talked, I learned that she was active in her church and occasionally listened to Billy Graham on TV. She believed what he had to say, but she was not a member of an evangelical church. I asked about her husband.

"Well, he doesn't have any use for church," she said. "But he is very spiritual."

Spiritual? What did she mean?

She meant what many people today mean by the word *spiritual*. She meant that her husband believed in an unseen world and was interested in it. The current fascination with the unseen represents a huge shift in our thinking. (The "X-files" would not have been a big show in the '50s because people were not as fascinated by the unseen.) For several centuries we have concentrated on what can be seen and measured: scientific facts and the human mind to figure it all out. But now it seems feeling is more important than thinking, unseen forces are center stage. "Spiritual" is in, and the most ungodly people are said to be spiritual. But is this what the Bible means by spiritual?

Biblical spirituality grows out of the nature and activities of God. God is a spirit-being, not material; we were originally created in His image. In this unit we'll consider what it means to be created as a designer model—fashioned after God Himself. God designed you to have a love relationship with Him, but to have such a relationship you must be God-compatible. God made you as a special designer model—created in some mysterious way in His likeness so you can experience intimate companionship with Him.

[Unit Memory Verse]

So God created human beings, making them to be like himself. He created them male and female.

—*Genesis 1:27, GNB*

[DAY 1] ················· WHAT DOES IT MEAN TO BE SPIRITUAL?

The Spirit of God has made me; the breath of the Almighty gives me life.
—Job 33:4

The word *spiritual* means generally three different things. It is important that we understand these three so that when people talk about *spiritual* we will know where they are coming from. The three attitudes include those who:

1. Deny that we even have a spiritual nature or that a spiritual world beyond the reach of science exists: Call it *naturalism.* Many people embrace the scientific method and believe anything you can't see is non-existent or irrelevant. According to this view, the spiritual must be limited to what can happen in the natural world. A naturalist would say that water is real because you can touch it and feel it, but God is not real because you can't see Him or feel Him physically.

2. Recognize our spiritual nature and dabble in the spiritual world: We call this spiritualism. Spiritualists don't limit themselves to biblical guidelines for dealing with spiritual reality. Today angels, magic, reincarnation, prayer, horoscopes, the occult, and life-after-death experiences fill the media. The interest may be from Eastern belief, New Age thinking, or as a result of science not solving our problems. Whatever the reason, spiritualism is effecting many people. This view recognizes the reality of the spiritual dimension, but it doesn't always distinguish between the good and the evil of that spiritual world. It denies the ultimate power of God.

3. Recognize our spiritual nature and the spirit world but choose to deal with the Spirit world only through relationship with the God of the Bible. I call this the *biblical worldview.* Those who believe the Bible recognize that the physical, visible world is not all that exists in life; it is not even the most important part. To believe that what we can see, hear, touch, or taste is the most important thing will sooner or later lead to disaster. Paul reminded the Corinthians of this in the verse in the margin. Christians recognize the spiritual world, and they deal with it through obedience to the God the Father, the Son, and the Holy Spirit.

We fix our eyes not on what is seen, but on what is unseen. For what is seen is temporary, but what is unseen is eternal.
—2 Corinthians 4:18

Naturalism denies or ignores the reality of the spiritual world. Spiritualism recognizes the reality, but runs a risk of deception by evil. Only the biblical view of the world provides a foundation for building a safe and effective spiritual life. I'm excited that people are beginning to recognize an unseen, "spiritual" realm, but we need the ability to determine what part of that unseen world is good and what is not. If we want to understand spiritual reality and to link up only with the good part, we need to get better acquainted with the source of all spiritual good, the Holy Spirit of God.

In Christ all the fullness of the Deity lives in bodily form.
—Colossians 2:9

THE CHALLENGE OF BALANCE

The Bible teaches many truths that we cannot fully understand. Some of them seem contradictory. For example, the Bible teaches that Jesus Christ is fully and completely human. It also teaches that He is fully God, dwelling in bodily form (see *Col. 2:9*). In life, as in studying the Bible, to take one truth to an extreme is easier than to keep these two truths in balance. I call this need for balance the "center of biblical tension." To stay at the center of biblical tension is to hold contrasting truths in balance.

We must maintain a biblical tension concerning the Holy Spirit. Since Jesus is the center of our faith, we can easily ignore and treat the Spirit as if He didn't exist. Or we may go to the opposite extreme and so focus on the Spirit that we forget that the Spirit was given to glorify the Son. We may try to use the Spirit, expecting Him to do things He never said He would, like keep us on a permanent emotional high. See the diagram in the margin illustrating the center of biblical tension concept.

Imagine the following: the President of the United States comes to speak at your local high-school. The band strikes up "Hail to the Chief" as the president walks to

Focus on Christ

Fellowship with the Spirit

the stage. The spotlight follows his every step. Suddenly the crowd, as one, rise and turn their backs to the stage and, pointing to the balcony, applaud the fine performance of the guy running the spotlight! Crazy? Yes, but it illustrates a truth about the Spirit. The Spirit glorifies—shines the spotlight on—the Son. The Spirit points people to Jesus, and Jesus glorifies the Father *(John 15:26; 16:13-14)*. Each member of the Trinity respects the others. They maintain a balance between individual personality and corporate identity. We need the same balance in our approach to the Spirit.

Accurate biblical understanding and proper living are always a matter of balance. We must not focus so completely on the person and work of the Spirit that we lose sight of Jesus Christ. We must also avoid the opposite extreme. We must not ignore the person and work of the Holy Spirit. Many churches and Christians treat the Spirit of God as if He did not exist. To ignore the Spirit is a tragic error.

We need the Holy Spirit to empower us for daily living. We'll see how Jesus depended on the Spirit for everything He said or did. We need the presence and power of the Spirit as much as Christ did. We don't have to go to either of these extremes. We can decide to live in the balanced center of biblical truth about the Holy Spirit.

 To go to an extreme is easier than to stay at the center of biblical tension. On the scale below place a check mark to show your relationship with the Spirit.

Ignoring   Excessive concentration
the Spirit   on the Spirit

|⎯|⎯|⎯|⎯|⎯|⎯|⎯|⎯|⎯|

Concentrating on or ignoring the Spirit is not just a mind thing. Unfortunately many people act as if all that really matters can be bought or sold, enjoyed by the body, or used to make them look good to other people. You might call such people unspiritual, since the realm of the spirit is not very important to them. To those who are spiritually minded, on the other hand, the realm of the unseen is all-important, and God is the most important person in life. Relating to Him is the most important relationship. In fact, a spiritual life is one controlled by the Spirit of God. Stop and think about this a moment. In which direction do you tend to actually live out your life—ignoring the unseen or constantly connected?

 On a scale of 1–10, mark the place which best describes how much you think about unseen realities. "I think of spiritual things...

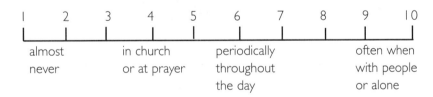

1 2 3 4 5 6 7 8 9 10

almost   in church   periodically   often when
never   or at prayer   throughout   with people
             the day   or alone

 When you think of "unseen realities," what specifically do you think about? What do you do? Check all that apply.
- ❏ I think about how good things are a gift of God, and I thank Him right then.
- ❏ When I face a problem or temptation I call on God to help me.
- ❏ When I fail, I ask God to forgive me. I don't wait until bedtime.
- ❏ I spend some time alone each day reading the Bible and talking to God.
- ❏ I go to church regularly and most times I feel that I really met with God.
- ❏ God seems nearby all the time, and I talk things over with Him throughout the day.

Center of Biblical Tension =
To hold contrasting truths in balance

"When the Counselor comes, whom I will send to you from the Father, the Spirit of truth who goes out from the Father, he will testify about me."
—John 15:26

When he, the Spirit of truth, comes, he will guide you into all truth. He will not speak on his own; he will speak only what he hears, and he will tell you what is yet to come. He will bring glory to me by taking from what is mine and making it known to you.
—John 16:13-14

Were you able to check each of the statements in the exercise above? If not, why not make those you couldn't check a set of goals for yourself?

KEEPING A JOURNAL

Since college days, I have greatly benefitted by keeping a journal. Often I write a prayer telling the Lord how I feel about my situation, praising Him for something about Him I especially appreciate, or calling on Him to help.

As I finish each day's lesson, I always tell the Lord my personal response to what He has been teaching me. Often I'll share my prayer response with you. If you feel the same sort of response and wish to use those prayers as your own, please do so. Or perhaps my prayer will trigger something you wish to talk to the Lord about. It would help to write out that response in your journal. Sometimes I will suggest something you may wish to talk to the Lord about. But whatever form your prayer response takes, be sure to close each lesson by talking to God about what you have been studying. (You may want to create your own journal or use *DiscipleHelps: A Daily Quiet Time Guide and Journal* available at your local Baptist Book Store or LifeWay Christian Store or by calling 1-800-458-2772 and asking for item # 7217-45.)

For today's lesson on spiritual realities, this was my response:

> Heavenly Father, Thank You that You are real and that Your unseen world, which goes beyond my senses and beyond scientific measurement, is more important than everything I see. Thank You for giving me Your Spirit. Through this study I want to know Him better and to experience His presence and power. Teach me all I need to know about the Holy Spirit, but especially help me learn to walk with Him all my days. In Jesus' name, Amen.

➤ **Write out *Genesis 1:27*, the memory verse for this week. Refer back to the unit introduction if necessary. Start trying to memorize the verse.**

➤ **Write in your journal something you understood or felt during this lesson—anything about your spiritual life or about your relationship to the Holy Spirit.**

[DAY 2] ························· WHO IS THE SPIRIT?

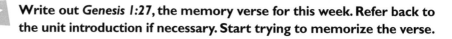

At Halloween our street is crowded with little "ghosts." But no matter how much we play ghost or joke about ghosts, the idea of unseen spirit-beings still seems spooky. We may get uneasy, for example, when someone speaks of the "Holy Ghost."

I have encountered each of the following ideas about the Holy Spirit.

• Some people today think of the Holy Spirit as a god-force, involved in all things and determining the course of human events.

• Some understand the Spirit not as an impersonal force but as a person, an agent sent from God to do His will, sort of like a chief angel.

• For still others, the Spirit is simply another name of the one true God, a name that emphasizes His invisible nature.

Each of these concepts seem true to certain individuals, but none of these are biblical views.

If a new Christian asked you to describe the Holy Spirit, how would you respond? Write in the margin your description of the Holy Spirit. Don't be scared by this exercise—it isn't a test!

My description of the Holy Spirit is...

LOOKING CLOSELY AT THE BIBLE

The Bible is the authority for answers about life in the Spirit. A primary question relates to the nature of the Holy Spirit. Is the Spirit a person or an impersonal god-force? Consider what the following verses say about the nature of the Holy Spirit.

> *I will ask the Father, and He will give you another Helper, that He may be with you forever—the Spirit of truth. The world cannot accept him, because it neither sees him or knows him. But you know him, for he lives with you and will be in you. ...But the Counselor, the Holy Spirit, whom the Father will send in my name, will teach you all things and will remind you of everything I have said to you (John 14:16-17,26).*

> *In the same way, the Spirit helps us in our weakness. We do not know what we ought to pray for, but the Spirit himself intercedes for us with groans that words cannot express (Rom. 8:26).*

 Is the Holy Spirit a person or an impersonal god-force?
❑ a person
❑ an impersonal god-force
Explain your answer: _____

The personal pronoun demonstrates that the Holy Spirit is a person rather than an impersonal force. He knows you, lives in you, teaches you, and prays for you.

 Read *Acts 5:3-4* and *I Corinthians 3:16* (in margin). How would you respond to someone who said the Holy Spirit is not God but is merely an agent of God?

Peter said, "Ananias, how is it that Satan has so filled your heart that you have lied to the Holy Spirit and have kept for yourself some of the money you received for the land? Didn't it belong to you before it was sold? And after it was sold, wasn't the money at your disposal? What made you think of doing such a thing? You have not lied to men but to God."
—Acts 5:3-4

You could point out to them that in many places the Bible speaks of the Spirit as God. In *Acts 5:3-4* Peter said Ananias had lied to the Holy Spirit. When Peter restated the charge, he said Ananias had lied to God. Paul said we are God's temple and we are the Holy Spirit's temple. These statements make sense because the Holy Spirit is God. You could also tell them of many passages that show the Holy Spirit is God because the Spirit has the power, attributes, and qualities of God. For example in *Psalm 139:7-10* the Spirit is all powerful and present everywhere.

Don't you know that yourselves are God's temple and that God's Spirit lives in you?
—I Corinthians 3:16

How do we know that the Holy Spirit is a person distinct from the Father and Son? For one example read *John 15:26* in the margin. The verse indicates that the Spirit goes out from the Father and testifies about Jesus.

"When the Counselor comes, whom I will send to you from the Father, the Spirit of truth who goes out from the Father, he will testify about me."
—John 15:26

 Below describe other examples that the Holy Spirit is a person distinct from the Father and Son. Remember the verses you read above.

You could have given many answers. *Romans 8:26* tells us that the Spirit talks to the Father. *John 14:17* says that the Father sent the Spirit. You may have remembered the story of Jesus' baptism. All three persons of the Trinity were present on that occasion, but they were separate and distinct *(Matt. 3:16-17).*

From these passages you see that the Holy Spirit is a person, and He is God; yet, He is distinct from the Father and Son. A division of responsibility exists between Father, Son, and Spirit. The Holy Spirit's role is to carry out the purposes of God.

THE ACTIVITIES OF THE SPIRIT

You have identified some key elements of the identity of the Spirit. The following activity will help you identify some of the Spirit's activities.

> **Draw lines matching the verses below on the left with the activities of the Holy Spirit in the right column. The verses are printed in the margin.**

1. *Genesis 1:2; Job 33:4*	brings about new life
2. *2 Peter 1:21*	spoke to men; gave us the Bible
3. *Luke 1:35; 3:22; 4:1*	gives clear direction; guides us
4. *John 3:5*	involved in creation

The Spirit is the One who created: *The Spirit of God was hovering over the waters (Gen. 1:2)*. He is the One who revealed God and gave us the Bible: *Men spoke from God as they were carried along by the Holy Spirit (2 Pet. 1:21)*. When the Son was to become man He was conceived by the Holy Spirit, and He taught and healed in the power of the Spirit.

In the same way the Holy Spirit works today. When God wants to act in our lives, He acts by His Spirit. God wants to relate to us personally to transform us into the likeness of Christ. He transforms us through the work of His Spirit.

> **Read the following passages in your Bible and describe four more activities of the Spirit.**

John 16:7-11 _____

John 16:13-15 _____

Galatians 5:22-23 _____

1 Corinthians 12:4,7,11 _____

The passages describe four more ways the Holy Spirit works in the lives of believers. He convicts us of sin, righteousness, and judgment. He teaches and instructs us, leading us into all truth. He produces the fruit of the Spirit in our lives, and He gives spiritual gifts—abilities for service.

> **Has today's study changed your understanding of the Holy Spirit? Look back at your original definition (p. 25) and add anything left off from your initial description.**

Now the earth was formless and empty, darkness was over the surface of the deep, and the Spirit of God was hovering over the waters.
—Genesis 1:2

The Spirit of God has made me.
—Job 33:4

Prophecy never had its origin in the will of man, but men spoke from God as they were carried along by the Holy Spirit.
—2 Peter 1:21

The angel answered, "The Holy Spirit will come upon you, and the power of the Most High will overshadow you. So the holy one to be born will be called the Son of God."
—Luke 1:35

The Holy Spirit descended on him [Jesus] in bodily form like a dove. And a voice came from heaven: "You are my Son, whom I love; with you I am well pleased."
—Luke 3:22

Jesus, full of the Holy Spirit, returned from the Jordan and was led by the Spirit in the desert.
—Luke 4:1

Jesus answered, "I tell you the truth, no one can enter the kingdom of God unless he is born of water and the Spirit."
—John 3:5

Descriptions are good, but let's get personal. How do you relate to the Holy Spirit? Check all boxes which apply.
- ❏ I love Him and He loves me.
- ❏ I rarely think about Him or sense His presence.
- ❏ He talks to me through the Bible, and I talk to Him in prayer every day.
- ❏ I can feel His presence often through the day.
- ❏ I'm not really sure how to relate to Him.
- ❏ I can see ways He is changing me into what I would like to be.

This would be a good time to pray. Reflect on your answers and talk to the Lord about them. Then reflect on the passages you studied about the Holy Spirit. Think about God and thank Him for each of the things about Him you appreciate most.

 In your journal write in your own words the memory verses. Practice saying them from memory.

MADE TO BE LIKE HIM ·········· [DAY 3]

"Just look at that boy! He looks just like his dad!"

I'm not sure how you feel when someone says you look just like your mom or dad. But that is exactly what we should want others to say about us: "They are the spittin' image of their Father—looks like Him, walks like Him, talks like Him." In some mysterious way we were made on the model of God Himself. In a planning session deep in eternity, the Father, Son, and Holy Spirit agreed, *"Let us make man in our image."* Read *Genesis 1:26-27* to get a mental picture of this momentous decision.

To know a person, watch what she does. In *Life in the Spirit*, we are concentrating on 10 activities of the Spirit. The first that impacts us daily is creation. God created us, in some mysterious way, to be like Him. That likeness we call the image of God. But what does His image look like? Some debate the meaning of *image*. Since the Bible doesn't give a concise definition, we have to draw from various passages of Scripture to find the meaning.

Then God said, "Let us make man in our image, in our likeness, and let them rule over the fish of the sea and the birds of the air, over the livestock, over all the earth, and over all the creatures that move along the ground." So God created man in his own image, in the image of God he created him; male and female he created them.
—Genesis 1:26-27

I have listed some of the meanings people have given for the image of God. Place a check by all those you think are included in human likeness to God.

- ❏ the human spirit
- ❏ ability to communicate
- ❏ ability to think clearly
- ❏ sexuality: male and female
- ❏ emotions, to love and be loved, to feel joy and sorrow
- ❏ ability to distinguish right from wrong
- ❏ the human body
- ❏ ability to choose
- ❏ character, attitudes, and actions like God

For each item on the list, a Bible scholar will agree that it is part of the image. Most of those listed are human characteristics that God made to reflect His character. This list may contain some exceptions, though. For example, a few educated people suggest that our bodies reflect God's nature in some mysterious way, but most would leave our bodies off the list. God is spirit and not physical, apart from the humanness of Jesus. Recently, some Bible scholars have added sexuality—male and female—to the characteristics of God. They believe that God combines in His being all the characteristics of both sexes, but most would not include sexuality in the list.

OUR DESIRE TO TAKE GOD'S PLACE

Alexander the Great, Caesar, King Nebuchadnezzar, and Herod the Great all had two things in common—each claimed to be God and each hated cats. They wanted all authority, and the cats were the only ones who wouldn't obey them! If you've ever had a cat you know what I mean.

Would all authority and power represent God's image? In this century we are rapidly achieving corporately what some of the ancients tried to achieve as individuals. With the assistance of computers we dream of accumulating all knowledge. With jets and telecommunications we think we can be everywhere—omnipresent. But these were not the aspects of God that He intended for us to share. Not omnipotence (all–powerful). Not omniscience (all–knowing). Not omnipresence (present everywhere). Notice that I included none of these characteristics in the last learning activity.

Of course, we do have high potential for knowing and doing, since we are modeled after God Himself. That's why so much human achievement in the arts and sciences is truly amazing, but God's infinities are forever beyond us. Yet, in one way God designed us to be just like Him.

Below list the ways in which you believe God intended you to be exactly like Him.

Scientists tell us that porpoises communicate with signals; but they've written no books yet. Pandas make tools—they break off a stick to dig out the food they want; but they've built no cars yet. Ants build complex cities, but no churches or temples have ever been found in those cities. Monkeys misbehave; but none have been known to be embarrassed by it.

When God created a special being in His own likeness, He designed one unlike the animals He had already created—one with a spirit who could communicate, create, know right from wrong, and, above all, love and be loved by God Himself. That is His "image," the stamp of the Designer. We are indeed a "designer model"—modeled after the Designer Himself. That was the work of the Holy Spirit in His first activity, creating us in God's image.

Some people have more intelligence, more authority, or more strength than others. In some very limited sense we might say these are more like God than someone with less intelligence, authority, or strength. But we are all far from God's infinite capacity.

Name a few people who have more authority, intelligence, strength, or skill than anyone else you know about (ex. athlete, entertainer, scientist).

Even the greatest among us falls way short of the authority, intelligence, and strength of God. Does being somewhat more intelligent, stronger, or having great power or unlimited money really make a person more like God?

God made us to be like Him, not in power or authority but, in our moral nature. He designed us to be loving, holy, trustworthy, fair, good, peaceful, and joyful. We share some of His non-moral attributes. For example, unlike the animals, we are capable of abstract thinking. But He designed us to be exactly like Him in His moral nature: *"Be holy because I, the Lord your God, am holy" (Lev. 19:2).*

 List the people you know who are most like God in His moral nature, people you would call very godly.

 In which of the above lists would you most prefer that people put you?
❑ known for my authority, intelligence, strength, or skill.
❑ known for my godliness.

You and I are designed on the model of the Creator. The joy of life comes from glorifying Him. We glorify Him as we more accurately reflect His character.

 Tell God how thankful and thrilled you are to have been designed after Him. Your journal is a good place to write that prayer. Are there other insights or experiences to note in your journal?

 Fill in the blanks of the memory verse. After you fill in the blanks, write the verse, then practice saying the verse from memory.

So God _____ human beings, _____ them to be

_____ _____. He _____ them male and female.

—Genesis 1:27, GNB

DESIGNED ON PURPOSE ························ [DAY 4]

Muriel was pretty, full of life, talented, fun, sold out to God—and in love with me! She agreed to be mine and everything we did was geared toward our wedding day. I was so in love with Muriel that I did many crazy things like only eating one meal a day so I could save money for the great day; and reading her love letters the minute they arrived, no matter that they usually distracted me in history class.

Shortly before the big day, some of my family and I borrowed my father's car and headed for Nebraska. In a long, sweeping curve a slow moving tractor backed up traffic for miles blocking our way.

Finally, my chance came. I could see around the curve, ahead of dozens of creeping cars, and no one was coming toward us. I whipped out into the left lane of that two-lane highway and put the accelerator to the floor—not very smart. But I was crazy in love. I had one objective: to get to the one I loved. Half-way around that curve, a speeding car appeared from nowhere, aimed right at us. I headed for the shoulder.

Oh, no! Why did they put that telephone pole there? The thought barely had time to flash through my mind. I closed my eyes and aimed at the narrow gap between the approaching car and the telephone pole. We left one of my father's fenders on that pole, but we limped on in to Beaver City. There in Beaver City Muriel and I began our lives together.

And now? Now Muriel lies in bed, unable to stand, walk, or feed herself. Knowing nothing really, a victim of Alzheimer's disease. But her contented smile sometimes breaks through the dimness and brightens my day.

People speak of my care of her as if it were something heroic—far from it. I love her more now than I ever did on that wild ride to Nebraska. When I'm away on a speaking engagement, I miss her more. I long to be with her, to feel the squeeze of her hand. But there is a big difference. Now the love flows mostly one way. The connecting point is gone.

We used to share our dreams, our work, our play, our children, our laughter, and our tears. And we drew ever closer to one another. We became more and more like one another, actually. But we're not much alike now. The two–way communication is almost gone.

Think about your best friend. How often do you talk or get together?

❏ Several times a day   ❏ Daily   ❏ Every Other Day   ❏ Weekly

Do you talk to your best friend about your dreams? school? future mate? love? hurts? joy? family matters? about *everything* in your life?

Now think about your relationship with God. How often do you talk with Him?

❏ Several times a day   ❏ Daily   ❏ Every Other Day   ❏ Weekly

Do you talk with God about your dreams? His dreams for you? school? future mate? love? His love for you? hurts? joy? family matters? about *everything*?

God created you to be like Him so you could share His life and His love. He had a mutually satisfying love affair in mind. The relationship started out so incredible, didn't it? But for many Christians, something has happened. Oh, He still loves them and lavishes that love on them daily. But how do they respond? Communication is occasional; love has lost its passion. Perhaps they can't even identify with Him, because they are so unlike Him now. Sad, isn't it? But that was never the Designer's plan.

THE DESIGNER'S PLAN

From all eternity God the Father, God the Son, and God the Holy Spirit were bound together in love, for God by nature is love *(1 John 4:7,16)*. From the overflow of His loving nature, He wanted people to whom He could show His love and who would love Him back.

For communication and love to flow freely, the people God made would have to be like Him. The relationship couldn't be like you and your dog. Fido may be a great friend, but communication is limited and he is not exactly a "suitable helper" to you, as God said of the mate He was creating for Adam *(Gen. 2:20)*. Fido is a different species, but Adam and Eve, that's another story. They were made for each other.

Just as God created Adam and Eve compatible with each other, He created us

Dear friends, let us love one another, for love comes from God. Everyone who loves has been born of God and knows God. And so we know and rely on the love God has for us. God is love. Whoever lives in love lives in God, and God in him.
—1 John 4:7,16

But for Adam no suitable helper was found.
—Genesis 2:20

to be God-compatible. If that compatibility weren't there, in-depth communication would not be possible, intimate companionship would be missing. That is why God the Holy Spirit created humankind on God's own pattern. As a result, Adam and Eve walked with God in the garden of Eden, sharing His presence and love. They were created to love God and be loved by Him. They were created in His likeness so they could experience that love.

 God's design determines your life's greatest purpose. What do you consider to be your supreme purpose in life? In the following list, check only one supreme purpose. I am here to—

- ❏ serve in the church faithfully
- ❏ become like Christ in my character
- ❏ be successful in my life's calling
- ❏ find a good husband/wife
- ❏ take care of myself
- ❏ lead others to Christ
- ❏ love and glorify God
- ❏ other _____

 Read *Matthew 22:37-38* in the margin. Circle what you consider to be the essential part of the passage.

Though the above list contains many worthwhile goals, the ultimate goal of our lives is to love and glorify God. Even becoming Christlike in character falls short of that supreme goal.

WHAT ABOUT CHRISTLIKENESS?

Becoming more like Jesus enables us to fellowship with God, but it is not the ultimate goal. The more like Christ we become, the more we will be able to love God and receive love from Him. Becoming like Christ is so important that the major emphasis of this study is how we become like Him, but keep in mind that becoming like Christ is not the final goal. The goal is to develop our love relationship with God. He created us on His pattern and provided the salvation process as a way for His image in us to be restored. He did all these things with the ultimate goal of loving us and us loving Him.

 List five ways in which those who know you best would say you are growing in Christlikeness—ways in which He is making you more like Himself.
1.
2.
3.
4.
5.

 List five ways in which you are least like Jesus, or ways in which people who know you best would say you least remind them of Jesus. If you fear someone may see this, you may want to list them in your journal.
1.
2.
3.
4.
5.

"'Love the Lord your God with all your heart and with all your soul and with all your mind.' This is the first and greatest commandment."
–Matthew 22:37-38

If you have the courage, sometime next week ask a close friend to answer those two questions about you. Ask someone who will tell you the truth. If you do this part of the assignment, write that person's answers in another color so you can see clearly the differences between your thoughts and those of the other person.

The great desire of the true lover of God is to develop a character that is just like Him so that His purpose in making and redeeming us can be experienced. We want to know the deepening love relationship that will bring Him joy and bring us joy, too!

End today's study talking with God about the following areas:
- Thank the Lord for what He has done to change you into Christ's likeness.
- Confess the ways you haven't changed, but want Him to change you.
- Thank God for loving you with an everlasting love, and tell Him how much you love Him.

Like the surge of joy I feel when Muriel responds with a smile, your Eternal Lover is waiting for your response.

Write the memory verse *(Gen. 1:27)* for this unit without referring back.

[DAY 5] · · · · · · · · · · · · · · · CAPACITY OF YOUR DESIGNER MODEL

We were window shopping in a huge computer mall. I discovered magical things like a program to landscape your yard. The program allowed you to plant shrubs and flowers and produce a picture of what it would look like six months later, a year later, or five years later. My son David, a software executive, was trying to explain things to me in simple terms so I could understand. Finally, he said: "Dad, your computer just doesn't have the capacity for that program."

His statement reminded me of our reaction to the Bible. We look through the Bible and see God's plan for a growing, mature Christian. To be an effective disciple sounds great, but do we have the capacity to run that program? Can I really live the kind of life the Bible describes?

Remember, we were designed on the model of God's own character. He created us with plenty of capacity. We ought to be able to live out any plan God gives for thinking or behaving like Jesus. But somehow, when we try to run the program we fail. We feel like the person at the computer who presses a button and gets a message that says, "Enter the password." We have no idea what word to enter or what to do next. What has gone wrong? Why can't we get the results God promised?

Adam and Eve could run the program. They knew right and did it. They also had the capacity to choose wrong, and they did. They disabled their "computer" so it could no longer run God's program successfully. Bible scholars have a special word for the damage done by the entry of sin into humanity. They call it *depravity. Depraved* means that "every human being has been damaged by sin." Can the damage be repaired? Can we get our original capability back? God's program for our lives looks something like this—
- showing love toward the unpleasant and our enemies;
- joy in the midst of bad circumstances;
- peace and hope when everything seems to be going wrong;
- patience with those jerks in our lives;
- kindness even to the unkind;

- choosing obedience when others are disobedient;
- faithful even when it is costly.

 Reread the seven statements above. After each statement write one word to describe how difficult or easy you find that part of God's plan.

THE NORMAL CHRISTIAN LIFE

We often use the word *normal* to mean "typical" or "average." Thus we consider the way most people live to be normal. God never intended for Christians to be average. So I use the word *normal* to describe the life God offers His children—the norm, so to speak, or the biblical standard for Christian living. For example, He designs us to overcome temptation, obey His commands, and grow in self-control, contentment, humility, and courage. He intends for us to be obedient to the Holy Spirit and gave us the example in Scripture so we can reflect the attitudes and the behavior of Jesus Christ. This is the normal Christian life.

In the normal Christian life, God has first place in our lives. We put others' feelings above our own desires. The growing Christian has the power for godly living and effective service in the church. Above all, he or she has the joy of constant companionship with the Lord.

 The next two paragraphs contain my evaluation of the spiritual condition of many church members. Read the paragraphs carefully. Then place a mark on the bar-graph that follows the paragraphs. Indicate to what degree you agree that my evaluation is accurate or disagree that my opinion is overly pessimistic.

The average church member thinks and behaves very much like morally upright non-Christians. They are decent enough but with nothing supernatural about them. Their behavior seems to come from things in their family, growing-up days, and present day experiences. They fall into temptation, lusting when their body craves it, wanting what they do not have, and taking credit for their accomplishments. The basis for their choices is selfishness, and though they have a love for God and others, broken relationships with others prove that the Spirit does not control their lives.

The average church member experiences little change for the better. In fact, many don't seem to expect or want much improvement. The Bible is boring, prayer is a joke, and helping out in the church comes out of selfishness. Above all, life seems to be empty, because it does not center around a constant, personal companionship with the Lord.

Agree   Disagree

⟵————————————————⟶

 Is your experience more like the average church member or like the normal Christian? Perhaps it would help in answering that question to read slowly and prayerfully the last five paragraphs again. Underline characteristics that describe you, whether found in the Great Designer's model described in the first three paragraphs or the more typical, average version described in the last two.

Each of us has our own strengths and weakness, some we are aware of, some perhaps not. But God knows, and when we acknowledge our need to Him, He will begin restoring our broken-down models to function as He designed them to operate *(1 John 1:5–2:2)*.

THE PRACTICAL QUESTION

"How, HOW, HOW can I ever live that kind of life?" A troubled graduate student scribbled the question on a scrap of paper and passed it to me after class. She had heard me talk about a Spirit-empowered life. She desperately wanted an answer.

Notice that in the passages (in the margin) the restoration process is in a Person, not a study, or a magic formula. The Master Repairman, can run the program as designed and restores our brokenness. The transforming presence and power of God the Holy Spirit will enable us to be what God designed us to be.

THE TRANSFORMATION CONNECTION

How do we connect to let His power flow? How do we move from an average to a normal Christian life? We connect with Him through faith. *The just shall live by his faith (Hab. 2:4,* KJV) was the only message of an Old Testament prophet that was repeated, not once, but three times in the New Testament *(Rom. 1:17; Gal. 3:11; Heb. 10:38)*. Faith is the uplink with divine power, whether for salvation or for being restored into the original design. God provides the power for living through the activity of the Holy Spirit. We respond to God's provision through faith. Faith releases the power of the Holy Spirit to work in our lives.

Faith means:
- believing what God has said;
- choosing to trust God by putting your life in His hands even when everything seems to be going wrong;
- placing your confidence in His love and knowledge of you and His ability to order your life for your greatest blessing.

God is the standard for our lives—we were meant to reflect His image. God also restores and empowers us to become like Him; the Holy Spirit can build character and make us more like Christ. We connect with God through faith. As you continue this study I pray that you will examine and experience those truths in all their exciting dimensions. Here is my suggested prayer:

> Thank you, blessed Spirit, that You have not left me alone. You have shown me a solid hope that You personally stand ready to show me the way, enable me to walk it, and stay with me to the end of it. Amen!

God is spirit. He created us on the same model—spiritual beings—so we could join His circle of love. We broke that relationship and damaged ourselves. But God chases us with an incredible love, wants to repair us, and change us into His moral likeness so we can again be God-compatible.

Share one item from your journal with your group or the partner you have chosen. This will strengthen your commitment, help others, and bring joy to the Holy Spirit.

Write *Genesis 1:27* from memory. Find a way to use the memory verse, or what the memory verse means to you, in conversation with someone today.

For those God foreknew he also predestined to be conformed to the likeness of his Son (Rom. 8:29).

We, who with unveiled faces all reflect the Lord's glory, are being transformed into his likeness with ever-increasing glory, which comes from the Lord, who is the Spirit (2 Cor. 3:18).

The new self...is being renewed in knowledge in the image of its Creator (Col. 3:10).

the GREAT UNVEILING

UNIT 3

Last week we learned that the Holy Spirit created us in the image of God. In this unit we will explore the role of the Holy Spirit in revealing truth to us so we may know God and knowing Him, love Him.

As a young adult I began to doubt the truth of the Bible. I grew up in a Christian home, accepted Christ as a young child, and attended a Christian college, but I began to doubt the basic truths of the Christian faith.

My doubts grew until I became a full-blown skeptic. I decided I would doubt anything I could not verify. I determined to be truly scientific—never to believe anything without proof. Since I couldn't prove the Bible scientifically, God was the next casualty of my "scientific" method. Remember, we called this naturalism in the last unit.

As my skepticism grew, my world became darker. I discovered that it was not just the Bible and God that I doubted. I began to feel that nothing was certain because I could never get all the evidence on anything. As a result, I believed less and less about more and more. I tried to convince myself that I was practicing "intellectual honesty," but trusting no one and no thing was a lonely existence.

Fortunately, I began to examine my own assumptions. If you are so "scientific," I asked myself, why have you ruled out in advance any investigation of the possibility of God? For the first time in a long while, I prayed. My prayer was simple, if a little arrogant: "God, if You exist, will You give me some objective evidence?"

In this unit we will examine *revelation* (not the last Book in the Bible, but the act of making things known), the second activity of the Spirit. The Holy Spirit broke into history to reveal to us the existence and nature of God. He has worked in the world throughout salvation history—the process of God revealing Himself. The Spirit inspired the writing of the Bible and was the power source for the ministry of Jesus. Apart from the Holy Spirit we cannot know about God or know God.

[Unit Memory Verse

All Scripture is inspired by God and is useful for teaching the truth, rebuking error, correcting faults, and giving instruction for right living, so that the person who serves God may be fully qualified and equipped to do every kind of good deed.

—*2 Timothy 3:16-17, GNB*

[DAY 1] ···························· CONFIRMING THE WORD

Out of frustration and without truth to live by in my life, I prayed a very honest prayer. I asked God to prove to me that He exists.

God had answered my prayer before I was even born. My search took me back to the Bible. I had come to believe that the Bible was full of mistakes, but the Holy Spirit began to use the Bible itself to build a foundation for my faith. For example, I realized that the Old Testament predicted when and where the Messiah would be born, what He would do, how He would die, and that He would live forever. These were predictions made hundreds of years before Christ was even born.

I began to slowly understand God with my mind. I was experiencing personally what God did through history—God revealed Himself. I call it the great unveiling. If God had not chosen to reveal Himself, He would remain forever a mystery to us. I have no doubt that the Holy Spirit was leading me into truth. That's His job. Jesus said, *"When he, the Spirit of truth, comes, he will guide you into all truth"* (John 16:13).

> **Many of us go through periods of questioning or doubting. If you've had a question or concern, write it below and describe how you dealt with it.**

God provided a written record of everything we need to know about Him so we can enter into relationship with Him. The Spirit of God led the writers of the Bible to communicate what we need to know to experience fellowship with God. But you may be asking these tough questions about the Bible (1) How do we know the words of the Bible are from God? (2) How did the Holy Spirit inspire Scripture? (3) Can we understand Scripture so that we know God's will?

Understanding the Bible and relating to God through His Holy Spirit go together. We cannot know God apart from Scripture, and we cannot understand the Bible apart from the Spirit.

> **Read *1 Corinthians 2:14*. In your own words explain why any person without the Holy Spirit is unable to understand spiritual things.**

The man without the Spirit does not accept the things that come from the Spirit of God, for they are foolishness to him, and he cannot understand them, because they are spiritually discerned.
—1 Corinthians 2:14

Several terms describe the relationship between the Bible and the Spirit. God made known truth about the universe, about humanity, and about Himself—truth that we would not know unless He made it known to us. We call this *revelation*. The Bible is our *authority* because it is the only completely dependable means through which God has revealed Himself to us. Just like the official rule book that decides how a basketball game will be played or a band contest will be judged. God gave His revelation through a process we call the *inspiration* of the Holy Spirit. We have the privilege and the responsibility to determine what each passage means through *interpretation*. For the task of interpretation we have the assistance of the Holy Spirit guiding us into all truth—the process of *illumination*.

Interpretation
Revelation
Illumination
Authority
Inspiration

> **Below are descriptions of the five terms related to the Bible that we'll learn this week. Match the description with the right term. Terms are listed in the margin.**
> _____a. how the Holy Spirit gave Scripture
> _____b. the Spirit's activity in helping me understand the Bible

_____c. the work of figuring out what the author meant in a verse
_____d. God communicating what I otherwise couldn't know
_____e. why I trust and obey the Bible

About the Bible Herschel Hobbs wrote: "Revelation is God's unveiling of truth. Inspiration is receiving and transmitting truth. Illumination is understanding truth *(John 16:13)*. In the biblical sense revelation and inspiration were completed with the close of the New Testament. But illumination is a continuing activity of the Holy Spirit."1 In the activity above, the answers were: a–inspiration; b–illumination; c–interpretation; d–revelation; e–authority. You might have reversed inspiration and revelation or interpretation and illumination because the words describe related concepts. When I began to recognize that the Bible was true, I began to trust and obey it.

THE NATURE OF AUTHORITY

If I were to tell you that a major earthquake will occur in California tomorrow you would have every right to ask, "Who are you?" Once you knew that I'm clueless when it comes to predicting earthquakes, you wouldn't leave the state. But if I were a leading seismologist (earthquake dude) who always makes accurate predictions, you might take immediate action. Why? The dependability of a statement depends on the speaker. So, the authority of the Bible depends on who said it. Because God said it, you can believe it. We call this Book—and only this Book—the Word of God. That's why it has absolute authority for our lives.

When I returned to God, I still had problems with some parts of the Bible. The doubts would set in my mind from time-to-time. After about 10 years of this, I decided to get this settled—to get in or get out. I went to a lonely beach and camped out for three days. I read the Gospels again and again.

The Holy Spirit used the Bible to change my life. Something blew through me—a sense of reverence towards this man Jesus Christ. Even if I accepted the arguments of the critics, there still remained a man that surpassed any other man, a unique revelation of God. On the third day, I had a sense that Jesus was with me, as if He put a hand on my shoulder and said, "Do you think you are smarter than I?"

"No!" I cried out, "I'm not smarter than You." The lights came on! The realization of who Jesus is and who I'm not cleared my doubts. That day on the beach, I settled the issue of the authority of the Word of God in my life. Because the living Word of God—Jesus Christ—is my authority, His written Word is my authority. From that moment, I decided to accept whatever Jesus said about the Father, heaven and hell, right and wrong—and the Bible. If He believed the Bible to be true—and He proved it as He lived on Earth—who was I to question some verses I didn't understand? All the struggles of the Christian life are not solved quickly or easily, but a solution begins by accepting the authority of Jesus and His view of the Bible.

 In the margin read the statements made by Jesus about Scripture. Then below circle the sentence that best reflects Jesus' view.
a. Jesus believed most of Scripture was true and enduring, but not all of it.
b. Jesus believed Scripture is true and lasting and necessary to spiritual life.
c. Jesus set aside the Old Testament to make room for the New Testament.

On the beach that day, I took the step of faith and chose Jesus as my authority. He viewed the Bible as God's Word. I'm not smarter than He is! If you cannot honestly agree that the Bible is the authority for your life, would you be willing to ask God, as I did 30 years ago, to show you what He thinks of Scripture? You may have to struggle with it as I did for awhile, but you will be demonstrating a willingness to change if He wants you to. In the activity above, I circled choice b.

*Jesus answered, "It is written: 'Man does not live on bread alone, but on every word that comes from the mouth of God.'"
–Matthew 4:4*

*"Do not think that I have come to abolish the Law or the Prophets; I have not come to abolish them but to fulfill them. I tell you the truth, until heaven and earth disappear, not the smallest letter, not the least stroke of a pen, will by any means disappear from the Law until everything is accomplished."
–Matthew 5:17-18*

➤ **What's your attitude toward the authority of Scripture? Check your description.**

❏ I can't believe some things in the Bible are true.

❏ The Bible is full of good stories, but it doesn't have divine authority.

❏ I believe the Bible is true, but I still want to choose my own values.

❏ The Bible is true in all its parts, and thus is the final authority for what I believe and how I behave.

❏ Other? _____

Now would be a good time to thank God for His authority in your life and for the Bible. Ask Him to empower you this week to understand the role His Word should play in your life. Write your response to God in your journal entry for today.

➤ **Paul gives at least five ways the Holy Spirit interacts with us in Bible study. Can you find them in *2 Timothy 3:16-17?* List them below, using your own words.**

1.

2.

3.

4.

5.

I worded my responses this way: The Holy Spirit (I) helps me understand the truths of God's Word; (2) corrects false beliefs or teachings; (3) convicts me of sinful attitudes and actions; (4) disciplines me in choosing a lifestyle pleasing to God; (5) helps me develop the skills and abilities I need to accomplish God's purposes for me. You chose different words, but check to see if the meaning is similar.

All Scripture is inspired by God and is useful for teaching the truth, rebuking error, correcting faults, and giving instruction for right living.
—2 Timothy 3:16-17, GNB

[DAY 2] ···································· 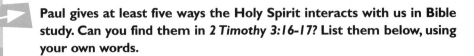 INSPIRING THE WORD

The Bible claims to be inspired by God, and that makes me curious. Exactly what did the Holy Spirit do to the Bible writers? How did He make sure they wrote what He wanted to say? Since He doesn't tell us, we try to figure it out. Some think the Spirit dictated the Bible to the authors like executives dictate to their secretaries. He obviously did dictate parts of the Bible like the Ten Commandments, but I don't believe much of Scripture was dictated in that way.

➤ **In the margin on the next page read the introduction to the Gospel of Luke. What does Luke tell you about how God inspired him to write?**

❏ God dictated the book to Luke.

❏ Luke just wrote what he "felt led" to write.

❏ Luke did careful research.

Some of the Bible comes from historical research, like Luke and Acts. On the human side, the experiences and writing style of each author are evident throughout Scripture. But in some mysterious way the writers were inspired *(2 Tim. 3:16-17)* by the Holy Spirit so that what they wrote was consistently called, "the word of God."

Many have undertaken to draw up an account of the things that have been fulfilled among us, just as they were handed down to us by those who from the first were eyewitnesses and servants of the word. Therefore, since I myself have carefully investigated everything from the beginning, it seemed good also to me to write an orderly account for you, most excellent Theophilus, so that you may know the certainty of the things you have been taught.
–Luke 1:1-4

Read *2 Peter 1:20-21*. Circle yes or no in response to the following questions:

yes   no   1. Bible writers thought up the ideas expressed in Scripture.

yes   no   2. Bible writers believed they were expressing God's thoughts.

yes   no   3. The Holy Spirit transmitted God's thoughts to human writers.

Above all, you must understand that no prophecy of Scripture came about by the prophet's own interpretation. For prophecy never had its origin in the will of man, but men spoke from God as they were carried along by the Holy Spirit.
–2 Peter 1:20-21

Though we may not know how the Spirit carried out this activity, we know from Scripture that He guided the writing process so that the human authors could use their own experiences and words and write what God wanted communicated. The Bible is the only book that this can be said about honestly. Other books may be called "inspired" because they inspire the reader, but none can be said to be God-breathed, as is Scripture. The Bible alone carries that guarantee. That's why we can trust it.

 Choose the idea about inspiration that is closest to your view.

❑ The Holy Spirit dictated the words to human authors, much as a person would dictate a letter to a secretary.

❑ The Bible is inspired like Shakespeare's work or any great piece of literature.

❑ The Holy Spirit influenced the minds of the authors so that they wrote in their own words exactly what He wanted to communicate.

❑ Scripture inspiration is a mystery I don't understand.

❑ Other _____

Since the Bible does not define inspiration, we might be tempted to take the option of calling it a mystery and letting it go at that! I hope you were able to select option three above. If not, let's think about the meaning of the other choices.

My son Kent, believing in the creation story of Genesis, first encountered an alternative view of human origins in the third grade. He decided to do his own survey: he asked each classmate, "Do you believe in human origins without God?"

Darwin, his best friend replied, "Of course I do." (He seemed to live up to the name his parents gave him!)

Kent then leveled his accusation: "Then you don't believe the Bible."

Darwin replied, "Yes I do, I just don't believe the part about creation." With wisdom, Kent asked, "Well, how do you choose which part to believe?"

 If you are uncertain about the reliability of the Bible, how would you answer Kent's question? "How do you choose which part to believe?"

Either the Bible is totally true or it's unreliable. If I say there is error in Scripture, then I put myself over Scripture. By deciding what to accept and what not to accept as true, I sit in judgment on the Book; I consider my understanding greater than the inspiration of Scripture, reducing the inspiration of Scripture to the size of my knowledge, and that's not a very impressive "revelation!" Paul assures us, in our memory verse that *All Scripture is inspired by God.*

 King Josiah of Judah believed the Scriptures were the inspired message from God to His people. Read the verses in the margin. Describe in your own words how Josiah reacted when he received the long-lost copy of the Book of the Law. How did the people react?

He went up to the temple of the Lord with the men of Judah, the people of Jerusalem, the priests and the prophets—all the people from the least to the greatest. He read in their hearing all the words of the Book of the Covenant, which had been found in the temple of the Lord. The king stood by the pillar and renewed the covenant in the presence of the Lord—to follow the Lord and keep his commands, regulations and decrees with all his heart and all his soul, thus confirming the words of the covenant written in this book. Then all the people pledged themselves to the covenant.
—2 Kings 23:2-3

What difference does believing that Scripture is the inspired Word of God make in a believer's life?

The Bible helps us by describing God's character so we may know Him; by telling us how to become a child of God; by giving us moral direction for our lives; and by assuring us of our final destination.

The Holy Spirit gave us a complete, reliable revelation of God's will for us. What a magnificent gift! He unveiled the character and purposes of God. We can know God! Knowing Him we will surely love Him. Love leads us to obedience as we seek to live our lives as Jesus lived His life on earth.

Let's stop right now and thank God for the things His Spirit does for us through the Bible. This is my prayer response as I think about the inspiration of the Word. Pray along with me or voice your own prayer concerning the Bible.

Father thank you for the gift of Your Spirit who has made known all truth. I want to know You, love You, and please You. Thank You that the Bible is true. Help me to understand it more clearly and obey its teachings more. Amen.

Write the unit memory verse by filling in the missing words below:

All Scripture is_____by God and is useful for _____the truth, rebuking_____, correcting _____,and giving _____ for right _____,so that the man who serves God may be fully _____and _____ to do every kind of _____ _____

—2 Timothy 3:16-17, GNB

[DAY 3] ·························· REVEALING GOD'S WILL

But these are written that you may believe that Jesus is the Christ, the Son of God, and that by believing you may have life in his name.
—John 20:31

Revelation means that "God has spoken." *Inspiration* means that "the Holy Spirit worked with the authors of Scripture so that they wrote what He wanted written." We have a Book we can rely on. But what is its purpose?

The Bible leads us to saving faith through Christ Jesus (*John 20:31*), the starting line for our lifelong journey toward Christlikeness. It also reveals what we will be like when we are spiritually mature (*Eph. 4:13*). It *is useful* for teaching us, rebuking and correcting us, training us in righteousness, and equipping us for every good work.

PRINCIPLES AND SPECIFICS

The Holy Spirit uses Scripture to guide us, but we often want specific—and simple—answers to our questions. The Bible does give do's and don'ts, but it is much more a book of principles than a list of rules. I'm glad the Bible gives both. I need specific instructions, but I especially need principles.

Unlike rules, principles can be used in all situations, but I may not understand how the principle applies to my life. So specific examples are also in the Scripture. *"Love your enemies," (Matt. 5:44)* is a principle that covers all relationships, but the Bible also describes specifics of how love will act. For example, when someone does

Until we all reach unity in the faith and in the knowledge of the Son of God and become mature, attaining to the whole measure of the fullness of Christ.
—Ephesians 4:13

something against me, if I love him or her, I'll go to the person alone and confront him or her *(Matt. 18:15-17)*. That's specific, but by giving the underlying principle of love, the Bible covers all potential attitudes, actions, and relationships. The Bible is a book of principles. We must rely on the Spirit to guide us as we interpret Scripture.

 First Corinthians 13 **describes loving behaviors without tying them to specific situations. For the following descriptions of love, give a specific example of a behavior that would demonstrate this quality:**

1. Love is patient *(v. 4)*. _____

2. Love is kind *(v. 4)*. _____

3. Love keeps no record of wrongs *(v. 5)*. _____

How long would the Bible be if it gave specific examples or precise commands covering every possible attitude and activity for all people of all time? Even if God put all that detail on some mega-computer, how could we possibly access the information for a particular situation and make the decision? No, the Spirit has given us something far better—principles to guide us in the decisions of life.

In the activity above, I listed these examples of love: I can be patient while waiting for my sister to get out of the bathroom in the mornings. I can be kind when I'm trying to work things out with a friend. I can choose to forgive and not hold a grudge against my parents. We also have situations like: Should I play in the band or take a job? What college should I attend? Should I run track or not? Even in those situations, the Bible provides principles for guidance.

God deals with us as individuals. His plan for your life is unlike any other person's. Even though their experiences differed, Abraham, Moses, and Jonah lived by the principles of God's Word. Their examples help us understand God's will for us.

GOD'S WILL REVEALED IN BIBLICAL EXAMPLES

The Scripture teaches both by commands and example. It states truth and it demonstrates the truth at work in the lives of people.

 Read each of the following principles. Write an example from the life of a Bible character that illustrates each principle. Many examples are possible; use your own examples or use the Scripture passages I suggest.

a. God loves everyone, even sinners *(Jonah 1:2; Rom. 5:8)*.

b. God disciplines His disobedient children *(Deut. 32:48-52; Heb. 12:6)*.

c. God wants us to trust Him even when we don't know how things will turn out *(Gen. 12:1; Heb. 11:39)*.

We could compare the Bible to a road map. It shows us the route from our beginning point as sinners without hope *(Eph. 2:12)*, then moving to our point of salvation where we accepted Christ as *"the way" (John 14:6)*. It leads us through the triumphs and pitfalls of everyday living to our ultimate destination *(John 14:1-3)*.

There will be a highway there, called "The Road of Holiness." No sinner will ever travel that road; no fools will mislead those who follow it.... Those whom the Lord has rescued will travel home by that road.... They will be happy forever, forever free from sorrow and grief (Isa. 35:8-10, GNB).

"Who is greater, the one who is at the table or the one who serves? Is it not the one who is at the table? But I am among you as one who serves."
—Luke 22:27

"As the Father has loved me, so have I loved you. Now remain in my love."
—John 15:9

Being found in appearance as a man, he humbled himself and became obedient to death—even death on a cross!
—Philippians 2:8

Although he was a son, he learned obedience from what he suffered.
—Hebrews 5:8

GOD'S WILL REVEALED IN SPECIFIC INSTRUCTIONS

Like any road map, the Bible has specific directions. I recall a trip Muriel and I took to London. We knew the sights we wanted to see. We talked with people who had been there, we watched videos, read travel books, and maps. We wanted to visit Tate Museum. But examples, descriptions, and principles would never have gotten us to the Museum. We needed specific directions.

The principles and commands of Scripture are never in conflict. You cannot justify violating a direct command by going with a broader principle. "I must lie," Tan says, "because I love Kristin and don't want to hurt her." No, the commands are God's official application of some principle and must be obeyed. My choice in applying a principle doesn't have God's authority and can't go against a clear command from God. The fact that no command covers a specific situation doesn't set us free to do as we please. We are still bound by the principles of Scripture. So we need both the principles and the commands to know God's will.

GOD'S WILL REVEALED IN JESUS

God didn't just make up rules. God's laws come from His own character. They express His will that we be like Him. We might not understand if He just sent instructions and gave us examples of Bible characters. He Himself came to show us what the Father is like *(John 14:7-11; Heb. 1:1-3)*. The exciting thing is this: Jesus in the flesh is our standard for life. He is God's supreme revelation of His will for our lives.

God's will is that we be like Jesus. Four Scripture verses appear in the margin. After each reference below write the characteristic of Jesus the verse describes. I have written the first response as an example. Put a check beside the attributes you want to develop more fully during this study.

❏ *Luke 22:27 Servanthood—Jesus served others regardless of their position in life*

❏ *John 15:9* _____

❏ *Philippians 2:8* _____

❏ *Hebrews 5:8* _____

God's revelation is more than truth about the unseen world, given to satisfy our questions. Revelation shows us what God wants us to be and do. The Holy Spirit enables us to become like Jesus; and Jesus is God's standard for the Christian. Seeing how far we fall short of reaching that standard can be discouraging, but if we don't first see our need, we'll never attempt to meet it! The characteristics of Jesus that I listed were servanthood, love, humility, and obedience.

Even with our map for living we will make wrong turns. But God always provides a way back! A serious disciple of Christ has at least two reasons to obey:
1. We want to know what will bring joy to the one we love. We want to please Him by doing what He wants. *"You are my friends,"* Jesus said, *"if you do what I command"* (John 15:14). Love makes obedience to God's rules a joy because the result is fellowship with Jesus.
2. Obedience is practical. I need direction and only the road that God has laid out for me will work. The Psalmist said, *Oh, how I love your law! (Ps. 119:97).*

In *Psalm 119:105* David said, *Your word is a lamp to my feet and a light for my path.* Give an example of how Bible study has guided your path.

In summary, God reveals His standard for Christian living in four ways. They all reinforce each other: (1) principles of Scripture; (2) example of Bible characters, whether good or bad; (3) direct commandments; and (4) the example of Jesus.

Has any truth become clear or especially important to you, perhaps demanding some response on your part? If so, you may wish to enter it in your journal for today.

 See if you can remember the key words in this Scripture and fill in the blanks.

All Scripture is _____ by God and is _____ ____ _____
the truth, _____ error, _____ faults, and _____
_____ for right living, so that the person who serves God may be fully
_____ and _____ to do every kind of good deed.
_____
_____

—2 Timothy 3:16-17, GNB

INTERPRETING HIS MESSAGE ·················· [DAY 4]

Do your best to present yourself to God as one approved, a workman who does not need to be ashamed and who correctly handling the word of truth.
—2 Timothy 2:15

Interpretation must be the most abused word in discussing the Bible. Many people believe that everyone's "interpretation" is valid, no matter how outrageously it twists the meaning of the Scripture. Curiously, the popular view of "interpretation," as if no objective truth exists, is most often used of the Bible. Can you imagine two teachers debating whether or not 2 x 2 = 4?

Interpretation always begins by determining what the author intended to communicate. Interpretation does not mean justifying my view of an issue by twisting the passage into a new shape. The writer may have used literal or figurative language, but the task is to understand the intended meaning, not impose our own "interpretation" on the written material.

 Can you name an issue which tempts you to make the Bible say what you want it to say? Write one or more examples below.

We all struggle with some issues in the Bible. When we read the Scriptures, our assumptions determine how we understand what we read. Our culture, life experiences, understanding of words and ideas come with us. Sometimes what we bring with us can lead us down the wrong path. Good interpretation uses principles to separate the message of the Bible from my own thoughts, opinions, and ideas; it is taking a look at Scripture objectively. If you wear sunglasses, you see the world through the shades you have in front of your eyes. To see what it really looks like you have to be willing to take the glasses off. That's what you must do in interpreting the Bible. Be willing to look at God's Word without whatever glasses you may have on.

THREE BASIC APPROACHES

The Bible is both a human and a divine book—*men spoke*, to be sure, but they were *carried along by the Holy Spirit* (2 Pet. 1:21). As is often the case, we tend to go to one extreme or the other. Some people understand Scripture strictly as a man-produced document, while others treat it as exclusively supernatural. Either approach will cause us to miss what God wants us to understand.

1. Those Who Treat the Bible as Purely Human

Some people reject any miraculous event recorded in Scripture as impossible. For example, they might say that the "feeding of the five thousand" was actually a story of sharing. A selfish crowd that had been hoarding their lunches gave after a boy shared his lunch. For people using this approach, miracles—like Jonah and the fish—are no more than mythological accounts given to teach spiritual lessons.

What are some problems with a purely human approach to the Bible?

With this approach, the interpreter's own natural reason sits in judgment on Scripture, filtering out the true from the false, the absolute from the less important. Many Christians, believe the authority of Scripture or even talk about "inerrancy," but refuse to believe or obey certain parts of Scripture because it doesn't fit what they want to do or have come to believe.

2. Those Who Treat the Bible as Exclusively Supernatural

Some interpreters treat Scripture as if it is only supernatural. Instead of working to understand the original meaning of a passage, they look for hidden meanings. They think the Bible is a mysterious, almost magical book. They use the Bible as a means of gaining insights, feeling impulses, or getting directions which may be completely unrelated to what the Bible author intended to communicate. This approach, though common, is magical; the reader looks for hidden, secret, or personalized meanings in the text.

I've done this myself. I wanted to be an overseas missionary but was a principal of a Christian school in the mountains of North Carolina. I considered it a temporary assignment. I kept thinking about the people in Japan needing a witness.

The problem was that no one thought we should go. Everyone said we should stay where we were. Wasn't God blessing the work? So Muriel and I went to the Bible to find guidance. We searched for verses that would tell us what to do. And we found them! We read *Deuteronomy 1:6 "You have stayed long enough at this mountain."* We did not realize that we were using the Bible like a Ouija® board, a magical divining rod. In those verses we were trying to get the biblical writers to speak to our current situation. Our "guidance" had nothing to do with the meaning intended by the authors. We were using a "supernatural" or magical approach to Scripture.

The Bible views itself as supernatural—God the Spirit is the Author behind the human writers. But the authors were inspired to communicate a specific meaning as the revealed truth of God. So even though the Bible may have some "picture language" in which the meaning is not obvious, the Bible is intended to convey meaning, not hide it. It is revelation. So our objective should be to understand the meaning the Author Himself intended to communicate.

List dangers of searching for a "magic text" to answer a pressing life need.

Several dangers exist, such as missing the Holy Spirit's genuine leadership and making wrong decisions, but the greatest danger may be in our relationship to God's Word. When we use the "magical" approach, we automatically stop looking for the real meaning of the Scripture; and that is a major mistake.

3. Those Who Treat the Bible as Divine/Human

Scripture is more than a human book from which we pick and choose or a magical book that grants our wishes. We need a balanced view that involves looking to Scripture as a divine revelation of things we could not otherwise know, but, as with any human communication, searching out the meaning intended by the authors. If we study the Bible, we'll discover that it's not meant to be a complicated puzzle. The Spirit wants us to understand the meaning He intended. With His help we can do it!

 Label the approach to interpretation you believe is being used in each of the following examples. (1) human; (2) magical; (3) divine/human.

____ "You have dwelt long enough at this mountain" means that I should move from my present location in the mountains.

____ Jesus didn't really die; He was drugged. On the third day he woke up and was able to free Himself.

____ "Go into all the world and preach the gospel" means that my church must take responsibility for world evangelization.

____ "If your brother offends you, go to him alone" means that I should not talk to anyone else about a person who has wronged me, at least not until I have confronted him and tried to solve the problem.

If our goal in Bible study is to find out what the Holy Spirit wants to say to us, we must treat the Book as both human and divine, not going to one extreme or the other. My answers to the exercise above would be 2, 1, 3, 3.

While serving as missionaries to Japan, we were asked to come to South Carolina, to lead Columbia International University; but our hearts were in Japan. We struggled with what we should do.

We scheduled time alone with God to seek His will for our lives. This time I wasn't looking for some personalized special hidden meaning in the Bible. Instead God guided us through the principles of Scripture. For example, I found that in Acts, God guided His servants on most occasions through His church. That suggested one way I should seek God's will would be to ask the church and my mission colleagues. I didn't want to go to my mission council because I knew they would never agree to my leaving, nor would the leaders of the Japanese churches. And the little church I was in the process of starting surely would not understand. But I gave in and agreed to follow the pattern I found in Scripture. To my amazement, the "church" was almost unanimous in urging me accept the call to Columbia as God's call. I had learned to use Scripture for what it was intended, treating it as a divine Book with God's own authority, but treating it also as a Book in human language that can be understood.

A BOOK AND A GUIDE

I have good news for you. We have more than a book, we have a Guide! The Holy Spirit guides us in understanding the Book.

 In the margin write out *2 Timothy 3:16-17* **from memory. Underline the key phrases you feel are speaking directly to you.**

ILLUMINATING MY MIND ⋯⋯⋯⋯⋯⋯⋯ [DAY 5]

Friends said I should get on the Internet so I could send and receive electronic mail. But I was scared. I'd used a computer for years, but had never read one of the manuals on my shelf. They might as well have been written in a foreign language. If I couldn't figure it out, instead of picking up a manual, I'd call an expert.

Some people approach studying the Bible the same way. The Bible sits on the shelf, so intimidating. How could I ever understand it? I'll just give the expert a call; I'll just wait to hear what the preacher says. The Bible was given to us to use. But like a computer manual, it takes effort to understand its message. The Holy Spirit, our personal guide, will guide us into all the truth we need *(John 14:26)*. I can't see the Spirit. So how does the Holy Spirit "illumine" my mind, throw light on the pages of Scripture? It's as mysterious as His activity in inspiring the Bible writers. How He does it, we may not know; but many of us experience it everyday.

DISCIPLINE REQUIRED

I haven't always had a hunger for God's Word. I once heard a Chinese evangelist say, "No Bible, no breakfast." I thought it made sense and started reading my Bible every day. But it was like eating sawdust. So I let it slide—the Bible, not the breakfast. Sometimes I'd have my "morning devotions," often I wouldn't. This went on for years. Finally, I was such a spiritual wimp that I became desperate.

At that point, I made a vow to the Lord that no matter what happened I would start the day with His "bread, milk, and meat," as the Bible calls itself. I thought He'd be pleased with that and work a miracle—the Bible would taste better than breakfast! But it didn't happen. It was still like eating sawdust.

I kept my vow, faithfully reading that Book each morning. Months later I noticed a radical change had come over me. It really happened without me noticing it. I suddenly had a huge appetite to study God's Word. If I had to miss the Bible or my breakfast, it would be no contest. I was a Bible junkie.

What had made the difference? I studied the Bible study and gave the Spirit the opportunity to teach me. The Spirit won't direct my life if I sit by waiting for His inspiration. Bible reading demands my best intellect, my best attitude, and my best time.

When is the best time for you to be alone with God? _____

What is the best place?_____

What "attitude adjustment" would make your time alone with God more productive?

_____

Would you like to make a firm commitment to read the Bible more often? Check your commitment:
❑ I will seek to read the Bible daily.   ❑ I will read the Bible on a regular basis.

If you aren't satisfied with your present relationship to the Bible, stop now and ask God to do a new thing in you. Share your experience in studying the Bible in your next group meeting, perhaps learning from the experiences of others.

ANOTHER SUBTLE DANGER

Growing disciples may face another challenge. Christians who have a life of intimate conversation with God may begin to think that what they understand about the Bible is perfect and that their understanding is as certain as the Bible itself.

We must never confuse the activity of the Spirit in inspiring Bible writers with His activity in illuminating our minds today. Both are part of His "revelation" activity—the Spirit gave us an accurate record of God's truth and He also helps us, subjectively, to understand it, but with a major difference. He inspired the Bible authors to write without error, but my understanding of the Bible's meaning is not without mistakes. I may mess up and when I do, I rarely know it. God does speak to us through His Word. He does lead us to understand the Word, but we need to beware of confusing our authority with that of Scripture.

To one there is given through the Spirit the message of wisdom, to another the message of knowledge by means of the same Spirit.
—1 Corinthians 12:8

We should have no disagreement on the virgin birth of Jesus. What's another major teaching on which most Bible-believing Christians would agree?

 To go or not go to movies may be a point of disagreement with some Christians. What's another doctrine or teaching Christians might disagree about?

 Why do you think there is not universal agreement on every point in the study of the Bible? Should there be? Explain your answer.

The Holy Spirit helps us understand the Bible. Each time you open it, ask God to help you understand its meaning. Christians agree on issues such as the divinity of Christ and the fact that He is coming again. We often disagree on details of future prophecy or the meaning of baptism. Maybe you've been helped by the Spirit more than you know.

 Review your journal entries. Underline five things about the nature of God or your nature, about your relationship to the Spirit or about His Book. Then answer the four questions in the margin.

1. What evidence do you find that the Holy Spirit is at work?

2. How hard have you been working to understand His self-revelation?

The Bible is a love letter showing us the face of our Beloved and pointing out what we'll be like when we become like Him. Here's my journal entry for today:

> Spirit of the Living God, thank You that in ancient times You unveiled God's character through the prophets and apostles, and that today You lift the veil of my heart to understand Your Book. I want to walk with You all the days of my life, listen carefully to Your whispers, follow the light You shine on my way, and bring You joy. Amen.

3. Do you make the time necessary to get better acquainted?

 In your journal express your response to the activity of the Spirit in giving you the Bible and in helping you understand it.

 Write *2 Timothy 3:14-16* from memory.

4. Are you committed to do what will bring Him joy?

---

[1] Hershel H. Hobbs, *What Baptists Believe* (Nashville: Broadman Press, 1964), 65.

a NEW CREATION

UNIT 4

In units 2 and 3 we studied the first two activities of the Holy Spirit. He originally created us in His image and then He revealed Himself to us in the Bible. In unit 4 we will take a look at the third activity of the Holy Spirit: God's plan for our redemption.

"Dad, I have terrible news. Bob has been critically injured in a diving accident. Please pray." Susan's voice at the other end of the line was controlled, though terror lurked around the fringes of her words.

I sat at my desk, stunned. I cried out to God to spare my son. Bob had just made a fresh commitment of his life to Jesus Christ. I thought of the conversation only three days earlier when he told me, "Dad, it's time for me to stop circling the harbor and launch out to sea." He was reaching the summit of his career as a photojournalist, his marriage to Susan was incredible, and I had just received another of his "Love Letters to Dad" he periodically wrote me. What a terrible time to die.

"Please, God," I cried. I felt so helpless; dared I even hope?

Ten minutes later the phone rang again. "Dad, Bob's with Jesus…." Hot tears flowed as if to wash away the pain, and friends gathered to comfort me; but the wound was too deep to be healed. Sons are meant to bury their fathers, not fathers to bury their sons.

In the following days I began to think about a father's love. I would have done anything to protect Bob. If given a choice, how gladly I would have taken his place. I would never choose to let him go, not for anyone. Yet, God did just that. He chose to give His Son for me. That's how much God loved me. I was not a family member, not even a friend. I was an enemy. And, unlike me, God did not have two sons left. He gave His only Son for me. Outrageous love motivated God to redeem a hostile, selfish, and angry world.

I had always thought of Jesus' love as supreme. Now I felt the impact of the Father's sacrifice. To give up one's own life is one thing, but the life of your son? I wondered if the pain I felt was like the pain of the brokenhearted God.

Unit 4 begins with the sacrificial love of the Father that made our redemption possible; His sacrificial love resulted in the death of His Son.

Unit Memory Verse

If anyone is in Christ, he is a new creation; the old has gone, the new has come!

—2 Corinthians 5:17

OUTRAGEOUS LOVE ·························· [DAY 1]

Through the work of the Holy Spirit, God sent Jesus to die—to become our Savior. What could motivate God to such sacrifice? When Bob died, I understood how much it cost God to love us. We will now explore the love that motivated redemption.

 "The Father's Cross" appears in the margin. Choose from the following list the statement you think best describes the main idea behind the poem.

❏ Sending Jesus to pay for our sins broke the heart of the Father.
❏ Only Jesus suffered on the cross.
❏ Giving His Son was more difficult for the Father than giving His own life.
❏ Out of love for us, God endured more pain than we can imagine.
❏ Other _____

The poem tells of the Father's love. I cannot imagine how God could love me enough to give His son to die for me. The learning activity asked for your opinion. You may have checked any but the second answer. Obviously, Jesus was not the only one who suffered on the cross. Perhaps you, too, have suffered a great loss. Would you have chosen to suffer that loss for the benefit of someone else?

 Think of the most painful loss you have experienced. From the list of words below, circle the word or words that best describe how that loss felt.

ALONE   FRIGHTENED   ANGRY
          DEVASTATED
AGONY   PAINFUL   HEARTBROKEN
          ACHE

Think about the greatest sacrifice anyone has ever made for you. Parents may send a son or daughter off to war, a firefighter may give life in a rescue attempt, but when do we sacrifice for an enemy? The Scripture says, *God has shown us how much he loves us—it was while we were still sinners that Christ died for us! (Rom. 5:8,* GNB).

 Tell God how very grateful you are that He loved you that much. Pause right now and write a prayer expressing your feelings to God.

LOST IMPACT

Once the word blood moved us. That single word summoned a vivid image of sacrifice and death. It stabbed our hearts with the pain of torture and senseless death. But no more. Movies and TV have so washed the screen with blood that the writers must work to invent fresh images of increasingly violent death to capture our emotions. We've also made blood very trivial when it comes to Christ. We sing about the blood in hymns and have no idea of what we are singing about. It doesn't have any effect on us. We don't understand the agony and suffering that Jesus endured.

The image of the cross also used to have a powerful effect. But today we have made the cross a piece of jewelry and have forgotten that it is a symbol of great suffering and agony. How do we regain the sense of loss, of outrage, of profound grat-

---

Redemption = "a release that occurs when a price is paid. Christ paid the price for our release from sin."

*The Father's Cross
Father,
What was your Gethsemane?
And when…
And where…
Did you decide,
Against all heart and reason,
To abandon your beloved one?
And that for me—
Oh, worthless substitute!*

*Like the piercings of a sword
We hear the cry,
"My God, my God, why
Hast thou forsaken me?"
"What love!" we say
And yet…
Was not the Savior's piteous lament
A mere echo
Of that broken-hearted cry
Reverberating down the endless
Corridors of heaven,
"My Son, my Son,
My beloved Son,
Why have I forsaken You?"*

*No greater human love,
Christ taught, than when one
Gives his life.
But Father's love explodes
Beyond the reach of
Highest, deepest, and most untamed
Flight of human thought—
God gave not life, but Son.
His only Son.
For me…*

itude when we speak of the cross? Before the crucifixion Jesus cried for a way out; His sweat poured to the ground like drops of blood. What was the agony for Him?

> **Read the story in *Luke 22:39-44* (also see *Matt. 26:36-45*). Write a brief explanation in your own words about how you think Jesus felt.**

Jesus went out as usual to the Mount of Olives, and his disciples followed him. On reaching the place, he said to them, "Pray that you will not fall into temptation." He withdrew about a stone's throw beyond them, knelt down and prayed, "Father, if you are willing, take this cup from me; yet not my will, but yours be done." An angel from heaven appeared to him and strengthened him. And being in anguish, he prayed more earnestly, and his sweat was like drops of blood falling to the ground."
—Luke 22:39-44

> **From the following list of possible reasons for Jesus' agony in Gethsemane, number your choices, beginning with the most likely reason for His deep struggle. Leave blank any emotions you think He did not feel.**
>
> ___ fear of death   ___ dread of a torturous death
> ___ horror of taking on our sin   ___ separation from His Father
> ___ terror of experiencing hell   ___ other _____

He may have feared death, especially so torturous a death, but I doubt that was His greatest struggle. Jesus knew His death wasn't permanent; He knew that He would rise again on the third day. He had predicted it. Maybe the identity with our sin was overwhelming to Him—experiencing the moral pollution of a whole world of sinners *(2 Cor. 5:21)*. Or perhaps something deeper caused the Savior's agony.

Have you ever been betrayed by a friend? Even more painful—have you been abandoned by someone you thought would stand by you no matter what? But at the critical moment that person was silent or absent. Perhaps you have felt such pain, not from a mere friend, but from a parent or family member.

THE DEEPEST AGONY

I believe the deepest agony of Gethsemane was not that Judas betrayed Him, nor that Peter would deny Him. The agony of Gethsemane was the horror of a break in the Trinity Itself. From all eternity, the Son was the delight of the Father's heart, the crowning joy of heaven. And now, the Son would bear our sin and the wrath of God would fall on Him instead of us. The heart of God, in a moment of time, would suffer an eternity of grief. *"My God, my God, why have you forsaken me?" (Matt. 27:46)*.

God made him who had no sin to be sin for us, so that in him we might become the righteousness of God.
—2 Corinthians 5:21

How do you feel about the cross, the blood? Have they lost their power? Tell God about your amazement that He loves you so much. Share with Him your love for Him and your gratefulness to Him. If you don't feel the joy, ask Him to restore it or, perhaps, to share with you this love for the first time.

> **Whatever your emotions—grief for His loss, gratitude for your gain, or just "the same old feeling"—isn't it time to tell Him? Whatever your heart's true condition, share your prayer with Him by writing it in your journal.**

> **In the space below, write the key words in the prayer you've already written in your journal, or perhaps you would like to write another prayer here.**

This course of study, doesn't focus on the activity of the Father and Son. But because God is inseparable, before we consider the specific activity of the Holy Spirit in our redemption, we need to be reminded of the sacrificial love of the tri-une God.

Write this unit's Scripture memory verse (located in the margin) on a card and begin memorizing it. If you have already memorized this and the other suggested memory verses, choose another verse you have read during this study. Write it on a card and memorize it along with the Scripture memory verses.

If anyone is in Christ, he is a new creation, the old has gone, the new has come!
—2 Corinthians 5:17

THE INCARNATION: GOD WITH US .... [DAY 2]

The unspeakable sacrifice of the Father and the Son amazes us, but what does the Holy Spirit have to do with the sacrifice? The Bible doesn't spell it out clearly, but it does give a hint: *Christ, who through the eternal Spirit offered Himself unblemished to God (Heb. 9:14)*. In some way the Spirit enabled Jesus to do what He did on the cross.

Scripture only hints about the Spirit's role in the crucifixion, but it goes into great detail about the role of the Spirit in the birth of Christ. We need to study the importance of the incarnation (God becoming human) to His whole plan of salvation. If the Spirit had not given human life to the eternal Son in the womb of a virgin, all the other activity of the Holy Spirit in our behalf would be meaningless.

Christ has always been a member of the Trinity, He is included in *Genesis 1:26, Then God said, "Let us make man in our image, in our likeness."* John's Gospel begins with the declaration that *In the beginning was the Word, and the Word was with God, and the Word was God. He was with God in the beginning (John 1:1-2)*. John credits Jesus with creation itself. He says, *Through him all things were made; without him nothing was made that has been made (John 1:3)*.

Incarnation = literally means "in flesh." Jesus came to us as God in flesh. "God with skin on."

 Paul agreed with John. Read *Colossians 1:15-17*. Based on these verses, who created all things?

Who holds all of creation together?

The Second Person of the Trinity, Jesus, has always existed, just like God the Father and the Spirit. Time is a part of our human experience, but God in some mysterious sense is beyond our concept of time. *"I am the Alpha and the Omega,"* says the Lord God, *"who is, and who was, and who is to come, the Almighty" (Rev. 1:8)*.

He is the image of the invisible God, the firstborn over all creation. For by him all things were created: things in heaven and on earth, visible and invisible, whether thrones or powers or rulers or authorities; all things were created by him and for him. He is before all things, and in him all things hold together.
—Colossians 1:15-17

GOD'S TIMETABLE
When did God decide to send Jesus to earth? Was the decision a last-minute attempt to straighten out the mess we had made of God's plan? Did God think up the idea in a moment of inspired daydreaming? NO! The Scripture tells us that Jesus becoming flesh was an accomplished fact long before mankind sinned.

 Read *Ephesians 1:4-5*. When did God decide to choose us as His adopted children through Jesus Christ?

Paul praised the Ephesian Christians for being among the first to put their hope in Christ *(Eph. 1:12)*. He affirmed that God's plan of redemption was put into place before the creation of the world.

For he chose us in him before the creation of the world to be holy and blameless in his sight. In love he predestined us to be adopted as his sons through Jesus Christ, in accordance with his pleasure and will.
—Ephesians 1:4-5

 In two other letters Paul affirms that the plan of salvation was in place before mankind sinned. In the margin, read *2 Timothy 1:9* and *Titus 1:2*.

This grace was given us in Christ Jesus before the beginning of time.
—2 Timothy 1:9

A faith and knowledge resting on the hope of eternal life, which God, who does not lie, promised before the beginning of time.
—Titus 1:2

Underline the phrase common to both verses that tell when God's plan was formulated.

God already knew we would sin and therefore needed a Savior. Man's sin did not create a need for the incarnation. Man's sin confirmed God's foreknowledge that a supernatural second birth would be necessary to re-create us in His image, capable of being like Him in His moral nature. God's plan was in place before time. *Revelation 13:8* describes Jesus as the *Lamb that was slain from the creation of the world.*

PROPHECIES OF THE INCARNATION

The Old Testament is the story of the preparation of Israel for the coming of the Messiah. The covenants with Abraham and Moses, the kingdom and the throne of David, the major and minor prophets, the fall of Judah and Israel, and the Exile—all show that *"man is not justified by observing the law, but by faith in Jesus Christ"* (Gal. 2:16).

The Old Testament prophets told of the coming Messiah. Isaiah introduced the Suffering Savior, who would bear our sins. (See *Isa. 53* and *61.*) Jeremiah, Daniel, and Malachi told about His life. Micah told us Jesus would be born in Bethlehem *(Mic. 5:2)!*

From your Bible, read the following verses from the Gospel of Matthew. Write the phrase common to all the verses. *Matthew 1:22; 2:17; 3:3; 4:14.*

Matthew wanted the Jewish people to know that the birth of Jesus happened just as the prophets said it would. Did you write *through the prophet?* I did. The last forerunner announcing the coming of the Messiah was John the Baptist, who was *"filled with the Holy Spirit even from birth"* (Luke 1:15). According to his father, Zechariah, John would *"go on before the Lord to prepare the way for him, to give his people the knowledge of salvation through the forgiveness of their sins"* (Luke 1:76-77).

Who first told you that Jesus Christ is the Savior of the world? Perhaps it was your parents, a youth leader, a friend, a teacher, or a neighbor. List their names in the margin. Pause and thank God for their ministry in your life.

THE ROLE OF THE HOLY SPIRIT IN THE INCARNATION

Both Matthew and Luke credit the Holy Spirit with the mystery of the incarnation. In Matthew's account, Joseph is told in a dream that he should take Mary as his wife because *"what is conceived in her is from the Holy Spirit"* (Matt. 1:20).

Luke tells us that the angel Gabriel told Mary that she would conceive. Mary asked: *"How will this be...since I am a virgin?"* (Luke 1:34).

The angel said, *"The Holy Spirit will come upon you, and the power of the Most High will overshadow you. So the holy one to be born will be called the Son of God"* (Luke 1:35).

The virgin birth is a supernatural event we'll never fully understand this side of heaven. Both Matthew and Luke clearly state that this miraculous event was the activity of the Holy Spirit. God's plan—in place before the beginning of time—was now put into motion. The holy child born in a manger in Bethlehem was named Jesus, *"because he will save his people from their sins"* (Matt. 1:21).

Why did Jesus come to earth in first-century Palestine? Paul said *the time had fully come (Gal. 4:4).* Many factors made this the right time and the right place for the birth of Jesus: (1) The Roman roads and postal system made the spread of the gospel possible. (2) It was a time of relative peace. (3) Greek was the universal language.

The most important factor, however, was that the legalistic Pharisees, the religious elite of their day, showed the impossibility of trying to keep the law in man-made systems. Paul explained the Jewish dilemma this way: *Before this faith came, we were held prisoners by the law, locked up until faith should be revealed. So the law was put in charge to lead us to Christ that we might be justified by faith. Now that faith has come, we are no longer under the supervision of the law (Gal. 3:23-25).*

 Read *Galatians 4:4-7* in the margin. What does the Spirit accomplish in the life of a believer? Complete the sentence below with these words: heirs, slaves, sons.

We are no longer _____ but _____

and _____.

But when the time had fully come, God sent his Son, born of a woman, born under law, to redeem those under law, that we might receive the full rights of sons. Because you are sons, God sent the Spirit of his Son into our hearts, the Spirit who calls out, "Abba, Father." So you are no longer a slave, but a son; and since you are a son, God has made you also an heir.
—Galatians 4:4-7

No longer prisoners of the law or slaves of sin, believers are rightful heirs of all the Son's inheritance. Today, thank God for the following: (1) His plan from the beginning of time to save you from your sins; (2) the work of the Holy Spirit in the incarnation of Jesus; (3) that you can be a child of God and an heir of all the riches of the Heavenly Father with Jesus Christ.

 Record in your prayer journal what being called a child of God means to you. List below some of the benefits you receive because you are a child of the King.

 Read the memory verse, *2 Corinthians 5:17*. Write it in the margin. Close your eyes and say it to yourself. Have a family member or friend check your accuracy. Write the verse one or more times to help you memorize it.

JESUS RELIED ON THE SPIRIT·····················[DAY 3]

All that Jesus did for our redemption, from birth to resurrection, the entire incarnation, was by the Holy Spirit's power. Let's look at ways Jesus depended on the Spirit.

 Do you remember the definition for *incarnation*? Write it in the space below. If you are having trouble defining it, look on page 51 to review the definition.

 From the list in the margin match the activity of the Spirit in the life of Jesus with the passage describing that activity.
___ 1. *Luke 1:35—The angel answered, "The Holy Spirit will come upon you, and the power of the Most High will overshadow you. So the holy one to be born will be called the Son of God."*
___ 2. *Luke 3:22—The Holy Spirit descended on him in bodily form like a dove. And a voice came from heaven: "You are my Son, whom I love; with you I am well pleased."*
___ 3. *Luke 4:1—Jesus, full of the Holy Spirit, returned from the Jordan and was led by the Spirit in the desert.*
___ 4. *Luke 4:18-19—'The Spirit of the Lord is on me, because he has anointed me to*

A. accomplished Jesus' sacrificial death

B. enabled Jesus to preach and minister

C. guided Jesus

D. healed the sick

E. brought about Jesus' birth

F. raised Jesus from the dead

G. testified to Jesus' identity

preach good news to the poor. He has sent me to proclaim freedom for the prisoners and recovery of sight for the blind, to release the oppressed, to proclaim the year of the Lord's favor."

____ 5. *Luke 5:17—One day as he was teaching, Pharisees and teachers of the law, who had come from every village of Galilee and from Judea and Jerusalem, were sitting there. And the power of the Lord was present for him to heal the sick.*

____ 6. *Hebrews 9:14—How much more, then, will the blood of Christ, who through the eternal Spirit offered himself unblemished to God, cleanse our consciences from acts that lead to death, so that we may serve the living God!*

____ 7. *Romans 8:11—If the Spirit of him who raised Jesus from the dead is living in you, he who raised Christ from the dead will also give life to your mortal bodies through his Spirit, who lives in you.*

The Holy Spirit worked in every event in Jesus' life. When Jesus healed, overcame temptation, taught, prayed, and endured His crucifixion—everything was attributed to the Spirit's power. Answers: 1. e, 2. g, 3. c, 4. b, 5. d, 6. a and 7. f.

If the powerful Son of God, Himself deity, needed the Holy Spirit's presence and power, how much more do you and I? Yet, we often try to live the Christian life as if the Spirit doesn't matter. Many parallels exist between what the Spirit did in Jesus' life and what He can do in ours.

Consider your life. In the exercise below, identify ways the Spirit works in you that parallel what He did in the life of Jesus. I have completed the first comparison as an example. Read the Scriptures listed if you need help.

How the Spirit Helped Jesus   How the Spirit Helps Me

1. Jesus' birth by the Spirit's power   my new birth
   (John 3:5)
2. Jesus' prayer life   _____
   (Rom. 8:26)
3. Jesus' service empowered by the Spirit   _____
   (1 Cor. 12:4-7)
4. Jesus' crucifixion enabled by the Spirit   _____
   (Rom. 8:13)
5. Jesus' resurrection by the Spirit's power   _____
   (Rom. 8:11)

You will find the answers to the last learning activity in the following two paragraphs. Circle actions of the Spirit in the life of the believer.

We must completely depend on the Holy Spirit from new birth to our own death and resurrection. Born again by the power of the Spirit, we gain any wisdom, live godly lives, pray, and minister with power only to the extent that He enables us.

In powerful picture language, Paul draws parallels between Christ's death and our own "death" to the old life. Our death marked our entrance into life. Paul says Christ's death also points us to how we are to continue that new life. The Apostle draws parallels between Christ's resurrection and our own—spiritually in the past and physically in the future. Jesus needed the Holy Spirit—we need the Spirit more.

Was Jesus able to do His Father's will because He was divine or because He relied on the Spirit's power? If it were because of His divine nature, then we can never hope to follow in His steps. Yet that is exactly what we are told to do by Paul: Follow my example, as I follow the example of Christ *(1 Cor. 11:1)*. Paul then explained how: If we live by the Spirit, let us also walk by the Spirit *(Gal. 5:25, RSV)*. Jesus said He was sending the Spirit for this purpose *(John 14:16-17)*. So we have exactly the same resource Jesus had to live His kind of life: the Holy Spirit within.

Jesus told His disciples it was to their advantage that He was going because only then would they receive the Holy Spirit (see *John 16:7-14*). Before He ascended to heaven, He said, *"You will receive power when the Holy Spirit comes on you" (Acts 1:8).*

 Read *John 16:7-14* in the margin and circle the things Jesus says the Holy Spirit (Counselor/Spirit of truth) will do.

Jesus attributed His powerful ministry on earth to the work of the Holy Spirit. *"The Spirit of the Lord is on me,"* Jesus said in *Luke 4:18*. Believers today have access to that same power source. Jesus intended that we live a victorious Christian life. He does not mean for us to be a prisoner of sin, to fail, or be defeated and discouraged, as though we had no Holy Spirit to set us free and empower us.

 Here's my prayer response to these truths. Join me in the prayer or tell God your thoughts, feelings, and concerns.

Holy Spirit of God, thank You for the gift of a Savior. For His life, death, and resurrection. You hovered over the Son, empowered Him, enabled Him. It's beyond my ability to understand, but You stand ready to do the same things for me. I don't have the words to let You know how thankful I am, but I want my life to prove my gratitude. That will happen only by Your work in me, so I now ask for that powerful work with confidence that You keep Your promises. Amen.

 Do you need to rely on the Spirit more in your life? Note it in your journal. Is there something you need to share with your accountability partner?

CONVICTION: WE NEED REDEMPTION ·············· [DAY 4]

The Holy Spirit touches me deeply and personally when He convicts me of my sin. All that Jesus did would be wasted, at least for me, unless the Spirit convinces me that I need a Savior. The rebirth experience Jesus spoke of to Nicodemus in *John 3* begins with the Holy Spirit convicting us of our sin. The Spirit must show me my sin so that I may repent, ask forgiveness, and receive salvation.

 Describe what the Scripture memory verse means as you now understand it.

Without conviction we would never become new creations in Christ. In *John 16:8* Jesus explained that the Holy Spirit would *"convict the world of guilt in regard to*

"I tell you the truth: It is for your good that I am going away. Unless I go away, the Counselor will not come to you; but if I go, I will send him to you. When he comes, he will convict the world of guilt in regard to sin and righteousness and judgment: in regard to sin, because men do not believe in me; in regard to righteousness, because I am going to the Father, where you can see me no longer; and in regard to judgment, because the prince of this world now stands condemned.
"I have much more to say to you, more than you can now bear. But when he, the Spirit of truth, comes, he will guide you into all truth. He will not speak on his own; he will speak only what he hears, and he will tell you what is yet to come. He will bring glory to me by taking from what is mine and making it known to you."
—John 16:7-14

If anyone is in Christ, he is a new creation; the old has gone, the new has come!
—2 Corinthians 5:17

"When he comes, he will convict the world of guilt in regard to sin and righteousness and judgment."
—John 16:8

It is to your advantage that I go away; for if I do not go away, the Helper shall not come to you; but if I go, I will send Him to you (John 16:7, NASB).

sin and righteousness and judgment." We can depend on the Spirit to show us our sin if we are open to His conviction. Even believers can shut out the Spirit and deny that they are sinning. Fortunately, the Spirit does not give up and go away, for the Father loves and disciplines His children *(Rev. 3:19)*. When we feel the conviction of the Spirit, we should rejoice—God loves us so much He doesn't want us to continue hurting ourselves or others. Conviction of sin is a blessing to a believer.

> **In *John 16:7*, look for why Jesus said His return to the Father was for your advantage. Check the best answer from those that follow the Scripture, or write your own response.**
> ❏ As long as Jesus remained, they wouldn't have the Holy Spirit in them.
> ❏ Having the Holy Spirit in you is better than having Jesus only with you.
> ❏ The Holy Spirit will not come to you until you turn from all your sins.
> ❏ Other _____

The first two statements are true, the third is false. We can't summon the Spirit by turning from our sins. The Holy Spirit comes to us first and shows us our sins.

THE WORLD'S RESPONSE TO CONVICTION

The work of the Holy Spirit can sometimes be painful. When the Spirit convicts me that I am a sinner or that a particular thought or behavior is wrong, I feel guilty. Many in our culture believe that guilty feelings are the "root of all evil." Their goal is to get rid of guilt feelings. But just as physical healing sometimes involves physical pain, the route to spiritual restoration involves confronting our own guilt and sin.

My friend had a disease causing him to feel no pain in his hands and feet. He caused himself serious injuries, eventually hastening his own death, because of his lack of feeling. He felt no pain, but the absence of pain was harmful rather than good.

> **Write your own moral to the story of my friend comparing our need to recognize our sin to his need to feel physical pain.**

If the Spirit doesn't convict us, we are something like my friend—only ours is a form of spiritual disease—our senses become dead to sin. The ability to feel guilt is a wonderful gift. We've been given a sense of soul-pain (guilt), a conscience to warn when we are spiritually ill. The greatest danger is to feel no pain of guilt. Guilty feelings are spiritual warnings, and we need to give immediate attention to what is causing our guilty feelings.

Search me, O God, and know my heart; test me and know my anxious thoughts. See if there is any offensive way in me, and lead me in the way everlasting.
—Psalm 139:23-24

> **Read *Psalm 139:23-24* (margin). Make these verses a regular part of your prayer life. Be sensitive to the Spirit as He convicts you of sin.**

THE OPPOSITE EXTREME

We can also have a sense of guilt when we actually are innocent. Spiritually sensitive people often confuse temptation for sin. For example, young men have come to me with a burden of guilt for the attraction they feel for a particular girl.

I explain that finding a girl attractive is not sin, but can easily become a temptation to sin. As long as you keep saying no to temptation, it stays temptation, not sin.

Satan likes to get in there and mix us up. If he can't trip us into sinning, he will make us believe we have sinned, because misplaced guilt is destructive. For example, many of us feel bad when we stand up to another person or say no. Christians often must face rejection for standing up for the truth. The price of obedience may include rejection or anger from those who disregard biblical standards. We may feel regret when we have been rejected but regret is not guilt.

 Have you suffered some kind of penalty because you stood for what you knew was right?   ❑ yes   ❑ no   Did you feel guilt or regret?

If what we did wasn't wrong, the feeling isn't legitimate guilt. A feeling of sadness about what we have done can come when we do the difficult but right thing, like confronting a person over a sin. Feeling bad about it, especially if we did the right thing poorly, is legitimate, but a feeling of guilt is not legitimate. These feelings may be the work of an over-sensitive conscience or the accusations of Satan.

How can you tell when guilt is appropriate and when it's not? The answer is the Word and the Spirit! Study the Bible and see how it defines the attitude or action in question. Our conscience can be our guide only if we have an informed conscience. Our moral judgment must be molded by what God has to say. We need both the Bible and the leadership of the Holy Spirit to guide our moral judgment. We humans can rationalize and excuse any selfish impulse or unworthy motive. We need the Holy Spirit to sensitize our conscience.

If we could go to a counselor who was always right, we would probably go see them often! We have access to such a counselor and He is free of charge. The word *Helper* in *John 16:7* (NASB) is also translated *Comforter* (KJV) or *Counselor* (NIV).

 Briefly describe a time when you felt guilt for something that was not your fault. Then briefly describe a time when you needed to feel deserved guilt.

I felt undeserved guilt when

I felt (or needed to feel) deserved guilt when

Most of us have experienced undeserved guilt. Some people struggle every day under a sense of personal worthlessness and shame. But ultimately every one of us has done wrong. We need to recognize our deserved guilt. When all the arguments of innocence and guilt are fully explored and the Judge gives the verdict, it is "guilty as accused." Every one of us is guilty of sinning against God and man. We are guilty of harming ourselves. I don't readily admit my guilt, even to myself, until the Holy Spirit sensitizes my conscience to see things truthfully. He was sent to *"convict the world of guilt in regard to sin and righteousness and judgment"* (John 16:8).

THE SPIRIT CONVICTED ME
At an early age I was desperately afraid of hell. My father, upon hearing my fear, asked me a question: "Have you sinned?" I nodded yes. Even worse, he asked, "And what was your sin?" That was my pain; I didn't even need to think about my answer.

Sobbing, I blurted out, "I lied." It was finally out. I was a confessed sinner.

"Any other sins?" I couldn't remember, but Dad helped me remember others.

Finally we prayed. I gave my life to the Savior. Since I was only a child, I could not begin to appreciate all that the Holy Spirit did in my life that day. I was sorry enough for my sin, but primarily I feared punishment. I had heard of hell, and I knew hell was for sinners. Jesus was for sinners, too. I ran to Him, opened my heart to Him and felt His warm embrace. With that embrace came peace.

"Son of man, I have made you a watchman for the house of Israel; so hear the word I speak and give them warning from me. When I say to a wicked man, 'You will surely die,' and you do not warn him or speak out to dissuade him from his evil ways in order to save his life, that wicked man will die for his sin, and I will hold you accountable for his blood."
—Ezekiel 3:17-18

Indeed, when Gentiles, who do not have the law, do by nature things required by the law, they are a law for themselves, even though they do not have the law, since they show that the requirements of the law are written on their hearts, their consciences also bearing witness, and their thoughts now accusing, now even defending them.
—Romans 2:14-15

What shall we say, then? Is the law sin? Certainly not! Indeed I would not have known what sin was except through the law. For I would not have known what coveting really was if the law had not said, "Do not covet."
—Romans 7:7

Those who sin are to be rebuked publicly, so that the others may take warning.
—1 Timothy 5:20

But it was many years before I fully understood the grace that I received that day.

I was asked to give a message on the death of Christ. As I prepared the message, for the first time in my life I felt sorrow that Jesus was on that cross because of my sin. My heart was broken by grief for what my sins did to Him. I mourned the hell I caused my Savior. That was the work of the Holy Spirit. Not everyone will have the same outward response, but the evidence of the Spirit's work is grief for the wrong I have done my Savior.

How did the Holy Spirit convince you of your sin when you first turned to the Savior? Was it through the painful consequences of some sin? your sense of weakness before a persistent temptation? Or not a sin, but a sense of loneliness or emptiness? Who helped you see your need? parent? preacher? teacher? book? Bible?

Below list all the ways you can remember that God used to make you aware that you needed a Savior.

In the margin read *Ezekiel 3:17-18; Romans 2:14, 15; Romans 7:7* and *1 Timothy 5:20*. As you read, underline any means the Spirit uses that were not part of your own experience.

Though it is the task of the Spirit to convince people of their sin and its consequences, the Bible does not teach all the methods He uses. It does tell us what the Spirit uses to bring conviction: the preached Word, one's own conscience, the Bible, and the example of those who sin, along with the consequences of their sin. In these ways and in direct whispers to the heart, the Holy Spirit does His convicting work. At the time of my rebirth I felt free and forgiven. Never again would God see me as a polluted, self-centered sinner. He sees me as clean and innocent as Jesus.

OUR RESPONSE TO THE SPIRIT'S CONVICTION

Have you heard the convicting whisper of the Spirit as you read? Do you have a repetitive sin that the Spirit continues to bring to your attention? If so, confess your sin, repent, and receive forgiveness before you continue this study.

Perhaps you are safe in Jesus and sure of it. For you, the Spirit's work of convicting the world of judgment to come is no longer your dread, but do you grieve over what your sin did to Jesus? Do you dread bringing Him pain again? Have you ever felt deeply what your sin means to Jesus? Perhaps today is the day the Spirit will break open your heart and let your love burst forth in grief and gratitude. Tell Jesus of your sorrow for whatever sin the Spirit may convict you of. If no moral sin comes to mind, consider the sin of running your own life for your own benefit. Thank Him for what He did to wash away the guilt. He will delight to hear what is on your heart.

In the margin or in your journal write this week's Scripture memory verse from memory if you can. Review your other Scripture memory verses.

[DAY 5] ⋯⋯⋯⋯⋯⋯ THE MAGNIFICENT RE-CREATION

The price Christ paid for our release from sin is called *redemption*. All the Spirit's activity since man's fall has been redemptive, God has taken the initiative to provide us with a way back into loving oneness with Him.

Jesus coming in person to pay the redemptive price and the Spirit preparing us through His convicting power to want salvation would come to nothing if something didn't happen to change us into a different kind of person: a God-compatible person. *If anyone is in Christ, he is a new creation; the old has gone, the new has come (2 Cor. 5:17).* Theologians call it *regeneration.* God the Spirit who "generated" us in creation, now "re-generates" us, transforming us into altogether different people. That's the turning point in our spiral down, away from God.

BIBLICAL DESCRIPTIONS OF SALVATION

Salvation is a word that encompasses all God ever did for us and all He ever will do. *Regeneration* describes one part of the total salvation process. Other words, such as *justification,* describe other aspects of our salvation.

 The following is a list of terms that describe parts of salvation. Describe in your own words each one as you now understand it.

Conviction _____

Faith _____

Repentance _____

Forgiveness _____

Justification _____

Regeneration _____

Read the following paragraphs describing what takes place when a person becomes a believer, watch for key words and phrases. Underline terms from the list above and circle any synonym I used in place of the technical word.

The Holy Spirit convinces us that we are sinners in need of a Savior. Finally He breaks through our denial, and we recognize our need of a Savior! We believe certain basic facts about Jesus and about our own condition. We feel sorrow for our sin. We turn from our sin in repentance and trust our lives to the Savior. I have just described complete or biblical faith. Biblical faith means more than simply believing.

When we respond to God in faith, He forgives our sins; He blots out the record of our sins and declares us righteous. This we call *justification*—just-as-if-I'd never sinned! At the same time, in some mysterious way God transforms us at the core of our nature into something new and different. We call this change *regeneration.*

If you are already a Christian, what happened when you were "born again" (regenerated, re-created). What changed? God changed something about every part of your personality—the way you think, how you feel, and what you choose.

 Below give an example of the major changes as you remember them, or as others saw them in you. If you were too young to remember, make your list from a later time in life when you may have recommitted to live for Him.

Your mind (how you thought)—what viewpoints changed? How did your thinking change about your values, priorities, and purpose?

Your heart (how you felt)—what attitudes changed? What changed in your likes and dislikes, who you liked to be around, who your heroes were? How did your feelings about yourself and God change?

Regeneration = "Being born again with a brand new life. A fresh start with God."

Justification = "to be made right before God."

Don't you know that all of us who were baptized into Christ Jesus were baptized into his death? We were therefore buried with him through baptism into death in order that, just as Christ was raised from the dead through the glory of the Father, we too may live a new life.
—Romans 6:3-4

Your will (your ability to make choices for God and against sin)—did bad habits stop, good habits start? Did you experience any changes in lifestyle?

A MAGNIFICENT NEW CREATION

You have just described a magnificent new creation. You! Regeneration sets in motion a great building project. Restoration begins when we trust in Christ and begin a continuing process of change that lasts a lifetime.

The doctor held a tiny creature by her heels. *Why is she so blue? I wondered. And why is she so silent? I thought babies started off with a cry.* Nurses hurried and the doctor whacked my baby across the behind! She let out a giant cry, startling me with her lung power, and bringing relief to a delivery room.

INCREDIBLE POTENTIAL

Who was this new creature? She was the same little person who had been residing for a time in her mother's womb. But now that she had been born, she experienced new dimensions of life! She could communicate, breathe on her own, develop loving relationships, and grow, without the restrictions of her former life.

The following paragraph describes three new potentials a believer receives that he or she did not possess before spiritual birth. Circle the three abilities I identify and write them in the margin along with any additional examples of how you would compare physical birth with the new birth.

Jesus taught that we must be born again *(John 3:3)*. When we experience the new birth, we are the same person physically as before. But what a radical transformation we have experienced! Now we can communicate with God, we can develop a relationship of intimate companionship with Him, and we can grow more like Him. We have become a new creation through the process called *regeneration*. We were originally generated through birth. Now we are re-generated, born again. You might identify other ways a believer receives new potential. Did you circle the opportunity to communicate, to develop a relationship, and to grow more like Him?

THE COMPLETION OF OUR TRANSFORMATION

The Bible compares the new birth to dying *(Rom. 6:1-11)*. I sat on the side of my bed, head bowed, tears flowing, grieving the loss of my eldest son, Bob. My youngest, Kent, stood by me, trying to comfort a heartbroken father.

"Dad," said Kent, "Bob is all you ever wanted him to be—and more. He is just like Jesus. He's free and fulfilled." The same Bob, who lay dying in a hospital one moment, now experiences new dimensions of life, new potentialities!

And so it is with us. The same person who lived out life in a dim shadow land, now has come alive in Jesus. We died, as it were, and have been resurrected to a new life. We don't know exactly how it was done or even exactly what happened, but we experience a radical transformation into a whole new dimension of being. *The old is gone, the new has come.* Sort of like a death. Or a birth. That's the work of the Spirit. The story of God's amazing grace never ceases to amaze. You know it well. But how would you tell the story to someone who came to you and said: "I really want to be a Christian. I want to be sure everything's OK between God and me"?

New Potentials We Receive

1.

2.

3.

Others:

Justification = "to be made right before God."

In the margin write out in non-technical words how you would answer, explaining God's plan of salvation and telling how to commit his/her life to Jesus.

Although your words may be different, did you list the following ideas? I am a sinner and deserve God's judgment. I can't save myself. Jesus took my penalty and died in my place. Jesus rose from the dead. Jesus demonstrated the Spirit's power to conquer sin, death, and hell. I receive Him by faith when I confess my sin and turn from it. I trust Him and make Him Lord of my life. He forgives my sin, makes me His child, and changes me into a new person, from the inside out. He is my daily companion.

Did the gospel story you wrote above include each of those actions on God's part and on yours? Circle any item you left out. Now the most important question of your life: Have you taken those steps?

A STORY OF NEW BIRTH

Yesterday I received a phone call from Kimie. My heart leaped for joy. For weeks Kimie has been asking questions about the Trinity, God's sovereignty and her choices, the deity of Christ, and the state of her father who recently died. She said she believed all I told her was true, and sometimes she was excited about it all. But she wasn't ready to turn her life over to Jesus, at least not unconditionally.

I said, "Kimie, you can study, pray, and attend church, but that will never make you a Christian." She was startled. She had been sure that by doing those things and trying hard to be a better person she would gradually become what she wanted.

"No, Kimie," I told her last week, "you can't grow into it. Sooner or later you must make a choice. You must decide."

"One of these days" she said and left for school in another city. That was last week. Yesterday she called to tell me, "I did it! I decided for Jesus!" And her joy had already begun to surge.

 Have you done what Kimie did? If not, I encourage you to do it now. Go back to what you and I wrote of God's plan of salvation and make that into a prayer of faith. Commit your life to Him unconditionally. Then thank Him that He's a promise-keeping God; He has indeed forgiven you and made you His child.

 If, on the other hand, you are sure that you have already made the salvation transaction with God, whether you can remember all the details or not, tell Him again how grateful you are for His great salvation, including remaking you into an altogether new person. The new you has all sorts of potential the old you never had.

 Practice saying the memory verse without looking. This week use the verse in a conversation you have with a friend, family member, or stranger. Tell someone how grateful you are for all that God has done for you.

 On the course-map on the inside front cover place a tiny check mark by the three activities of the Spirit that we have studied.

CLOSE CONNECTION

In this unit we will learn how to keep the close relationship with the Spirit that comes with regeneration.

Jim, the school bully, stalked me after school every day, week after terrifying week. Like some evil presence, he haunted my life by day and my dreams by night. Finally I ran out of ways to evade him. I lingered in the school building long after everyone else had gone home. Everyone but Jim, that is. From the second floor window I could see him by the front entrance. Suddenly, my eyes glimpsed someone familiar. Walking down the sidewalk was the most wonderful sight I had ever seen—my father!

Down the stairs and out the door I ran. My comforter had come. What relief! Holding my father's hand, I marched bravely past Jim and waved cheerily, "Hi, Jim!" What strength! What joy!

We may not be 10 years old, but we, too, are haunted by the evil presence of an enemy set on destroying us. We have experienced a lifestyle of worry—about a job, date, car we have or don't have, about our families or friends, about our looks or popularity. We have been ambushed by greed or booby-trapped by an explosive tongue. The Bible and church are supposed to help, but the enemy just keeps stalking us.

To cope with the enemy, we try one thing and another, but nothing works for long. Then down the street comes help. The Comforter has come! *(John 14:16, KJV)* The name Comforter means "the one called alongside," but He doesn't just shepherd us through the crisis of the moment. Unlike my father, the Holy Spirit is with us forever. Better than that—the strong Comforter doesn't just walk beside us; He resides inside us! Greater is he that is in you, than he that is in the world *(1 John 4:4, KJV)*.

I will pray the Father, and he shall give you another Comforter, that he may abide with you for ever; even the Spirit of truth; whom the world cannot receive, because it seeth him not, neither knoweth him: but ye know him; for he dwelleth with you, and shall be in you (John 14:16-17, KJV).

The Spirit acts in me, however, only to the extent I respond. The connection is faith. He acts, but I must respond for the power to flow. So there are two parts to the "close connection"—His part and mine. These two activities—His work inside me and my faith response—are our themes in this unit. The Holy Spirit takes up residence inside me and I keep a close connection through faith.

[Unit Memory Verses]

Do you not know that your body is the temple of the Holy Spirit, who is in you, whom you have received from God? You are not your own.
   —*1 Corinthians 6:19*

The just shall live by his faith.
   —*Habakkuk 2:4, KJV (also Rom. 1:17; Gal. 3:11; Heb. 10:38)*

THE "IN" RELATIONSHIP ··························· [DAY 1]

God's Spirit within us supplies what we need for successful Christian living. What a mystery! He whom the heaven of heavens cannot contain, the infinite One, everywhere present, in some mysterious way lives inside me.

 The Holy Spirit is not the only one who lives in us. Read the verses in the margin and complete the following.

John 14:16-17—The _____ lives in believers.
John 14:23—The _____ and _____ live in Christians.
Ephesians 3:17— _____ resides in the believer.

The Bible teaches the Father and the Son also live in the believer. The relationship we call the Trinity is our human minds' attempt to understand God. We see from Scripture that God relates to us as three persons, but He is only one God. So in this amazing love relationship the fullness of the Godhead—Father, Son, and Holy Spirit—all love and live in the believer.

Does God—the Trinity, what Bible scholars call the Godhead—live somewhere inside my body? Perhaps a key to unlock the mystery is the way the Bible uses the word *in*. The focus is not on the physical. Jesus speaks almost interchangeably of being in us and our being in Him (*John 14:20; 15:4-5*). They seem to mean the same thing. Obviously we are not in Jesus in a physical sense.

 In your Bible, read *John 15:1-17* and circle every "in" you can find.

Most but not all of these "in's" speak of our being in Christ and Christ being in us. However, in *verses 7, 9-11* we find a different perspective. Check the items below that Jesus said we are to have in us.

❏ His love ❏ His joy ❏ His commandments ❏ His words

Jesus is talking more about a relationship than a physical location. He intends for His words (*v. 7*) and His joy (*v. 11*) to remain in us. He wants us to remain in His love. In bypassing the physical aspect, which is a mystery we may never fully solve, Jesus moves on to something far more important. He speaks of a relationship.

The Theological Dictionary of the New Testament calls the "in Christ" relationship the "in" of fellowship.[1] We might call it closeness—a relationship with another Person so close the only way to describe it is to speak of His being in us and we in Him. Believers share with Jesus an identity of life, a deep love (*v. 9*).

Have you ever been so deeply in love that you couldn't think about anything but the person you loved? The human experience of love is a mere shadow of what this spiritual in-love-ness was meant to be. God's love of us dwarfs any human example.

The only good way to describe the love relationship God intends with us is to say it's the way the Father and the Son relate (*John 14:9-10*)! The Father and the Son love each other. They love me. They are in each other and they are in me. The Father, the Son, and the Spirit—one God—is in me, and I am in Him!

God has planned my life around Himself—uninterrupted companionship with the greatest Lover who ever lived! I don't have to take a number and wait my turn, and He doesn't just put up with me. Outrageous mystery—God actually wants my company! He wants to be best friends. That's a hint of what it means to be "in Christ"

God actually wants my company!

and for Christ to be "in me"—a new relationship that can't be fully understood by us. While we wonder about the mysterious physical part of us as God's home, we can rejoice in the mystery and focus on building the relationship between us.

WHAT THE SPIRIT DOES INSIDE

The Holy Spirit of God has always been at work. In the Old Testament He worked primarily in an external way. Since Jesus' death and resurrection, however, the Spirit has a new relationship. Now He lives inside us.

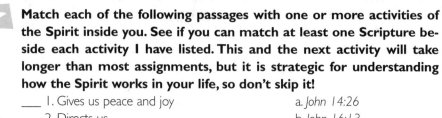

Match each of the following passages with one or more activities of the Spirit inside you. See if you can match at least one Scripture beside each activity I have listed. This and the next activity will take longer than most assignments, but it is strategic for understanding how the Spirit works in your life, so don't skip it!

___ 1. Gives us peace and joy	a. *John 14:26*
___ 2. Directs us	b. *John 16:13*
___ 3. Assures us that we are His	c. *Acts 13:2*
___ 4. Guides us into the truth	d. *Acts 16:6-7*
___ 5. Calls us to serve Him	e. *Romans 8:14-16*
___ 6. Teaches us the thoughts of God	f. *Romans 14:16-17*
	g. *1 Corinthians 2:10-11*
	h. *1 John 4:13*

Look up the following Scriptures and write in your own words how they describe the activity of the Spirit in your life.

Psalm 51:11-12 _____

Ephesians 3:16,20 _____

Ezekiel 36:27; Galatians 5:22-23 _____

Zechariah 4:6; Matthew 10:20; Acts 1:8 _____

1 Corinthians 12:7,11 _____

Ephesians 6:18; Jude 20 _____

The Spirit whispers to my spirit, "Remember, the Heavenly Father is your daddy and we—the Father, Son, and I—will be here forever, no matter who is after you" (see *Rom. 8:15-16; 1 John 4:13*).

The Holy Spirit is the Master Teacher, helping our minds to understand all the truth we need to know about God and His will for us (*John 14:26; 16:13; 1 Cor. 2:10-14; 1 John 2:20*). He helps us understand Scripture and guides us in our personal decisions. Sometimes He impresses us with the way to go; sometimes He blocks the way we planned to go (*Acts 16:6-7; Rom. 8:14*).

His name is Comforter because that is what He does. When we're in trouble He gives peace and joy that can't be explained in terms of our early environment or present circumstances (*John 14:16; Rom. 14:17*). When we stumble, even falling like David into gross sin, the powerful Spirit of God lifts us up and recommissions us. He never abandons us (*Ps. 51:11-12*). He strengthens us with the same power He used when He loosed Jesus from the grip of death (*Eph. 1:19-20; 3:16,20*). The Spirit energizes us for godly living (*Ezek. 36:27; Gal. 5:22-23*), for powerful ministry (*Zech. 4:6; 1 Cor. 12:7,11*), and for bold witnessing with wisdom (*Matt. 10:20; Acts 1:8*).

God's Spirit even assists us in our prayers (*Eph. 6:18; Jude 20*). Often we don't know how, or what to pray (*Rom. 8:26*). But He knows and inspires our prayers. Even inspired prayers may fall short, and that's when the Spirit goes straight to the throne and tells the Father exactly what we needed to pray.

I've given you several activities of the Spirit in the preceding four paragraphs. Reread them and underline each activity you identify. Circle the two activities you appreciate most.

With the Spirit, nothing can stop you! A successful life in the Spirit is no fantasy, nor is it just for the spiritually elite. Effective Christian living is here, now. God the Spirit lives in you in such a close relationship that everything He promises is within your reach.

 Tell the Comforter how much you appreciate Him. If you've never called the Spirit by name in prayer, why not now? Tell Him how much you love Him, how grateful you are for what He has done, is doing, and will yet do. Ask Him to develop those areas of your life that you are struggling in. Jot down your thoughts of today's encounter with the Spirit in your journal.

INDWELLING AND BAPTISM BY THE SPIRIT ·············· [DAY 2]

The Spirit brings about the "in" relationship—Jesus in you and you in Him.
• How does a person get into the "in" relationship?
• How can I be certain that I have such a relationship?

BAPTISM BY THE SPIRIT

The New Testament talks about the "in" relationship with the phrase baptism by the Spirit. Read *1 Corinthians 12:13* in the margin. Confusion exists when people use it to describe different aspects of the Christian experience.

 Briefly describe what the phrase *baptism by the Spirit* means to you. Then read the following paragraphs labeled 1, 2, and 3, describing three ways people use that phrase. Circle the paragraph or phrases that are similar to what you wrote.

We were all baptized by one Spirit into one body—whether Jews or Greeks, slave or free—and we were all given the one Spirit to drink.
—1 Corinthians 12:13

In this study I seek to avoid controversial issues in order to focus on the central theme all believers can agree on—that God provides a supernatural quality of life by His Spirit to all who surrender to, obey, and trust Him to do what He promises.

Each of the three interpretations of *baptism by the Spirit* contain an element of practical truth. Different believers use the term in different ways trying to describe their experience of the Christian life.

1—At some time in their life many Christians drift away from a close relationship with the Lord. Some believers then experience a profound turnaround as if they have been saved all over again. When unbelievers turn to Christ, we call the experience *repentance and faith*. When a believer experiences repentance, we might call such a turnaround yield and trust. We experience a deeper level of repentance through such an experience. Some Christians say this is *baptism by the Spirit*.

2—The second description uses *baptism* in a way that some Christians use the term *filling.* The people understand the baptism or filling of the Spirit to be a one-time experience like salvation. After salvation a person seeks the additional experience of baptism by the Spirit. This baptism provides the power to live a more-effective Christian life. Some Christians who hold this understanding believe spirit baptism is accompanied by sign gifts, particularly speaking in tongues.

This view is not the kind of "filling" Paul tells us to have when he says, "keep on being filled with the Spirit" (literal translation of *Eph. 5:18*), or the kind of fresh "anointing" of courage the disciples received by being filled with the Spirit a few days after their filling at Pentecost (*Acts 4:31*). Scripture uses the term filling to refer to different experiences with the Spirit as we shall see in a later unit.

3—The third view describes the salvation experience only.

Approaches one and two describe some people's personal experiences. The only way the Bible actually uses the phrase *baptism by the Spirit* is to describe entry into the original salvation relationship. Carefully read again *1 Corinthians 12:13*.

The phrase in biblical usage refers to initial regeneration by the Spirit. That's because the term baptism was commonly used to mean "initiation" or "act of joining." When you are initiated into Christ, you are "baptized" by the Spirit into that relationship. As I understand *Romans 6:3-5* the act of water baptism demonstrates in a visible way what the Spirit of God has already done in the life of a new Christian.

Since the Bible uses the phrase *baptism by the Spirit* to describe regeneration, am I saying that those who use the term differently are wrong? No, I personally prefer using the term to refer only to the salvation experience, but those who use the term to describe a life-changing, after-salvation experience also have a point. Remember that we are dealing with picture words. They draw on another use of the term baptism. The word is sometimes used to mean "suffused with," as in a baptism by fire, or an overwhelming experience like the crucifixion—*"I have a baptism to be baptized with,"* said Jesus (*Luke 12:50*, KJV). Since the Bible never uses it to describe a second encounter with the Spirit, it may be confusing to use it that way, and that's why I avoid using it.

BAPTISM AND FILLING

The term *filled* is a picture word, like baptism, and therefore capable of conflicting interpretations. *Filled,* rather than baptism, is the picture word the Scripture uses to describe how the Spirit works in the life of Christians. Because being filled with the Spirit is so important, unit 8 will be devoted to living a life filled with the Spirit.

BAPTISM AND INDWELLING

Since I am using the phrase *baptism by the Spirit* to describe your entry into the Christian life, baptism is the beginning of a life with the Holy Spirit living in you. We can use the term *indwelling* to describe the same reality. *Indwelling* means "to live in." When we have been regenerated or baptized by the Spirit, the Spirit lives in us.

In *Romans 8:9* (margin) circle the phrase that speaks of indwelling. Below write the meaning of the verse in your own words.

According to Paul, who is indwelt by the Spirit? ❑ all Christians
❑ only certain Christians

All Christians are baptized by the Spirit in the sense that I use the term and in the sense of *1 Corinthians 12:13*. Not all Christians, however, are led by, filled with, or controlled by the Spirit. Since Paul was so clear that every Christian has the Spirit

We were all baptized by one Spirit into one body—whether Jews or Greeks, slave or free—and we were all given the one Spirit to drink.
—1 Corinthians 12:13

Don't you know that all of us who were baptized into Christ Jesus were baptized into his death? We were therefore buried with him through baptism into death in order that, just as Christ was raised from the dead through the glory of the Father, we too may live a new life. If we have been united with him like this in his death, we will certainly also be united with him in his resurrection.
—Romans 6:3-5

You, however, are controlled not by the sinful nature but by the Spirit, if the Spirit of God lives in you. And if anyone does not have the Spirit of Christ, he does not belong to Christ.
—Romans 8:9

dwelling in his or her life, why do so many seem to experience defeat? Unbelief prevents the Spirit from also guiding and controlling us.

 We have two Scripture memory verses this week *1 Corinthians 6:19* **and** *Habakkuk 2:4.* **Practice writing the verses in the margin. Check your work on page 62. Say the verses from memory.**

PRACTICAL EXPERIENCE: THE HAZARD OF UNBELIEF ·········· [DAY 3]

The Spirit lives inside me. He has all the resources of heaven to empower me. But what's wrong if I don't seem to experience a supernatural quality of life? A key source of difficulty comes from the connection between us. The current doesn't flow automatically. I have to throw the switch, and the "switch" is faith. *"The just shall live by his faith."* Not only are we justified by faith, but we also live out the Christian life by that same faith. The Holy Spirit within does His work when we throw the switch of faith.

When the Spirit of God confronts us with the challenge to believe, we must make a choice. We choose to practice either belief or unbelief. We need to look at our attitudes and actions. When we choose to disbelieve we don't obey Him. Our disbelief and disobedience say significant things about our attitude toward God.

 Before you continue, you may want to pray the prayer in the margin.

WHAT UNBELIEF SAYS ABOUT GOD

The father was distraught. Jesus' disciples had failed to live up to the advertisements. They couldn't cure the son's terrifying condition. Then Jesus came and the father said, "If you can, heal my son!" (*Mark 9:22*). "If you can?" What kind of question is that?

 By his statement, what was the boy's father saying about Jesus?

The crowd knew death when they saw it. So they scoffed and pointed at the visiting preacher, "Some healer he is! He doesn't even know the kid's dead. We know better!" (*Luke 8:53*). You know better? What kind of talk is that?

 By their laughter, what were they saying about Jesus?

The wind blew and the waves lashed over their boat, terrifying the fishermen. But one passenger on board leaned back against a pillow and went to sleep. "Enough of this!" The fishermen shook their leader awake. "Teacher, don't you care if we drown?" (*Mark 4:38*) "Don't you care?" What kind of question is that?

 By their question, what were the disciples saying about Jesus?

These people were making statements of unbelief. The father wondered if Jesus could handle his situation; the crowd believed more in their own judgment than His; and the disciples accused Him of being uncaring. These three stories startled me with

They laughed at him, knowing that she was dead.
—Luke 8:53

Jesus was in the stern, sleeping on a cushion. The disciples woke him and said to him, "Teacher, don't you care if we drown?"
—Mark 4:38

Without faith it is impossible to please God (Heb. 11:6).

what I was actually saying about God. I saw my "innocent" flirtations with unbelief as actually calling into question the very character of God. I was insulting Him!

 In the margin describe a time when you have allowed, or are now allowing unbelief rather than faith to control your thoughts and actions.

When we don't trust God we are actually questioning His power, His wisdom, or His love. We're saying, "You're not strong enough to handle my situation, to help me with my impatience, to meet my needs while I'm in school." We're saying, "I'm not sure You're smart enough to get me out of this jam, to guide me in the best way. I think I know a better way." Or we're saying, "You're powerful and smart enough, You just don't care about me." We call into question the character of God.

WHAT UNBELIEF DOES TO GOD

The first problem with unbelief is that it displeases God. God is displeased when we don't trust Him; He has been dishonored, and by a family member at that!

 According to *Hebrews 11:6*, what is absolutely essential to please God?

WHAT UNBELIEF DOES TO ME

When we don't trust Him, it makes God sad. Our unbelief doesn't block God's unconditional love, but it does prevent God from working in our lives. Because God chooses to respect our freedom, unbelief hinders God's activity in us.

The tragedy of unbelief does more than just hurt God—it hurts us. Unbelief short-circuits the flow of divine energy—the Holy Spirit won't act freely in the life of one who doesn't trust Him. For salvation, for growth, for success in the Christian life, for power in ministry, faith is the connection through which God's power flows. Is trusting God difficult in some areas of your life? your family? your health? your job? your school? your friends? your habits? your future?

 List your main areas of fear, defeat, or worry. Then, to the right of each note the characteristic of God you need to trust: His power, wisdom, or love. In other words, why are you unable to trust God? If you have been calling into question, by your responses to the Holy Spirit, more than one of those characteristics of God, list both or all three. I have given you an example.

MY AREAS OF FEAR, DEFEAT OR WORRY
My temper

GOD'S CHARACTERISTIC THAT I NEED TO TRUST
His power to control situations

_____ _____

_____ _____

_____ _____

My wife Muriel called herself a chain worrier. With six children she thought, *What's a mother for, but to worry?* One night our daughter was out in a storm. What has happened? An accident? Will the state highway patrol call? At that point, the Lord spoke to Muriel: "Do you really want to keep on like this the rest of your life?"

"Oh, no," she cried out. "Please, Lord. I don't want to live this way. Deliver me."

God heard her prayer. As she turned our children over to the Lord, He made a basic change in her personality. She trusted God with our children instead of seeking to do His work for Him. In the days after her prayer she wrote this couplet:

Anything, anytime, anywhere,
I leave the choice with You;
I trust Your wisdom, love, and power
And all I need You'll do.

Muriel began identifying the characteristics of God she needed to trust. She expressed her fears to God, and spent time focusing on His attributes rather than concentrating on her fears. Muriel experienced deep, lasting, worry-free change.

 Analyze Muriel's experience with worry. From the list below, check the best description of how God changed her pattern of thinking, feeling, and acting.

❏ Muriel chose to change, and she made the change in her own power.

❏ God challenged Muriel, and she responded in obedient faith.

❏ God enabled Muriel to see what she was doing to herself. She then chose to trust Him and began practicing different behavior.

❏ God simply acted, Muriel had nothing to do with the change.

Life-change involves two parts—His and ours. The Spirit confronts us with our need and supplies the power to obey. We must choose to obey. The second or third response is correct. The third response more completely explains the process.

 Try to say the Scripture memory verses from memory. Ask your parents or a friend to listen while you repeat the verses to them sometime today.

HOW MUCH FAITH IS ENOUGH? ·················· [DAY 4]

The prophet, Habakkuk, said, "All justified people live by faith." Life is to be lived in the power of the Holy Spirit. But, how much faith do we need to live a spirit-powered life? Do different people have varying levels of faith?

 Read the following passages that appear in the margin and describe the level of faith Jesus saw in these different—and unlikely—people.

The disciples in *Matthew 8:26* _____

The foreign woman in *Matthew 15:28* _____

The Roman army officer in *Luke 7:9* _____

Little. Great. Greatest. The disciples asked for more faith. Jesus' response appears in the margin.

 According to *Luke 17:5-6* (in the margin), how much faith does a person need for God to work in great power? ❏ little ❏ great ❏ greatest

Jesus taught that if you had faith as large as a tiny seed, you could say to this mountain, "Up! Into the sea," and it would jump (*Matt. 21:21*). Jesus says, "If you have

He replied, "You of little faith, why are you so afraid?" Then he got up and rebuked the winds and the waves, and it was completely calm."
—*Matthew 8:26*

Then Jesus answered, "Woman, you have great faith! Your request is granted." And her daughter was healed from that very hour.
—*Matthew 15:28*

When Jesus heard this, he was amazed at him, and turning to the crowd following him, he said, "I tell
(continued on next page)

you, I have not found such great faith even in Israel."
—Luke 7:9

The apostles said to the Lord, "Increase our faith!"
He replied, "If you have faith as small as a mustard seed, you can say to this mulberry tree, 'Be uprooted and planted in the sea,' and it will obey you."
—Luke 17:5-6

It's not how much faith you have but what your faith is in.

Suggested Prayer:
Spirit of the Living God, like the father with a demon-possessed son, I cry to You, "I do believe. Help me overcome my unbelief." I want to be strong in faith so that Your power may flow freely and effectively to help me to be all You designed me to be. I commit to You my body and my mind. Guide me in the directions You plan for me to go. Amen.

ever-so-little confidence in Me, you're connected to all My resources."

Let's think back to those three Bible stories at the beginning of yesterday's lesson. **Jesus acted anyway:** Notice that, though they doubted, Jesus acted anyway. **Jesus responded to a little faith:** The father's timid faith was enough: he cried out, "I do believe; Help me overcome my unbelief," (Mark 9:24) and his son was set free. **Jesus acted in response to belief:** The mourners standing around didn't believe; but Jairus, the religious leader whose daughter had died, did believe and the little girl rose to embrace her father. **Jesus acted on behalf of His disciples:** The disciples were in fear of their lives during the storm. Jesus rebuked them for their low-level faith (*Matt. 8:26*), but He stilled the raging seas anyway. In a sense, the issue is not how much faith you have but what your faith is in.

HOW CAN I TELL IF I HAVE ENOUGH FAITH?

How can I tell whether or not I have any faith at all? For example, how do I know I have enough faith when a broken relationship tears me apart?

The difference between hesitant faith and sinful unbelief occurs at the point of choice. Do I choose to follow God's way no matter how fearful my timid steps, or do I choose to say no to Him and go my own way? The evidence of faith or lack of it is obedience. Do I believe Him enough to do what He says? Bible scholars differ as to whether obedience is part of faith or simply the evidence of faith. Either way, Scripture teaches that we can't connect with God while saying no.

Faith is the only human response that connects with God. It lets the life of the Spirit flow to us and through us. Successful Christian living is trusting God to do what He says. So how is your Faith Quotient? average? above average? painfully low?

▷ **Ask the Spirit of God for a strong faith. Use the suggested prayer in the margin.**

▷ **Fill in the blanks of the memory verse. In the margin write out your memory verses for this unit, referring back to page 62 as necessary:**

Do you not know that your body is the _____ of the _____ _____, who is in _____, whom you have received from _____? You are not _____ _____.
—1 Corinthians 6:19

The _____ shall live by his _____.
—Habakkuk 2:4, KJV

[DAY 5] ·················· THE "SPIRIT" OF FAITH: OBEDIENCE

A friend of mine knows that moving in with her boyfriend is against God's will, but she does it anyway. Why?

▷ **From what you studied in day 3, what are three possible things about God that my friend may be having difficulty believing?**

1.
2.
3.

She might believe that God isn't powerful enough to provide her a life partner or to empower her to live a full life on her own. She may believe God isn't smart enough to know what's best for her, or she may think He doesn't care enough about her to work things out for her best interests. So she chooses to disobey God.

What might have happened if she chose to obey God even though she felt miserable and abandoned? She would have acted in faith. Timid, faltering faith, to be sure. But that obedience would be evidence she had enough faith to connect with the powerful Spirit of God.

 In the margin, read what James wrote about the relationship between faith and obedience. Write in your own words what these verses mean.

"Faith" and "deeds" are so intertwined that James says you can't have one without the other. A body without a spirit is a human body, but it's dead. James says our connection with God is the same. Faith that doesn't obey is no more than a corpse.

TWO COMPLEMENTARY TRUTHS IN SCRIPTURE

The Bible uses hard or challenging words like *repent, obey,* and *confess.* Those words emphasize the importance of positive, active effort on the part of the believer.

 Remember the Principle of Balance? If the hard words of Scripture are taken alone or to an extreme, what kind of Christian lifestyle and attitude develops?

The hard words show the responsibility of the Christian. Taken by themselves, they can lead to a "works" view in which we think we must earn God's favor. They lead us to become rigid and self-righteous like the Pharisees in Jesus' day.

The Bible also uses soft words like *love, trust,* and *surrender.* Those words emphasize God's activity rather than our effort.

 If the soft words of Scripture are taken alone, what kind of Christian lifestyle and attitude develops?

By themselves the soft words of Scripture can lead us to think, I just have to believe; I don't have to do anything, mentality. Good theology and Christ-honoring living always involve balance. Let's see how these hard and soft terms contribute to a balanced view of faith and obedience.

 We sometimes speak of the hard words as "lordship" and the soft words as "salvation." The following list contains words and phrases that describe aspects of our Christian experience. Draw an arrow pointing each concept either to the soft list (salvation) or the hard list (lordship).

Hard words/   Soft words/
Lordship   Salvation

1. grace
2. obedience
3. sanctification
4. repentance
5. no conditions
6. once for all
7. law as guide
8. moment by moment rather
   than once for all

We see the importance of balance—Scripture uses both concepts. We are to

What good is it, my brothers, if a man claims to have faith but has no deeds? Can such faith save him?

You believe that there is one God. Good! Even the demons believe that—and shudder. You foolish man, do you want evidence that faith without deeds is useless?

As the body without the spirit is dead, so faith without deeds is dead.
—James 2:14,19-20,26

Repent = "Turn from sin to live God's way of life."

Obey = "Follow God's commands."

Confess = "Admit your sins to God."

believe and emphasize both salvation and lordship. I drew arrows to salvation from numbers 1, 4, 5, and 6. I connect numbers 2, 3, 7, and 8 to lordship. You might choose differently. The important fact is that we recognize the balance present in Scripture.

 Practice a little self-examination. Do you tend more toward the hard (law) or the soft (grace) words of Scripture? On the scale below place a check for where you see yourself.

LAW   ←————————————————→   GRACE

SAVED BY GRACE

In your Bible, read *Ephesians 2:1-10*.

In what way does Paul's view of faith/works seem to differ from the view expressed in *James 2:14, 19-20, 26*?

James said, "Faith works." Obeying God is how I show that I have faith. And what does Paul say? I paraphrase *Ephesians 2:8-10* this way: "By grace you have been saved through faith, a gift, not earned by your own effort. That salvation is accomplished by the work of the Spirit who re-created you to do good. That was God's original plan."

Paul rejoices in God's grace—God's free gift of full salvation to those who have earned hell. You can't *earn* a bit of grace, he says. But notice that Paul ends up in the same place James did: faith works. In fact, Paul seems to say here that the purpose of salvation is a changed life.

If my salvation depended on how good I acted or was, I'd always be wondering, *Have I done well enough to make it?* I know I'd never make it! "Jesus paid it all, all to Him I owe!" Salvation is by grace alone through faith.

SANCTIFIED BY GRACE

The Bible speaks of our salvation in another way. Through our salvation we were "sanctified." The word *sanctified* literally means "set apart." When God saved you He set you apart from sin for Himself. Sometimes the word is translated "holy," so we are called a holy or "set-apart" people. Other times the word is translated, "saint," so all believers are called saints. By new birth I've been sanctified—that is, made holy—set apart from sin and it's consequences to God and His use.

The term *sanctify* has another meaning the way it is most commonly used. I may be officially declared a saint on the merits of Christ, but am I saintly? *Saintly* means to be like Jesus. So the second use of the term *sanctification* is the activity of the Holy Spirit in me from the time of my initial salvation till I reach heaven. As a Christian, I continually change from what I was by natural inclination to what God desires for me to be. I become more like Jesus. This second use of the word *sanctification* is the term that best describes the whole process of living life in the Spirit.

The case studies below picture what happens when we get law and grace out of balance. Write either "law" or "grace" beside each case study.

- John lives by the creed, "I'll work 'til Jesus comes." He lives with continual self-evaluation, always asking "Have I done enough?
- Jill's not a consistent Christian. Her motto is "God loves me anyway."
- Andy excuses his lack of discipline with a shrug, "Nobody's perfect," he says.

Balance is the key. In the case studies above, John is out of balance on the law while Jill and Andy are out of balance on grace.

What does it profit, my brethren, if someone says he has faith but does not have works? Can faith save him?

You believe that there is one God. You do well. Even the demons believe—and tremble! But do you want to know, O foolish man, that faith without works is dead?

For as the body without the spirit is dead, so faith without work is dead also.

—James 2:14, 19-20, 26 (NKJV)

Salvation is by grace alone through faith alone!

Sanctified = "Set apart. Holy. Saint."

Saintly = "To be like Jesus."

REPENTANCE FOR SALVATION, OBEDIENCE FOR SANCTIFICATION

Just as saving faith included repentance or turning away from sin as well as believing what He promised, so sanctifying faith includes obedience as proof that we really do trust Him. There's no way to succeed in the Christian life than to trust and obey.

 Trust and obedience both involve learning and growing. Think of any skill you have developed—from learning to walk to using a difficult computer program. In the margin describe the process you followed to develop that skill.

Did you write how others taught you, trying and failing, learning from mistakes, and practicing to develop skill or knowledge? In exactly the same way we develop our ability to trust and obey God.

 Read *Romans 6:16* that appears in the margin. How does offering ourselves and becoming "slaves" fit the process of developing any life skill? Check all that apply.
❏ The more I practice, the easier a behavior becomes.
❏ Learning includes failing and trying again.
❏ My daily choices have little effect on my life.
❏ Difficult actions may lead to a life of greater meaning and purpose.

Discuss this verse in your group session. I checked the first and fourth response.

THE LAW AS GUIDE

Galatians 5:25 says, Since we live by the Spirit, let us keep in step with the Spirit. But how does He guide me in my walk and tell me the difference between right and wrong?

God's will is written out for us. The Spirit and the Bible work together to guide us. The Spirit gave the law to convict us and bring us to our senses. By the law we understood how sinful we were, so that we would run to the Rescuer *(Gal. 3:24)*. Once we recognize our sin and run to Jesus for grace, we no longer have to fear the law. *Therefore, there is now no condemnation for those who are in Christ Jesus (Rom. 8:1).*

The law has another duty. To the believer it is a guide, showing the attitudes and actions that are pleasing to God. Nothing the Spirit suggests to my spirit can be opposite to what He revealed in the Bible. He spotlights God's will written in Scripture. To the sinner, the law is like a light showing the dirt to be removed, condemning. To the saint that same law is like a flashlight, showing us clearly the way to go.

 Read David's *Psalm* in the margin. Are you transitioning from fearing the law to loving the law? On the scale below place an "S" to indicate how you felt about God's law as a new Christian and an "N" to show how you feel now.

FEAR   LOVE

To fear the Word of the awesome and holy God is an appropriate response. When we first come to know Him fear may be our only response to the law. Then, as we grow in grace and obedience, we learn that the law is for our benefit; and we come to love the words God has given us.

God's part of our "close connection" is so incredible and so beautiful. It isn't just a set of instructions we try to follow, but the Holy Spirit coming to be an intimate, inside companion! Our part is incredible, too—to trust God! That's the beginning and end of the Christian life—oneness with God through faith.

Don't you know that when you offer yourselves to someone to obey him as slaves, you are slaves to the one whom you obey—whether you are slaves to sin, which leads to death, or to obedience, which leads to righteousness?
—Romans 6:16

Oh, how I love your law! I meditate on it all day long.
—Psalm 119:97

¹ *Theological Dictionary of the New Testament*, Vol. 2 (Grand Rapids, MI: Wm. B. Eerdmans Publishing Co., 1964), 543.

SPIRALING UP

This week we'll look at how the Spirit leads us to become more and more like Jesus—
how He leads us on the upward spiral of spirit-filled living.

"What's wrong, Matsuyama San?" I asked.

"I'm not a Christian." He explained, "I was drunk, got in an argument with some guy, and chased him with a baseball bat. I'm no Christian."

Matsuyama, a skilled electrician, had been saved from a life of drunkenness.

"Did you ever get drunk and fight before you became a Christian, and then feel bad about it?"

"Only if I got beat."

"Don't you see, Matsuyama San? Since the Holy Spirit lives in you, when you sin you're miserable. Your misery because of your sin is evidence that you really are a Christian!"

Six months later Matsuyama arrived at church with shoulders sagging. "What's wrong?" I asked.

"I really chewed out a man who works for me. A Christian doesn't blow up like that."

A year later, on New Year's Day, Matsuyama wasn't a happy man even though by then he owned a leading electrical contracting firm. When I asked him what was wrong he replied, "The check bounced." In Japan people commit suicide when they can't pay their bills by December 31. He owed many people and was counting on being paid for his work on a major project. Finally, paid by check on the 31st, he rushed to the bank. But the check was worthless.

"Did you beat up the contractor?" I asked.

"No. But my stomach is standing up" (that is, "I'm very angry").

A year later in church Matsuyama told this story: "Two of my employees had been deceiving me for months. They called in sick, took a company truck, and drove to another town to moonlight, drawing sick pay for the times off. So I planned to surprise them when they returned to town. As I sat there, planning the violence about to happen, I thought about Jesus, how Jesus forgave me of a lifetime of evil, and how much loss Jesus had suffered to provide that forgiveness. As I sat there, thinking about Jesus," Matsuyama said, "I choked up and went home."

That Sunday morning we celebrated the incredible victory of the Holy Spirit in the life of a sinner saved out of Buddhist idolatry, from hopelessness to hope, from failure to success, from bondage of an explosive temper to freedom and power. Matsuyama was developing Christlikeness. I encouraged him to deal with his employees, but I knew he would do it with compassion and a forgiving spirit.

Review the course map on the inside front cover. This week gets us to the beginning of the spiral that represents our growth into Christlikeness. Many verses in Scripture describe this upward spiral in different ways, but one of my favorites actually reads like a spiral. It's a little longer than most of our memory passages, but the verses are short and it really does flow upward in a beautiful spiral toward likeness to Jesus.

Unit Memory Verse

For this very reason, make every effort to add to your faith goodness; and to goodness, knowledge; and to knowledge, self-control; and to self-control, perseverance; and to perseverance, godliness; and to godliness, brotherly kindness; and to brotherly kindness, love. For if you possess these qualities in increasing measure, they will keep you from being ineffective and unproductive in your knowledge of our Lord Jesus Christ.

—2 Peter 1:5-8

TURNING POINT: A CRISIS IN LIFE ···············[DAY 1]

In this study we are dealing with the believer's faith walk. The spiral begins with the salvation experience. From that point believers move either toward Christlikeness or away from Christlikeness by lifestyle choices.

Matsuyama was on a spiral, and so are you! In fact, every believer is. The only question is whether the spiral is going up or down. We are not all spiraling at the same rate—some are on the fast track and others on the slow track, either up or down. This spiral represents our movement toward or away from Christlikeness.

The spiral does not picture our standing with God in terms of salvation. Rather it pictures our change into the character of Jesus. Believers have the opportunity to *work out your salvation with fear and trembling (Phil. 2:12)*. When we experience regeneration, the process of sanctification begins. We begin to grow in faith and grace day by day. Now we are on the spiral, moving toward or away from Christlikeness as we make choices for or against Christ's Lordship.

 To help picture the spiral, here are some descriptions of people with certain characteristics: faithful, cheater, prideful, peaceful, ill-tempered, loving, hateful, moral, humble, worldly. List these words under the appropriate heading below:

Spiraling Away from Christlikeness

Spiraling Toward Christlikeness

How do I tell if I'm on an upward spiral? I'll begin to display these character traits:
• loves unlovable people more each year,
• has joy and peace in the midst of life's storms,
• endures difficult times with strength and grace,
• gentle with those who are hurting,
• humble about personal accomplishments,
• rejects sinful impulses with increasing strength.

I have described the fruit of the Spirit *(Gal. 5:22,23)*! That's how to tell whether I'm on the upward spiral. Do I feel, think, act, and react more and more like Jesus?

 To get an initial feel for your own spiral, go back and rate yourself on each of the characteristics in the last paragraph. In the margin beside each characteristic, put an "F" by any fast growth items, "S" by any slow growth items.

Sometimes I'd like to think I'm in neutral or a spiritual holding pattern—not growing, but not spiraling down either. But that's not possible. We're always on the move, either up or down.

 Read *Matthew 12:30* in the margin. In the space below explain what the verse teaches about being in a spiritual "holding pattern" or in neutral.

Fruit of the Spirit = "outward expression of the inner person—love, joy, peace, patience, kindness, goodness, faithfulness, gentleness, and self-control."

"He who is not with me is against me, and he who does not gather with me scatters."
—*Matthew 12:30*

If I think I'm in neutral, I'm actually rolling backward downhill. If my sails aren't raised to the wind of the Spirit, the tide is pushing me toward enemy territory.

ANALYZING THE PROBLEM

What's the basic problem in the life of believers who aren't "being transformed from one degree of Christ's glorious likeness to another?" They are either (1) ignorant of some basic truth essential to growth, (2) living in rebellion against God, or (3) not trusting God.

1. _____

2. _____

3. _____

In the margin see if you can summarize in a single word each of the three problems just described.

God gives us the ability to choose. We can consciously choose to move away from His revealed will, or we can drift away unconsciously. Either course is movement away from the abundant life Christ came to give us. I wrote ignorance, disobedience, and unbelief, but any synonyms for these words will do.

Are you spiraling up to greater likeness to Christ? Can your family and friends see it? If you have some uncertainty, or at least you're not satisfied with your present rate of progress, reflect for a moment on which of the three problems contributes most to the slow growth or decline.

Check the word or words you feel describe what is hindering your progress.
❏ ignorance   ❏ disobedience   ❏ unbelief

REVERSING THE DOWNWARD SPIRAL

God's plan is for the newborn Christian to keep growing. While none of us leads a sinless Christian life, our lifestyle should reflect an upward journey. But for many of us, because of ignorance, disobedience, or unbelief, our Christian life is not one of growth. We slip into a downward spiral, getting out of touch with the Spirit.

When we realize that we are on a downward spiral away from God, we need to make a U-turn. Bible scholars call this a "crisis" experience. The basic meaning of the word crisis, both in the dictionary and in biblical teaching, is simply "a turning point." And without that, no one spiraling downward will ever spiral upward.

Though no one in my father's family or church would have guessed it, he was fighting a losing battle in his attempts to spiral upward toward God. Then came the turning point. Challenged by a dramatic turnaround in the life of a friend, he went to his room and one-by-one yielded to God each part of his life. Everything. As a result of that experience, his life was transformed. He said there was no special emotion, no vision, but from that time on doing the will of his Lord became his first priority.

Like my father, a person can have a crisis, a turnaround, that is a rational transaction with God. The intensity of the experience may depend on one's personality, expectations, or the time and the way he or she has resisted the will of God.

Have you had a turning point since your initial conversion? If so, briefly describe it in the margin.

Once we have made the decision to turn around, the Holy Spirit is free to begin the process of transforming us into greater likeness to Jesus.

Where are you in life's spiral? In which direction are you headed? Check one response: ❏ **upward**   ❏ **downward**   ❏ **not sure**

Wherever a person may be on the spiral of life, the way to change direction from downward to upward is to turn around. We call that turn-around "repentance." Repentance means a change of mind that results in a change of behavior. Without this turning, the only direction possible is down.

Jesus wants to be Lord of our lives. He has to be Lord if we are moving upward in the spiral. We can choose between two masters: Christ or sin. Notice we cannot choose to put ourselves in control. When we think we are in control, sin is our real master. Of these two choices, which do you want to control you: Christ or your sin nature?

Are you ready for the big turnaround? If you are, now is the time to settle the direction your life is headed. In repentance, acknowledge the factors that have led you away from God. Yield to Christ's control. Ask for the Spirit's guidance as you seek to carry out your commitment in the days ahead.

 On the graphic below, list the "add-ons" from our memory verse, beginning with "faith" and ending with "love".

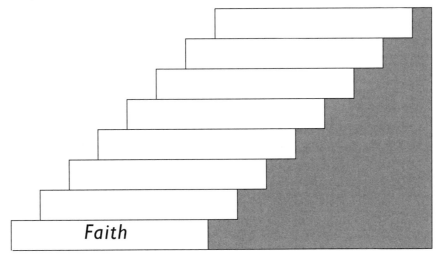

Faith

 What, in your own words, does our memory verse say will result if we don't keep spiraling?

KEEPING STEP WITH THE SPIRIT ················· [DAY 2]

"If you have come into life by the power of the Spirit," says Paul, "by that same Spirit keep on walking" (*Gal. 5:25*, my paraphrase).

The Spirit invites us to companion with Him all day every day. Companionship with the Spirit is not just a mystical, internal experience. In the process of transforming us, moving us up the spiral, the Spirit gives us resources we can see, touch, and experience. These resources are called *means of grace*. We use these means of grace to participate with the Spirit in His work of remodeling our lives.

THE DEVOTIONAL LIFE: COMPANIONING WITH GOD

The devotional life is one key resource for spiritual growth. The term devotional life includes anything that increases our fellowship with God. Prayer and Bible study are the basics of a devotional life. God is our source of power. Intimate communication with Him is the only way to live a victorious Christian life.

Jesus said, "I am the vine; you are the branches.... apart from me you can do nothing" (*John 15:5*). The only way to avoid a dry, lifeless Christian life is to consistently abide in Christ by meditating on God's Word and talking with Him in prayer. Companionship with God, walking with the Spirit, is not confined to just a daily devotional time.

So I say, live by the Spirit, and you will not gratify the desires of the sinful nature. For the sinful nature desires what is contrary to the Spirit, and the Spirit what is contrary to the sinful nature. They are in conflict with each other, so that you do not do what you want. But if you are led by the Spirit, you are not under law.
—Galatians 5:16-18.

Companion (v.) = "united in fellowship; to spend time with; to befriend."

Means of grace = "resources from the Holy Spirit including our devotional life, prayer, Bible, church, and adversity."

Each of us can be aware of His abiding presence and turn to Him spontaneously throughout the day. We can share our gratitude when things go well and call on Him to help when they don't. We can develop the habit of sharing our hearts with our Best Friend who is always there. I'll never get over the wonder that the Heavenly Father actually desires my companionship!

Check each item that plays a major role in your devotional life.
❑ I have a set time each day for devotional activities.
❑ I read and meditate on Scripture.
❑ I praise God and give Him thanks for my many blessings.
❑ I confess my sins to Him when I fail.
❑ I pray for my own and family needs and for other individuals and causes.

A Christian can routinely read the Bible, offer praise, and pray without any real awareness of God's presence. The devotional life can be mechanical, something to check off a list of good things to do. Going through the motions can lead to spiritual pride and self-righteousness. The big question is, What is the quality of your encounter with God? What kind of fellowship do you experience with Him?

On a scale of 1 (a dull routine, mostly just going through the motions) to 10 (an intimate, exciting companionship with God). Rank what your recent devotional times have been like by circling the number on the scale that most closely matches your devotional times.

1	2	3	4	5	6	7	8	9	10
Dull									Intimate

I, like you, want to develop more intimacy with God. I'll share my approach to the devotional life, but remember that my way isn't the only way. After I explain my devotional routine, I'll share some other ways that might fit you and your schedule.

MY APPROACH

I tried to have a personal quiet time after I made my big turn-around at age 12, but more often than not I skipped it in favor of more sleep or breakfast. At age 21, I told the Lord I'd read the Bible daily whether it had meaning for me or not, just as an act of obedience. Things didn't change except that I kept that promise faithfully, week after week. Then one morning I realized I had changed. I couldn't get along without that time with God. In fact, the Bible had come alive to me. It's been that way ever since.

My quiet time is every morning at 6:00. Why morning? Well, David said God would hear his voice every morning *(Ps. 5:3)*. Jesus set a powerful example by praying early in the morning, and a friend of mine once said he couldn't see tuning your violin after the concert was over! Some say they just aren't morning people, but it's important to have a set time or other things crowd out your time with God. The Enemy sees to that! I prefer early morning because there aren't many interruptions.

How much time should I set aside for my "date" with God? For some it may be 15 minutes a day alone with God. Many Korean pastors say for them 4 hours is necessary. For myself, I set aside an hour, and it is always too short! One thing's for sure, a hasty salute toward heaven isn't sufficient for building a meaningful relationship with God. The goal is companionship, not dutiful routine.

First, I sing aloud a couple of hymns. Singing sets my mood. No wonder the Bible contains so many commands to sing (See *Ps. 146:1-2; Col. 3:16*).

That's how I get started. How do you do it? This would be a great time to decide on your approach and then set some goals if you would like to change.

	Present Practice	New Plan
• Time and place of appointment	_____	_____
• Length of time spent in your "quiet time"	_____	_____
• How you begin	_____	_____

SCRIPTURE READING

After singing, I ask the Spirit to speak to me through His Word, then I turn to the Bible. I use a different translation each time I read through the Bible to keep it fresh and gain new insights. I read consecutively through each book. As I read I underline verses that give me a new insight about God, comforts my present heartache, convicts me of sin, or shows me a principle of life I didn't understand or had neglected.

Then I go back through and think about the parts I underlined, often praying these back to the Lord in His own words or asking Him to work them out in my life. If the underlined portion is something I want to be sure not to forget, I type it on a three-by-five-inch card and rotate those on my "refrigerator collection." That way I can memorize them.

That's my approach to devotional Bible reading. What's yours? Again, note your present practice, and set some goals if you desire to change:

	Present Practice	New Plan
• How often do you read the entire Bible?	_____	_____
• From what version(s) do you read?	_____	_____
• How do you "capture" what God is saying?	_____	_____
• How do you reflect on what you read?	_____	_____
• How do you memorize key passages?	_____	_____

PRAYER

Thanking God for His blessings, rejoicing in His beauty, and worshiping Him with adoring praise often come naturally through the songs or passage of Scripture. If not, I spend some time in worship, not asking for anything, just focusing on God.

Then I turn to "intercessory" prayer. I commit each plan for the day to the Lord, asking Him to use me for His purposes in each encounter and each activity, planned or unplanned. I talk to God about everything in my life—He invites us to, but I don't want to be selfish in prayer. I also pray for the needs of others.

I have a prayer list of people who are a special concern, divided by categories: unsaved, Christians in spiritual trouble, people with health needs or sorrow, and a catch-all of those making hard decisions, or having special ministry opportunities. Some people I pray for daily—family, close friends, and others for whom I have assumed a prayer responsibility. Others I pray for less frequently. Finally, I pray for the nations and for missionaries seeking to reach them. I want to be a world Christian on my knees! God loves the world; I want to love it also.

> **How would you evaluate your prayer life?**

	Present Practice	New Plan
• Is there a vital time of praise/worship/thanksgiving?	_____	_____
• Do I routinely confess sin?	_____	_____
• Intercession for personal needs?	_____	_____
• Intercession for others?	_____	_____
• Other prayer activities	_____	_____

> **Review each of the plans in the right-hand columns, pause now and commit those plans to the Lord. Don't feel you need to change everything instantly. Just take a step at a time—that's what spiraling upward is all about. Talk with the Lord about your desires and plans.**

> **The memory verse for this unit speaks of the spiral. Commit it to memory if you haven't already and write it out in the margin.**

[DAY 3]  PARTNERING: HOW THE CHURCH FITS THE SPIRAL

Instead, speaking the truth in love, we will in all things grow up into him who is the Head, that is, Christ. From him the whole body, joined and held together by every supporting ligament, grows and builds itself up in love, as each part does its work.
—Ephesians 4:15-16

We want to be on the upward spiral, growing daily to become more like Christ and to experience loving companionship with Him. We've seen how important our personal devotional life is, but we are mistaken if we think private prayer and Bible reading alone can make us all God intends. God has given us the fellowship of believers to support us in our upward spiral. Paul constantly reminds us that a major purpose of the church is spiritual growth—to "build up" believers. Church life is an essential ingredient of spiraling upward.

PURPOSES OF THE CHURCH

Any activity done by a group of God's people to honor God can be used to strengthen each member of the body, but Scripture emphasizes five major purposes of the church: worship, fellowship, discipleship, ministry, and evangelism. We'll study ministry and evangelism in later units.

Worship.—Public worship is directed toward God, bringing Him joy, but it also helps each person who participates to spiral upward. When we worship, we remind ourselves who God is. We think about His love and commitment to us.

> **In the margin list some of your experiences of growth through public worship.**

Did you list the spiritual joy you felt in singing together with other Christians? Or how it felt to understand a Scripture passage you never really understood before? Or a surge of faith as God's people united in prayer for a special need? Were you inspired to make an important decision?

Fellowship.—Fellowship in the early church was more than visiting for a few minutes after church, or even more than a "fellowship supper." Fellowship meant a family unity in which each member was committed to others in a caring relationship. Many of us would list fellowship as one of the major ways the church meets our needs. *Fellowship* means "supporting each other as you travel toward the same place." In God's family we are on a spiritual journey where we may encounter many obstacles. I'm glad to have the companionship of fellow believers on that journey.

 Can you identify a time when the fellowship of your youth group has been particularly important in your life? ❑ **Yes** ❑ **No If so, describe the circumstance.**

Fellowship means more than just company. Fellowship includes elements of accountability and guidance as well.

Discipleship.—Discipleship means to spiral up! It means to become a more faithful disciple of Jesus. Ways to disciple include preaching, teaching, small-group studies, and one-to-one relationships. The church as a whole also disciples through accountability and guidance.

• *Small group discipleship*—serves many purposes, both for fellowship and for discipling. Special benefits result from meeting in smaller groups, benefits not available to a large group. Think of your study group for Life in the Spirit, for example, or your Bible study class. These groups focus on discipling believers.

 List in the margin how you felt motivated toward discipleship as a result of your small-group meetings recently.

Maybe you wrote that you have been encouraged by your small group, or helped with a specific situation, or realized that others in your group have the same problems that you have. In a small group members strengthen and help each other, and small groups help hold each other accountable.

• *One-to-one discipleship*—A key element in serious discipleship involves having a relationship with someone for mutual accountability. Do you have a Christian best friend you can talk to about anything? I can't get along without mine. A prayer partner is the most common one-to-one relationship in the church body. Many people have chosen to go even deeper by enlisting an accountability partner.

Accountable = "Accepting responsibility for one's own actions."

Jason was in high school. He was a Christian who wanted someone to hold him accountable so he could grow spiritually. He asked a friend to meet with him once a week. His friend was startled when Jason gave him a list of very pointed and personal questions he wanted his friend to ask him every week. Here's his list:

• Ask me about my time each day with God—the content of my prayers, the truths I've learned from Scripture, the amount of time spent.
• Ask me about my language and thought life and how I've reacted when I've been angry.
• Ask me to list the amount of time spent with TV and what specific programs I've watched.
• Ask me how much time I've spent with my family and my attitude toward them.
• Ask about what I've done to combat sexual temptation; probe to see if I have done anything to feed an unhealthy sexual appetite. Ask about my relationship with the attractive girl whom I'm dating.
• Ask me about my motives in friendships.

Jason was serious about "spiraling upward"! Are you serious about it?

> **What questions would you want an accountability partner to ask you? Write out questions that would expose every area of your life in which you think God wants you to grow. Be honest and thorough.**

"If your brother sins against you, go and show him his fault, just between the two of you. If he listens to you, you have won your brother over. But if he will not listen, take one or two others along, so that 'every matter may be established by the testimony of two or three witnesses.' If he refuses to listen to them, tell it to the church; and if he refuses to listen even to the church, treat him as you would a pagan or a tax collector."
—Matthew 18:15-17

Did you know that the fellowship you enjoy with your church friends could be withdrawn? The New Testament is clear on the role of the church in the individual member's life: The organized church has spiritual authority over me. If I sin and refuse to repent, or if I teach false doctrine, the church's responsibility is to discipline me, bring me back into line. Paul rebuked the church in Corinth for failure to discipline a sinning member *(1 Cor. 5)*. Many churches, like Corinth, are defiled and weak because they don't do the hard work of disciplining those who are sinning, first by counsel and rebuke, and ultimately by separating from the fellowship if the gentler methods don't work.

The main purpose of church discipline is to restore the one who failed. We need the discipline of the church to help us grow spiritually. We must be open to our church's responsibility and authority in holding us accountable.

• *Discipleship for guidance*—The church assists each member to understand what God intends for him or her. I call this *guidance*. The Spirit revealed His missionary purpose for Barnabas and Paul to the church at Antioch when they met in prayer. The Spirit didn't speak directly to Paul, but to the church about Paul.

Early in my ministry I was responsible for a Christian school. The board did not always agree with me on the direction we should go. Gradually, through painful experience, I began to have more confidence in the leading of the Holy Spirit through our responsible body than through my own independent judgment.

We need to make our ministry choices by seeking guidance from God's church. God doesn't save us and put us on a lonely pilgrimage. The Holy Spirit is our constant companion, but He provides touchable companions, too. Paul gives a magnificent description of how this happens in his letter to the church at Ephesus.

It was he who gave some to be apostles, some to be prophets, some to be evangelists, and some to be pastors and teachers, to prepare God's people for works of service, so that the body of Christ may be built up until we all reach unity in the faith and in the knowledge of the Son of God and become mature, attaining to the whole measure of the fullness of Christ.

Then we will no longer be infants, tossed back and forth by the waves, and blown here and there by every wind of teaching and by the cunning and craftiness of men in their deceitful scheming.

Instead, speaking the truth in love, we will in all things grow up into him who is the Head, that is, Christ. From him the whole body, joined and held together by every supporting ligament, grows and builds itself up in love, as each part does its work.
—Ephesians 4:11-16

> **Read *Ephesians 4:11-16* in the margin. Underline every word or phrase that sounds like spiraling up.**

Among others I underlined built up, reach unity, and become mature. You may have selected different phrases, but altogether I counted eight images that fit the spiral.

> **Now circle every word in *Ephesians 4:11-16* that tells who helps you spiral toward maturity, toward perfection in Christ.**

Did you include your helping others to grow? You're part of "God's people." "Every supporting ligament" and "each part" means we are important to each other. Reread the verses once more as a prayer of thanksgiving, adding words like, "Thank You Lord that…" Make it personal, "I praise You Lord for giving me…" Or a petition, like, "Please use me, Holy Spirit, to…"

ADVERSITY, THE FAST-TRACK FOR SPIRALING UP ·············[DAY 4]

Today we'll learn about a means of grace we prefer to avoid—*adversity*. Through hard times we learn lessons in discipleship that we would never master if we only experienced good times.

Adversity = "hardship, trouble, setback."

HOW TROUBLE STRENGTHENS US

Colin greeted me with a big smile, hug, and a happy "Praise the Lord!" She was, cooped up in the hospital room with her husband who was unable to talk or make sense, uncooperative, and belligerent due to Alzheimer's disease.

"Why so happy?" I asked. She told me about a mother she met in the hall of the hospital. This mother had traveled from a distant city to watch her son die. Colin, forgetting her own situation, befriended her and led that distraught mother to find hope in Christ. Both were filled with unexpected happiness as they hugged and cried.

The previous week Colin's husband broke down the door of their home to get out of his "prison." He collapsed in the front yard. Colin couldn't lift him, but before she called for help she cleaned and dressed him to save his dignity. She spent the night with her husband in the hospital, rescuing the nurses from his odd behavior. The next morning her son arrived with bad news: "Mom, your house is on fire!" A few hours later I entered that hospital room and received a warm hug from that courageous lady who whispered in my ear, "Praise the Lord!"

 Not everyone responds to trouble like Colin. Some emerge from hard times better people, some bitter. Why? Put a check by each of the following that you think might contribute to differing outcomes. Then circle the one you feel is most important for explaining the differences.

❏ Some people inherit a stronger makeup than others.
❏ Some people have a more traumatic childhood than others.
❏ Some people face more tragic events than others.
❏ Some people have more faith than others.
❏ Some people have a stronger support network of loving people.

Did you check all of them? I did. The difference is not in the circumstances, but in our response to them. Lack of faith lets the circumstances put a wedge between God and me. I become a weaker person, less like Jesus than before, perhaps discouraged, sad, depressed, even bitter, or at least a miserable, complaining person.

Faith in God keeps the circumstances outside, pressing me closer to God; and I become a stronger, better person, more like Jesus. Remember, it's not the quantity or even the quality of our faith, but the object of our faith—a trustworthy God—who can transform our trouble into strength and purpose.

WHERE TROUBLE COMES FROM

Sometimes it's quite clear who or what caused me pain. Other times trying to figure out who's to blame can be a frustrating and futile task. Some people always blame someone else for their troubles. The object of blame may be a family member, friend, teacher, society stacked against them, or the devil himself. Still others tend to blame themselves for everything, guilty or not. Have you ever fallen into the "blame" trap?

Even if my blame-laying is on target, that truth has little power to deliver me from my problems. Indeed, the blame hunt itself may make me a more angry and bitter person, less like Jesus. The effort to fix blame can be self-destructive.

No matter where the problem comes from, I can always recognize one basic truth about trouble. God knows every hair on our heads, so ultimately God is responsible. Of course, the tragedy in your life that is the result of another person's sin is not God's will. He didn't cause it, but He did permit it—no harm can touch the child of God unless it first passes through Jesus' nail-scarred hands. To know that God is aware of every grief of mine and could have supernaturally intervened to stop it may create some anxiety, but at least it simplifies the search for the responsible party!

Once we understand this truth about suffering, we don't need to devote our energies deciding who is guilty and making that person pay for it. God has our best interests at heart, and He plans to bring good through it. He can use the most painful circumstances to shape our lives and our characters. The pain is temporary, but the character He develops in us is eternal.

THE REASONS FOR PAIN

Why do we experience pain? One or more of the following seven reasons may contribute to our suffering.

1. **Consequences of sin**—(2 Sam. 12:13-14; Jer. 11:10-11; 1 Cor. 11:30-32; John 5:14). No believer will face punishment for sin in eternity, but while still here on earth Christians may suffer as a result of sin. In the past when tragedy struck, people asked, "Which of my sins is God getting me for?" Today we ask, "What's wrong with God? Why me? I deserve better." In searching for the purpose in my grief, it doesn't hurt to ask the old question. God allows us to suffer the consequences of our sin so we and others can learn from them.

2. **Discipline**—God disciplines those He loves (Heb. 12:5-11). Like the shepherd searching for the lost sheep, our Heavenly Father seeks to bring His children back to the right way (Ps. 119:67,71). Discipline corrects and restores us.

3. **Warning**—God may discipline a sinning child as a warning or example to others to be careful (1 Cor. 10:11). The sudden deaths of Ananias and Sapphira certainly served to warn early Christians against dishonesty (Acts 5:1-11).

4. **Guidance**—Sometimes God allows hard times to get us to go somewhere or do something we otherwise might not consider (Acts 8:1-4; Matt. 10:23). Jonah refused to obey God until he was swallowed by a fish (Jonah 3:3).

5. **Service**—Suffering prepares a person to help others (2 Cor. 1:3-4). Suffering makes us more compassionate toward others.

Although one or more of these five reasons may be God's purpose for our suffering, two reasons are always present in every trial. They are: God's glory and my growth.

When I respond to trouble with confidence in God, people see and give God the credit. Sometimes they see His deliverance (John 9:2-3). Sometimes they see Him supply strength in the midst of suffering (2 Cor. 12:7-10). Suffering can always bring glory to God (Ezek. 20:9,14,22). Suffering also has the purpose of growing me up into Christ's own likeness. Trials come to test us and refine us, to purify us as fire purifies gold (1 Pet. 1:7). Every circumstance in life is an opportunity to become more like Jesus. How do I make sure adversity actually brings glory to God and growth to me?

Read James 1:2-4 in the margin. Faith is the key! When I pass the faith test I become stronger. Endurance leads to maturity, which produces the character of Christ in me. But, if I think God is unable to deal with my problem, or not smart enough to know what's best for me, or doesn't care enough to see me through, then I spiral downward. I fall apart in self-pity and give up, or I grow hard and gloomy. I may even become mean-spirited and hostile.

Faith will transform that same trouble from a stumbling block into a stepping stone. Without the testing we would remain spiritually flabby and quite unlike the *One who learned obedience from what he suffered (Heb. 5:8)*. When we respond with

---

If we judged ourselves, we would not come under judgment. When we are judged by the Lord, we are being disciplined so that we will not be condemned with the world.
—1 Corinthians 11:31-32

It was good for me to be afflicted so that I might learn your decrees.
—Psalm 119:71

When all kinds of trials and temptations crowd into your lives...don't resent them as intruders, but welcome them as friends! Realize that they come to test your faith and to produce in you the quality of endurance. But let the process go on until that endurance is fully developed, and you will find you have become men of mature character, men of integrity with no weak spots.
—James 1:2-4, Phillips

childlike trust in a loving Father, we can join Colin in saying from the heart that we still have cause to "Praise God!"

 Make a list of five major problems, trials, or sources of pain in your life now.

1.
2.
3.
4.
5.

For each of the problems you identified, write in the margin a response that could cause God to be honored and a response to help you grow.

Are you ready to move on faith? Stop and thank God for how the Spirit is going to transform each problem into His glory and growth in you. Write your prayer of thanks in your journal. Turn it over to God, thanking Him that He is wise enough, strong enough, and cares about you enough to use that problem for eternal good.

 Using 2 Peter 1:5-8 as a guide, write the growth pattern on the stair steps below. Begin with "faith" at the bottom.

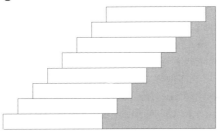

A STORY OF SPIRALING UPWARD ·················· [DAY 5]

God is working to transform my life. I committed my life to Christ when I was 12 years old, but I didn't automatically begin to grow. I was sincere enough but didn't develop a strong devotional life or learn to follow the direction of the Spirit. I knew nothing of the biblical pattern of mentoring—learning from a more mature Christian. I did not know what I needed to advance up the spiral. Jesus was dear to me, but the Holy Spirit was a stranger. Ignorance blocks progress. I did not understand myself, much less the many aspects of my life I needed to commit to Christ. Some were more difficult for me than others.

 The following Scriptures list aspects of our lives we may find difficult to commit to God. Read each Scripture. Put a check by those items you have difficulty turning over to God.

❑ Reputation—*Philippians 2:3-11; Luke 14:11*
❑ Talents, abilities—*1 Corinthians 4:7*
❑ Family, friends—*Matthew 10:37*
❑ Everything you have—*Luke 14:33*
❑ Entire self—*Romans 12:1-2*
❑ Future—*Matthew 6:33-34*
❑ Possessions—*Luke 12:33-34*

List here or in your journal any other areas of your thought life, relationships, activities, talk, or habits that you need to yield to God.

At age 18 I wanted to overcome sin in my life. I listed items for daily prayer and on that list I put "T & T," my code for tongue and temper. I sometimes got into fights. In college, when I was seeking to be more like Jesus, that never happened. But my tongue hurt people, and I began to feel the pain. That's why "T & T" stayed on my list.

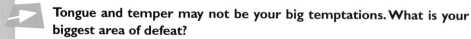

Tongue and temper may not be your big temptations. What is your biggest area of defeat?

To yield to God in biblical terms is not just a passive cry of "uncle—I quit, God, you win." Yielding to God is positive, aggressive, an active desire for God and good, an attitude of going for the goal of likeness to Jesus. This desire became an obsession with me. On the spiral I had turned around and was headed up. Still I didn't seem to be making very rapid progress.

MY "AH-HA!" MOMENT

I had tried to live the Christian life in my own strength. Then a preacher said, "The key to the victorious Christian life, is surrender and faith." Suddenly I realized the meaning of Christ living His life through me.

In *2 Corinthians 3:18* the Greek word, *transformed*, is from the word *metamorphosis*—a transformation of nature. God transforms believers. We cannot accomplish the metamorphosis in our own power. I began to replace *try* with *trust*. I realized that the means of grace tools were not part of my self-improvement project. God uses these tools to transform Christians into the image of Christ. They were the instruments God used to perform needed surgery in my life.

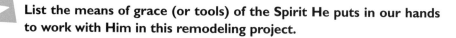

List the means of grace (or tools) of the Spirit He puts in our hands to work with Him in this remodeling project.

God began changing me from a short-fused, shoot-from-the-lip person into someone more like Jesus as I began to cooperate with Him. I didn't struggle against Him as He used the means of grace: God's Word, prayer, the church, and adversity.

- The Word preached taught me and gave me confidence of what could be.
- My daily prayer focused on a cry for deliverance from my spiritual failure.
- The church—At that point I didn't know about small-group accountability, and I didn't have a spiritual friend. My father, however, was the most powerful Christian example to me. I wouldn't have made it on my own. He instructed me, was always available, and modeled the life I longed for.
- Adversity—To answer my prayer for mouth-control and a patient spirit, God used the circumstances of life, adversity! Troubles were God's severe mercies, designed to make me more like Jesus. Paul calls suffering a grace—the same word used of salvation, an unearned gift for our welfare, a "means of grace."

God continues to use the circumstances of life to shape my character and develop the fruit of the Spirit in my life. In fact, I seem to be in a post-graduate program in patience, caring for a dear wife who suffers from Alzheimer's and whose needs change daily. So far I have been in this advanced school of patience for 18 years.

That's a bit of the story of one man in his spiral up. Whatever growth I have experienced is the grace of God, the work of the Spirit. Part of His grace is to put "tools" in my hand to participate with Him in the reconstruction project of my life. Those tools include prayer, Scripture, the church, and adverse circumstances. Your story is different from mine, but the grace of God is the same!

Christian Life = "Surrender and Faith."

We, who with unveiled faces all reflect the Lord's glory, are being transformed into his likeness with ever-increasing glory, which comes from the Lord, who is the Spirit.
—2 Corinthians 3:18

You have been given the privilege of serving Christ…by suffering for him.
–Philippians 1:29, GNB

We … rejoice in our sufferings, because we know that suffering produces perseverance; perseverance character; and character, hope.
—Romans 5:3-4

God disciplines us for our good, that we may share in his holiness. No discipline seems pleasant at the time, but painful. Later on, however, it produces a harvest of righteousness and peace for those who have been trained by it.
—Hebrews 12:10-11

List the four means of grace we have studied in this unit in the order of their strength in changing your life.

1.

2.

3.

4.

We need to aggressively use all the tools God supplies. When we do, the Spirit of God does His transforming work, making us into working models of Jesus to attract people to Himself.

How has He been transforming your life? Are you changing from impatience toward patience, from lust toward purity, from overeating toward self-control, from materialism toward contentment, from self-centered thinking toward concern for others, from doubt toward confidence in God's promises? Or maybe it has been something else God has been working on.

 List a few key areas in the blanks below.

What I was	What I am	What I want to be
_____	_____	_____
_____	_____	_____
_____	_____	_____

Write these out in your journal if you prefer, but be very honest with yourself and the Lord about it. If you can't truthfully see any progress toward Christlikeness, maybe the time has come for the great turn around, the surrender of your will to the will of the Father.

If we aren't in a growing mode, maybe we haven't used one or more of the tools of the Spirit. Our memory verse, says that we have to work at spiraling up. Why do some people work and get few results? As we have seen, it could be from ignorance of God's plan for transforming them; it could be from a basic unyielded sticking point; or it could come as a result of immature faith. But it could also be that some work hard at spiraling, at using the "means of grace" or "tools of the Spirit" while others don't. Decide today to get on the fast track and give it all you've got. What joy it will bring the Spirit, and you, too!

 Fill in the blanks below. Practice saying and writing *2 Peter 1:5-8* from memory.

For this very reason, make every effort to add to your faith _____; and to goodness, _____; and to knowledge, _____ - _____; and to self-control, _____;
and to perseverance, _____; and to godliness, _____ _____; and to brotherly kindness, _____. For if you possess these qualities in increasing measure, they will keep you from being ineffective and unproductive in your knowledge
of our Lord Jesus Christ.

—2 Peter 1:5-8

Every circumstance in life is an opportunity to become more like Jesus!

EXPECTATIONS

What can I expect from my life in the Spirit? Total victory over all sin? Some victory but mostly defeat? Something in between? In this unit we'll consider why we need realistic expectations of life in the Spirit—biblical expectations.

Marguerite, my sister, had high expectations. She had been so miserable with her failure to measure up that in desperation she turned to Jesus and invited Him into her life. She thought, *Tomorrow everything will be different. I won't get angry with Robertson anymore.* When she told me her story I responded, "And I gave you plenty of cause to be angry." Marguerite said, "No, Not just you. I was mad at lots of people."

Why did she think her temptation to get angry—and all those other miserable temptations that held her in their grip—would disappear? Because they seemed to have disappeared for her father. Robert McQuilkin preached all over the world about the victorious Christian life. He wrote about it in articles and books read by tens of thousands, but he did more. He lived that life right before us in the home. To outward appearances, a flawless life full of love, joy, peace and all the fruits of the Spirit. How was Marguerite to know that she was comparing her insides to her father's much more mature outsides?

Marguerite awoke to great disappointment the morning after her conversion. As she put it, I "smart mouthed" her, she blew up just as she always had. In addition, none of her other temptations or failures disappeared. "I was so disappointed," she said. "At first I struggled and fought the temptations, just like I always had. Finally, I gave up. For me the Christian life didn't work." For years Marguerite settled for spiritual defeat. She struggled to be good with sometimes modest success, often with failure to be and to do what she longed for.

When were Marguerite's expectations of her Christian life too high? When were they too low? After several years overseas, I returned home to discover a beautiful person, one of the most godly people I've known. Under the bitterest of circumstances, she lived a life of quiet patience and tireless service for others. What had she found?

Is there a middle way, a more biblical way? We'll search out that fundamental puzzle of Life in the Spirit, looking first at the low expectations many settle for, then the high expectations many cling to, and finally the biblical expectations you and I may experience in daily life.

[**Unit Memory**
Thanks be to God! He gives us the victory through our Lord Jesus Christ.
—*I Corinthians 15:57*
Verse]

WHAT CAN WE EXPECT? ·····················[DAY 1]

Let's be encouraged about what we can expect of our new life in Christ. All Christians agree that the Holy Spirit is to make saints out of sinners. However, many of us disagree about the outcome of His activity in this present life.

 Read through the following examples. Mark A by those you fully agree with, D by those you disagree with, and U by those you're uncertain about.

___ Jason is convinced that both he and all Christians sin consciously and deliberately every day.

___ Virginia was baptized by the Spirit last year; her sin nature was eliminated and she no longer sins.

___ Mary has given up on any miracle deliverance from her many troubles and relies on her therapist to help her cope.

___ Evan is composed of two natures, an old one that can't do right or improve and a new one that can't do wrong. His vote determines which will win out at any moment in time.

Today we'll identify biblically-based views of what we can expect from our life in the Spirit. First, what can we become in the Spirit's power? Second, what means does the Spirit use to transform us into Christlikeness? Third, what is our responsibility in the process? As we search for biblical truth, we'll study what to guard against.

WHAT IS OUR GOAL?

To answer the question, What can we become in the Spirit's power? let's look at two extreme positions. Some people expect either bondage and defeat or perfection.

Emphasizing bondage and defeat limits the degree to which the Spirit can overcome our sin nature. Therefore we wake up each morning with the expectation of sinning, because we see failure as inevitable. The opposite view expects perfection in this life. If we believe we can or must be perfect, we either deny that we have a sin nature, or we believe that the power of the Spirit makes us incapable of sin.

 What does the Bible tell us about a life of bondage and defeat? Read the three short Scriptures in the margin indicating Paul's belief. Circle the words he used to describe the practical experience of the believer.

I circled *conquerors, triumph,* and *live.* The Old Testament foretold this good news: *Put your hope in the Lord, for with the Lord is unfailing love and with him is full redemption. He himself will redeem…all their sins. (Ps. 130:7-8, GNB).* The New Testament emphasizes the same theme. Jesus commanded us to be perfect *(Matt. 5:48). Peter says that if we aren't godly we are shortsighted, even to blindness (2 Pet. 1:9, NKJV),* and John assures us that if we live sinful lives we aren't children of God at all *(1 John 3:6-10).* No, we're not condemned to a life of spiritual failure. We must resist those who would push us back into a feeling of defeat.

 What about those who hope for perfection? Read the words of the apostle Paul in *Philippians 3:12-14*. Circle statements that indicate he wasn't sinless.

John spells out our imperfection clearly: *If we claim to be without sin, we deceive ourselves and the truth is not in us. If we claim we have not sinned, we make him out to be a liar and his word has no place in our lives (1 John 1:8,10).*

In all these things we are more than conquerors through him who loved us (Rom. 8:37).

Thanks be to God, who in Christ always leads us in triumph (2 Cor. 2:14, RSV).

If you live according to the sinful nature, you will die; but if by the Spirit you put to death the misdeeds of the body, you will live (Rom. 8:13).

I do not claim that I have already succeeded or have already become perfect. I keep striving to win the prize for which Christ Jesus has already won me to himself. Of course, my brothers, I really do not think that I have already won it; the one thing I do, however, is to forget what is behind me and do my best to reach what is ahead. So I run straight toward the goal in order to win the prize, which is God's call through Christ Jesus to the life above. (Phil. 3:12-14, GNB).

Life in the Spirit =
- *win out over temptations*
- *grow toward greater likeness to Jesus*

God doesn't expect absolute perfection in this life, though He does promise just that when we reach heaven—*We shall be like him for we shall see him as he is* (*1 John 3:2*). In the meantime, what can we expect? What does the Spirit mean by speaking of our being *more than conquerors* (*Rom. 8:37*) and being always caused to triumph (*2 Cor. 2:14*)? When we live life in the Spirit we can expect to win out over temptations and grow steadily toward greater likeness to Jesus in our attitudes and actions.

WHAT DOES THE SPIRIT USE?

We may have warped expectations about what can be achieved in the Christian life, and also about how we achieve the goal—is it all human effort or all God's doing?

"It's hard being a Christian," moaned our five-year-old Kent. He expressed the sentiments of many grown-ups who try to be good, relying on their own willpower and effort. At the other extreme, others see in Scripture the hope of victory by the power of the Spirit and retire to watch God take over their responsibilities for them.

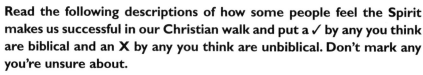 **Read the following descriptions of how some people feel the Spirit makes us successful in our Christian walk and put a ✓ by any you think are biblical and an X by any you think are unbiblical. Don't mark any you're unsure about.**

____ 1. It's a hand and glove relationship. The Spirit is the hand, you're the glove, so "let go and let God" work in and through you.

____ 2. It's a relationship in which you are invited to companion with God, and the closer you stay to Him the more He empowers you.

____ 3. It's the substituted life—just as Christ died as your substitute, now let Him live as your substitute.

____ 4. It's pretty much up to you—your willpower, determination, hard work. God will assist you as you ask His advice.

____ 5. You'll know when the Spirit comes—you'll experience a surge of spiritual energy like you've never had before and, if you'll let Him, He'll keep you on that high plane, free from struggle and failure.

Though most of those approaches have an element of truth in them, all but the second and last options above have dangerously misleading elements. Approaches 1, 3, and 4 emphasize God's action but neglect our response. They can lead to a passive kind of irresponsibility. God doesn't want you to become the spiritual equivalent of a vegetable. He wants to have a mutual relationship with you. Response 4 clearly goes to the opposite extreme of depending on human effort.

WHAT IS OUR RESPONSIBILITY?

We can become unbalanced in our Christian lives by having false expectations about our goal—what we can achieve spiritually. We also can get off track by having false expectations about the means—the part God plays in reaching the goal. But we can also be confused about our part in the process.

- **Grin and Bear It**—At one extreme are people who have a grin-and-bear-it resignation to their fate—whatever happens, happens.

- **Severe**—Some don't just endure tough times, they create them! They believe in severe self-denial, taking vows to remain single and to own nothing.

- **Expect Good Life**—Others believe God has promised what, in fact, He hasn't. They think, *If I'm not enjoying life free from failure and full of only good stuff, it's because I don't have enough faith.*

Remember that faith connects us with Holy Spirit power. Fake forms of faith—ideas, or attitudes that just look *like* faith—will never connect with Holy Spirit power. Biblical faith keeps us centered between the ditches of severe self-denial and effortless abundance. Biblical faith focuses on continually being in Christ, from which we draw our strength.

 Read the Scripture memory verse in the margin. Rewrite the verse as a prayer thanking God for specific victories in your life.

Thanks be to God! He gives us the victory through our Lord Jesus Christ.

—1 Corinthians 15:57

DON'T AIM TOO LOW ························· [DAY 2]

"We confess, Lord," the man in the pulpit prayed, "that we Your people turn our backs on You and shake our fists in Your face every day of our lives." Would you agree with that prayer or do you think he's aiming too low? In a the book, *Less Than Conquerors,* the author argues that the best we can expect in the Christian life is struggle and failure. He says that anyone who claims more is either misled or a fake.

 Circle those statements below that you think are true.

Nobody's perfect.	God understands when I fail.
God loves me unconditionally.	God accepts me just the way I am.

Did you circle all of them? I did! But I'm a little uneasy and maybe you are, too. Perhaps it's because the thoughts are incomplete. I'd worry about what conclusions the reader would draw from these statements. For example, it's true that God is inviting me to come just as I am. But if by saying, "He accepts me just the way I am," we mean, "God accepts me, so don't expect me to change," the point of salvation is missed. He accepts me as I am to transform me into what He designed me to be.

Some people have expectations for the Christian life that are too low because they have been discouraged by their own and others lack of progress. They just don't believe God changes human beings all that much in this life.

BROKEN CHOOSERS

The church is full of hurting people. Most of us could use help toward healing, some by a skilled counselor. When a person is—
- blind to his own sinful behavior, or
- her choice ability "chooser" is so damaged it can't function, or
- his "truster" is so violated he thinks he can't get through to God—

a trained counselor may be able to help him see himself, others, and God in clearer perspective. Then that person can begin to trust God and choose God's alternative. However, when we begin to use human brokenness as an excuse to disobey God and remain in our patterns of sin, we do ourselves and others a severe disservice.

VASTLY DIFFERING EXPECTATIONS

A lowered expectation of what the Holy Spirit can do may come from treating people as victims, rather than as responsible individuals. Americans often believe less and less in sin and guilt, and more and more in a battered psyche that needs healing. We believe we are no longer guilty sinners needing salvation, but victims of someone else's hurtful behavior and need restoration of a healthy self-image. We could picture the difference in viewpoint this way:

Biblical idea of the human predicament and the way out:

Sin ▸ Guilt ▸ Repentance/Faith ⟶

⟵ **Growth ◂ Restoration ◂ Forgiveness** ⟵

⟶ **Freedom and Fulfillment** (of God's purposes)

Victim model of the human predicament and the way out:

Injury ▶ Damaged Self-Image/Illness

Healing (Restored Self-Image) **◀ Therapy**

Freedom and Fulfillment (of my purposes)

The victim model contains a critical flaw. We are self-centered rebels against God. We choose to disobey Him and dishonor ourselves in the process. Though the victim/therapy model may get some people part of the way to a life of effectiveness, it can never deliver the spiritual energy for a life of victory.

If we buy into the victim syndrome of viewing ourselves and others, we may block ourselves and others from God. The view of self as a hurting person, damaged by wrongs inflicted by others, may lead persons away from taking responsibility for their feelings or actions. We deny our own guilt and personal responsibility to choose right.

Scripture bases its promise of salvation and power-filled Christian living on the assumption that we can respond to God in faith. We can choose His way. Some of us may need more help from the outside than others, and the church should provide that help. But the power of the Holy Spirit can give us the will and the way so that we can work out our salvation with fear and trembling (*Phil. 2:12*).

The failure syndrome and the victim syndrome are two major paths to expecting less of the Christian life. If I choose to believe that I can't become an overcomer, that I can't experience miracle intervention by the Spirit of God, surely my belief will prove self-fulfilling. Paul describes Holy Spirit potential in the life of every believer.

Read *Romans 8* slowly and soak up the glory of what God promises for your Christian experience. Now go back and circle every time the Spirit is mentioned.   How many did you find? _____

1.

2.

3.

4.

5.

Jot in the margin your five favorite activities of the Spirit in empowering your life, identified in *Romans 8*. Check out verses *28* and *29* and verses *31-39* which don't mention the Spirit, but are glorious promises for a victorious Christian life.

By the way, the NASB, NIV, and KJV translations mention the Spirit 21 times.

Don't settle for too low an expectation of what your Christian life can be. Listen to Paul's great proclamation of victory: *Sin shall not be your master* (Rom. 6:14). He gives thanks to God who causes us to triumph (2 Cor. 2:14) and exults in the assurance that *we are more than conquerors* (Rom. 8:37). *Thanks be to God,* Paul says. *He gives us the victory through our Lord Jesus Christ* (1 Cor. 15:57). Incredibly, he promises a life filled by the Spirit to *all the fullness of God* (Eph. 3:19). In another verse he describes the Christian life as *attaining to the whole measure of the fullness of Christ* (Eph 4:13)!

These reflect the mood of the entire New Testament from the promise by Jesus of abundant life (John 10:10) and a bumper crop of Christlike characteristics (John 15) to the promise of Peter that we can escape from the world's corruption and experience abounding godliness (2 Pet. 1). John draws the curtain on the final act, "He who overcomes will inherit all this, and I will be his God and he will be my son" (Rev. 21:7). Such is the destiny of the overcomer.

Write out your prayer in your journal or in the margin. Be honest. If your expectations are low, tell Him. But don't leave it there; ask for wisdom to understand what Scripture really teaches about what you ought to expect. Pray for the gift of faith to believe His promises. If you are excited about the possibilities, tell Him so. He's delighted to see His children free and fulfilled!

DON'T AIM TOO HIGH ···················· [DAY 3]

We've seen some of the dangers of aiming too low in our Christian life. But the opposite can get us too. Start this lesson with a prayer, use the one in the margin.

Some see the grand promises of Scripture and think they mean we can become sinlessly perfect in this life—perhaps even instantly, through a particular experience. One such preacher, Boris, said God had eliminated his sin nature. Another preacher testified that he had not yet attained perfection *(Phil. 3:12)*. Paul struggled with temptation and weakness. He was sometimes filled with fear, for example, and had more than one fuss with his colleagues. How do we read the same Bible and come up with such different answers? By the way we define sin or perfect.

DEFINING SIN

 The following are common definitions of sin. Check the one that you think best represents the biblical definition of sin.

❑ 1. A sin is an action, not a feeling or an attitude, that violates God's law.
❑ 2. Sin is transgression of the law.
❑ 3. Sin is any failure to measure up to the moral character of God.
❑ 4. To sin is to knowingly violate God's will. Attitudes and misbehavior I don't know to be wrong are part of my human nature, not sin.

I checked 3 because the biblical standard is to be just like God morally *(Matt. 5:48)*. Yet, all have sinned and fall short of the glorious character of God *(Rom. 3:23)*. You may have checked 2 also because it is a biblical statement *(1 John 3:4)*, but it was not intended as a comprehensive definition of sin. Other attitudes and actions also fail to measure up, such as failing to think or do what I ought. I did not check 4. Although to sin knowingly is indeed sin, it is nevertheless sinful to have attitudes or actions that are not Christlike, whether I am aware of them or not. We call them "sins of ignorance," but we are not innocent when we sin in ignorance.

Option #1 is misleading because Christ carefully designated wrong attitudes as sin *(Matt. 5:21-30)* as well as the outward acts. Some say anger or sexual desire is wrong only if you act them out, that emotions are morally neutral, but Jesus compared some types of anger to murder, and lust to adultery. If we lower the standard, then it's easier to reach it! If I'm guilty of sin only when I deliberately violate what I know is the will of God, maybe it's possible to live a life relatively free of sin. Christians differ on the definition of perfection because they differ on the definition of sin.

DEFINING PERFECT

Linked to one's definition of sin is the definition of perfect. How do you define perfect?

 The following examples contain a common use of the word *perfect*. Beside each example write the letter(s) that corresponds with one of these synonyms:

RG—really good   M—mature
H—healthy   WS—without sin

__ The Smith's new baby is perfect!   __ Be perfect as God is perfect.
__ Gifts of ministry enable God's people   __ This ice cream is perfect.
to grow up into perfection *(Eph. 4:13)*.

We would have no problem if people who teach the possibility of perfection in this life meant healthy (like the Smith's new baby) or mature (as in *Eph. 4:13*) or really good (like ice cream). The Bible uses the term perfect in all these ways. The problem comes when some speak of sinless perfection, without flaw, in the moral sense.

Scripture says a person who says he is without sin is self-deceived or, even worse, makes a liar of God. The only way a person can be sinless is to redefine sin, to make it something less than any failure to attain God's moral perfection. Thus when people speak of sinless perfection, the difference is often a difference in wording; the term sin is defined with limitations. If I promise a life free of deliberately choosing to disobey God, for example, maybe perfection is within reach. But if I promise a flawless life, free from all wrong attitudes and actions, full of God's perfection, I am promising more than the Bible teaches.

No doubt to aim too high and fall short is better than to aim too low and hit the target! In fact, Paul prays for the perfection of the Christians in Corinth and tells them to aim for it! (*2 Cor. 13:9,11*)

> **Brainstorm for a moment. What might result from a person seeking to live with unrealistic expectations? Write your answers in the margin.**

Boris said that he was perfect, but don't ask any of the people around him about that evaluation. They were fearful of his explosive rages. The slightest thing that didn't go his way could set him off. What was his problem? He no doubt considered his anger "righteous indignation" and so he remained "perfect." Boris' definition resulted in a life of self-deception and ineffectiveness.

Some people who believe in perfection aren't like Boris at all. They know they fail; they just talk like they don't. They are in danger of hypocrisy. For many, however, the danger is discouragement in not being able to achieve or maintain what they expect. Many become so discouraged they just quit. Here are the hazards of unrealistic expectations:

- Self-deception, especially by redefining sin or a particular sin so we no longer acknowledge it as sin
- Hypocrisy from knowing they fall short but claim otherwise
- Discouragement from expecting perfection and failing to achieve it.

Expectations may be too low or too high, but a strange combination of the two exists. This odd combo is common in Christian practice. Some say, "I don't sin as much as most people" and think that's good enough. Some Christians pray, "forgive us of our many sins," but don't think of any specific wrongs that they personally need to right. Both may be jealous of a classmate or critical in spirit. They are satisfied with their own level of achievement. Their expectations are too low by biblical standards, but their evaluation of themselves is too high!

Before pressing on to *take hold of that for which Christ Jesus took hold of me (Phil. 3:12)*, we need to accept the biblical limitations on our expectations. In this life we'll never be absolutely perfect as God is, without sin, though when we see Jesus *we shall be like him (1 John 3:2)*. We praise God for the bad news of limited expectations. In the margin is my prayer.

Suggested Prayer Response:
Thank you, blessed Spirit, for releasing me from the drivenness and disappointments of unrealistic expectations. Help me to accept my own limitations and those of others. And please, don't let me swing to the other extreme and settle for less than You intend. I want to be all a redeemed human being can be. And that's for Jesus' sake—not just for mine. Amen.

> **Fill in the blanks of the Scripture memory verse. You can check your work on page 88. Now write the entire Scripture memory verse in the margin.**

_____ be to _____! He _____
us the _____ *through our Lord Jesus Christ.*
—1 Corinthians 15:57

TWO KINDS OF VICTORY .... [DAY 4]

If expectations of a Spirit-filled life can be too low or too high, what can we expect? Somehow our expectation of spiritual success seems linked to our view of sin.

VARIETIES OF SIN

Many of us have far too limited an understanding of sin. The Bible uses several models or concepts to describe sin. When I first saw the biblical distinction among sins, it became a liberating truth that gave birth to hope for my personal life in the Spirit. I want to focus on three different categories of sin.

Notice in *Numbers 15* (in the margin) the distinction between intentional and unintentional sin. When a person knew the law and deliberately chose to break it, the sin was intentional. When a person sinned unintentionally, there was that sin could be forgiven.

As Christians we're no longer under condemnation, but we can learn from the example in *Numbers 15*. We can recognize that not all sin fits in the same category. Some sin is willful and deliberate—we know better, and we just choose to do what is wrong. Some sin grows out of our warped belief systems—we may not even know that we are sinning, but we are. Some people's racism is an example of this second category of sin. We might call these two types of sin *deliberate sins* and *sins of ignorance*.

We can look at the issue of sin in another way. *Galatians 6:1* speaks of someone who is *caught in a sin*. The context would seem to be speaking of a fellow believer. Christians and unbelievers can be caught or trapped in patterns of sin.

 Read *Ephesians 5:18* that appears in the margin. Circle the big, technical-sounding word in the verse.

Debauched means "to be lured away from duty or virtue." The word implies to be without strength, to be whipped. A result of sin is to be so overcome by it that we become slaves. Read *Romans 6:16* in the margin. We can see three different distinctions of sin (1) deliberate and willful, (2) result of ignorance, (3) result of weakness or slavery. Remember all types of sin are still just that—sin. While nothing excuses sin, we may be better able to understand ourselves by seeing these distinctions.

 Try to write an example of each kind of sin.

sin that is the result of defiance _____

sin that is the result of ignorance _____

sin that is a result of slavery _____

To distinguish sin isn't always easy, but I thought of the following examples:
• Deliberate—lying about a homework assignment.
• Ignorance—not recognizing my own prejudices.
• Slavery (want to stop but can't seem to)—yelling at my brother in anger.

This distinction between sins may help solve the mystery of two passages in the New Testament. *First John 1:8* says: *If we claim to be without sin, we deceive ourselves and the truth is not in us.* Then only a bit later in the same letter John wrote: *No one who lives in him keeps on sinning. He who does what is sinful is of the devil...No one who is born of God will continue to sin, because God's seed remains in him; he cannot go on sinning, because he has been born of God (1 John 3:6,8-10).* Those two teachings can't be contradictory; they are by the same author only a few verses apart. The Apostle didn't slip up, he meant

"The priest is to make atonement before the Lord for the one who erred by sinning unintentionally, and when atonement has been made for him, he will be forgiven. But anyone who sins defiantly, whether native-born or alien, blasphemes the Lord, and that person must be cut off from his people. Because he has despised the Lord's word and broken his commands, that person must surely be cut off; his guilt remains on him."
—Numbers 15:28,30-31

Do not get drunk on wine, which leads to debauchery. Instead, be filled with the Spirit.
—Ephesians 5:18

Don't you know that when you offer yourselves to someone to obey him as slaves, you are slaves to the one whom you obey—whether you are slaves to sin, which leads to death, or to obedience, which leads to righteousness?
—Romans 6:16

both basic truths. But how do they fit together?

Recognizing different kinds of sin might help. *John 1* is talking about any and all sins, including anything that falls short of God's glorious character, deliberate or not. If you claim to be without any kind of sin you're badly deceived. But in the third chapter he uses a continuous action verb that is not clear in some English translations: if anyone keeps on sinning, he says. If you deliberately choose to violate the known will of God and stick at it, John says, you're not a Christian at all! And Paul says the same thing *(1 Cor. 6:9-10; Gal. 5:19-21)*. The writer of *Hebrews 12:14* agrees.

You'll notice these verses apply differently to the three types of sin. Everyone commits sins of ignorance. We all have a less-than-perfect belief system, so we make sinful choices. The challenge of being a disciple includes building a biblical belief system. As disciples we cooperate with the Spirit as He renews our minds. Probably everyone struggles with patterns of sin like temper, gossip, or overeating. The first category of sin—deliberate and willful—is the key. What do we do when we recognize some thought or action is sin?

Mark the following with a D for deliberate and willful, an I for based on ignorance, or an S for slavery. This exercise won't be your easiest!

__ __ 1. Peter "borrows" a little from the cash box at work.

__ __ 2. A friend hurt Mary. Mary wonders if she'll ever trust again.

__ __ 3. Everyone else comes to church in really nice cars and Harry is always upset about the old clunker he has to drive.

__ __ 4. Sandra and Lou aren't married, but they're in love, so they live together.

__ __ 5. Dean is an alcoholic, trying hard to be a good Christian. Last night he drank some alcoholic drinks.

__ __ 6. Seems like everyone but Helen knows how critical she is. But she's no gossip, she says, she just tells it like it is.

__ __ 7. Ben isn't cruel or abusive, but he is domineering in relation to his family. After all, Paul said he's supposed to be head of the house.

I know it's difficult to decide on some of those situations because you don't know all the motivations, but I put a D by 1, 4. I put S by 2, 3, 5. I labeled numbers 6 and 7 as possible examples of ignorance.

TWO KINDS OF VICTORY

A yielded and trusting Christian can expect to win over temptations. Hubert understood that. In our Sunday School class we were discussing our failures when Hubert finally spoke up: "Well, whenever I was born again I quit sinning." Every head whipped around toward Hubert. We knew he was a godly man, but quit sinning altogether? He continued, "Since I was born again I never deliberately choose to do wrong." Right idea! A Christian ought never deliberately choose to do wrong.

But what does the Bible offer for victory over the other kinds of sin, sins based on ignorance or bondage? Sometimes there is instant deliverance from that kind of sin. When we find ourselves in a spiritual failure, we should cry out for total deliverance. But sometimes it doesn't happen that way, but there can be a pattern of growth.

VICTORY AS GROWTH

The New Testament teaches that Christian life is growth. We are to grow in all ways, but Peter says to grow in two specific ways: grace and knowledge *(2 Pet. 3:18)*.

1. Grace. Grace is a gift given to one who hasn't earned it. You can't get it no matter how hard you work, like salvation. When we grow "in grace" we receive more and more Spirit power for godly living. The Spirit's bank of grace is unlimited, but our capacity to receive His gifts is limited. The more we use grace, the

We do not dare to classify or compare ourselves with some who commend themselves. When they measure themselves by themselves and compare themselves with themselves, they are not wise.
—2 Corinthians 10:12

Grow in the grace and knowledge of our Lord and Savior Jesus Christ.
—2 Peter 3:18

more we'll have. For example, Mary, from the previous exercise, needs to grow in her capacity to love her classmate.

2. Knowledge. We must grow in understanding what the will of God is. Ben, in the previous exercise, seems unaware of his sin, but he needs to learn what a godly husband and father is. He needs to grow in loving his family like Christ loves the church family—to the point of laying down his life for them *(Eph. 5:25–6:4)*.

SIN THAT GROWS FROM WEAKNESS AND IGNORANCE

Sin can be unplanned rather than deliberate for two distinct reasons—weakness or ignorance. I know it's wrong to be impatient, and I don't plan to lose my temper. But suddenly I find myself upset over the way someone speaks to me. I need God's enabling grace. On the other hand, I keep discovering racial prejudices that are buried so deep I had no idea they were there. I need to correct my belief system with knowledge—of myself and of God's view of right and wrong.

 In the margin by each of the examples on page 96 mark a *G* (grace) for those whose need is for strength to use God's grace and mark *K* (knowledge) by those who need to learn what sin is. If you're uncertain, you could put both.

Judging clearly in every example, or even in our own lives, may not always be easy. But usually, we know the difference.

 Are you aware of any sins in your Christian life, things you struggle with, things you need to change? Create three lists, in the margin. Be very honest and thorough. Once you've been honest about it, you can choose to quit or start pleading for God's resources (graces) to overcome.

DELIVERANCE FROM UNKNOWN SIN

Did you have trouble with the sin of ignorance list? Of course! How can you change a behavior or attitude if you are not even aware of it? You have three helps available to help you grow: the Bible, prayer, and true friends.

• Stay sensitive in your daily reading of the Word of God so you can hear Him when He wants to alert you to something you've been blind to or insensitive about. Stay teachable so you can learn when the Bible is taught by others.

• Through prayer ask the Spirit to reveal your true self to you. If you do, you may be surprised how quickly the events and people in your life begin to direct your attention to that characteristic the Spirit wants you to acknowledge and begin to change. Stay sensitive to hear His whisper when your attitude or motive hurts Him.

• A true friend helps you see things you were blind to. An accountability partner is helpful. Periodically I ask my family and coworkers, "If you could change one thing about me, what would it be?" Look out! It might hurt. But what a means of growth!

 Here's a tough assignment for this lesson: Ask at least one person the above question before your next group meeting. Pray about the answers and if God seems to be speaking to you about change, put it on your permanent prayer list—a list of things you want to be reminded of to pray about daily.

For items under slavery, consider a stronger, more focused form of accountability. God intends that we overcome areas of spiritual or physical bondage. Enlist a "specialist" accountability partner or group, a Christ-centered person or group who has overcome that specific form of slavery. To quit smoking or overcome anger, get someone

Defiance
_____
_____
_____

Ignorance
_____
_____
_____

Slavery
_____
_____
_____

who has successfully dealt with the problem that focuses on the issue.

> **Are there any temptations under defiance that you know are wrong but you keep choosing anyway and trying to rationalize away? If so, confess and forsake those sins. You will experience no growth until you choose to obey.**
>
> As for those areas of slavery, why not present each of them in order to the Lord, telling Him you're truly sorry and thanking Him that He is strong enough to give you the victory. Ask Him to give you greater grace (capacity, strength, wisdom) to spiral up. Ask that He daily give you more understanding of yourself. Make these three areas a regular part of your prayer life.

[DAY 5] ······················· THE SPIRIT'S ACTIVITY

Do you not know that the wicked will not inherit the kingdom of God?
—1 Corinthians 6:9

The acts of the sinful nature are obvious: sexual immorality, impurity and debauchery; idolatry and witchcraft; hatred, discord, jealousy, fits of rage, selfish ambition, dissensions, factions and envy; drunkenness, orgies, and the like. I warn you, as I did before, that those who live like this will not inherit the kingdom of God.
—Galatians 5:19-21

Make every effort to live in peace with all men and to be holy; without holiness no one will see the Lord.
—Hebrews 12:14

How can we expect to win out consistently over temptations? How can we grow in likeness to Jesus? We know the answer has something to do with the Holy Spirit—the quality of our love relationship and how freely we allow Him to work in us.

Review the activities on the course map. Several of the activities are both past historical actions and present ongoing actions. For example, the first activity of the Spirit is creating. The Spirit was instrumental in the creation of the universe (past) and the Spirit created you and me (ongoing). The second activity is revealing. The Spirit's work of revelation includes inspiration (past) and illumination (ongoing). The third activity, redeeming included the ministry of Jesus (past) and the work of regeneration (ongoing). The fourth activity is indwelling, and the fifth activity is sanctifying believers. We summarized the sanctifying work of the Spirit the word *transforming*.

> **Briefly explain how each of the following activities relates to Christian living. You could give several good answers for each, but here's a sample possibility:**
> 1. Creation: *Created as spiritual beings in God's likeness we can know and be like Him.*
> 2. Revelation: inspiration: _____
>   Revelation: illumination: _____
> 3. Conviction: _____
> 4. Regeneration: _____
> 5. Indwelling: _____
> 6. Sanctification: _____

CREATION

> **To review some of the important implications of the way the Spirit designed us, answer *T* for the following statements which are wholly true and *F* for those you believe false or not wholly true.**
> ___ A person with an interest in the unseen world is therefore a spiritual person by biblical standards.
> ___ God's ultimate purpose for us is to be like Him in moral character.
> ___ God's ultimate purpose for us is loving oneness with Him.
> ___ Though theologians differ on how free our will is, the Bible is clear that God expects us to make choices, to choose Him.

Mere interest in the unseen world will not make us spiritually mature. You may have marked T for the second option, being like God, but God's original purpose in creating us was to have fellowship with Him. The ultimate goal is loving oneness with God. It's certainly true that our transformation starts when we choose God, trusting Him with our lives. My answers would be F,F,T,T.

REVELATION: INSPIRATION AND ILLUMINATION

Those who know the Spirit trust the Bible He gave. They expect Him to make it plain to them; they study it to know His will; and, they are prepared to obey it fully.

 Is the Bible sitting on the shelf of your life, or is it your actual working guide? In the list in the margin underline the attitudes or activities God expects of believers.

I underlined the first two and the last. If we are ever to spiral up into likeness to Christ we have to know what the Bible says, understand, trust and obey it.

CONVICTION

People will never turn to God until they feel the need to. No one will feel the need deeply enough to turn unless the Holy Spirit does the work He was sent to do. Jesus promised if He went away He would send the Holy Spirit to *"convict the world of…sin and righteousness and judgment" (John 16:8)*.

 Circle the word in Christ's promise above (John 16:8) that indicates the convicting work of the Holy Spirit is universal.

In the mysterious connection between God's sovereign initiative and my responsibility to respond, the Bible constantly points to my responsibility. Some people harden their own hearts through resisting the convicting power of the Spirit. In fact, it's possible to close down completely and not hear the Spirit, but He's still at work. I circled world. God loves the world, as a result of that love the Spirit convicts the world of sin, of righteousness, and of judgment to come. (see *Rom. 1:18-31; 2:14-16*).

REGENERATION

Those who know the Spirit view themselves as new creations, with incredible new potential. The new Christian has been so radically transformed that the Bible uses many word pictures to describe the change.

 Circle the phrases below that most closely describes your understanding of the biblical picture of your new life in Christ.
1. "You were dead, you're now alive" means:
   a. You were incapable of doing anything good, but now you can do good.
   b. You were disconnected from God and His power; now you're connected.
2. "You died and are now resurrected" means:
   a. You're "dead" to the old temptations—they no longer even appeal to you.
   b. You've been changed to a new kind of person with new potential you never had before.
3. "You've been born again" means:
   a. You've been changed so radically you could compare the change to physical birth.
   b. Though basically the same, you've changed direction, gotten a new start in life.
4. "You're a 'new man,' having put off the old man means:
   a. "Man" means "nature" and you now have two, an old one that can't improve and a new one that can't sin. Always vote with the new one!
   b. "Man" means "self" and you are recreated, a new person with new capabilities to grow in likeness to Christ.

1. Study the Bible daily, working toward a mastery of its teaching.
2. Be willing to obey every Bible teaching.
3. Know the theme of every book of the Bible.
4. Memorize a verse a day.
5. Be humbly obedient to every church tradition—if a new idea comes along that differs from our way of doing things, reject it.
6. If a new idea comes along, believe in progress and accept it.
7. When people differ on what is right or wrong, eagerly search out all the Bible teaches on the subject.

Jesus calls it a new birth *(John 3)*. You have been changed from what you were—disconnected from God, unable to consistently choose right. You are an altogether new person, connected with Holy Spirit life and able to be transformed into the likeness of God! You did good things before you were reborn, but you couldn't consistently choose the right—didn't even want to. You can sin now, but the new you has the power to resist evil. Now you can grow in an ever-increasing spiral of love for, companionship with, and obedience to God.

INDWELLING

Those who know the Spirit maintain a close relationship of surrender and faith. Even the new me could never live the Christian life successfully, so God Himself comes to live with me. And if I stay faithful to Him, I'll start being more and more like Him. I can find real meaning in life only by developing this intimate love relationship.

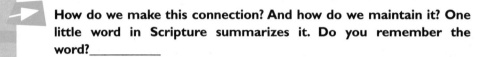 **How do we make this connection? And how do we maintain it? One little word in Scripture summarizes it. Do you remember the word?**_____

The word is *faith*. By faith we enter spiritual life and by faith we grow to maturity. Faith connects with God-power. There are two sides to faith. We repent, yielding to God's will and we trust Him to do what He promised. Faith is the key to both salvation and sanctification.

SANCTIFICATION

Those who know the Spirit will faithfully use the tools He provides, working with the Spirit to spiral up.

Important Tools

_____

_____

_____

_____

 In the margin name the three or four important tools the Spirit uses to work in our lives.

Prayer and Bible study can be joyous, church can be fun, but we would avoid all suffering if we could. When we respond correctly, adversity can be a tremendous opportunity to grow. If I believe God can use suffering to bring honor to Him and growth in me, the pain can press me closer to Him. Faith is the key. Our response to suffering determines if we draw closer to God. Allowing suffering to harden our hearts toward God separates us from God and wastes our opportunity to grow.

The Spirit's activity gives us life and grows us toward Christlikeness. The key to whether we grow is our personal relationship to Christ. The closer we stay to Him, the faster we spiral up! The more we trust and obey the more He empowers us to grow. The more we grow the more we love Him. The more we love Him the more we trust and obey and become more like Him. The more like Him we become the greater capacity we have to love and trust. "We ... *are being transformed into his likeness... which comes from the Lord, who is the Spirit" (2 Cor. 3:18).*

Thank God that as you grow spiritually you can expect transformation into His very likeness. Write this week's Scripture memory verse in the margin.

FILLED FULL

In this unit we will learn what it means to be "filled with the Spirit," how the Spirit fills us, and how to remain filled.

"Do you remember me?" The bright-eyed teen looked at me eagerly. I couldn't bring myself to say no, so I stalled. I asked if she was from Birmingham. I knew a large group from Birmingham was at the youth conference. I heard how God had moved in the local high school. Starting with a couple of girls in a prayer meeting, dozens had come to Christ; the spiritual awakening impacted the whole campus.

She continued. "Do you remember last year, after that last meeting of the conference when we sat on that stone wall over there?"

The memory came back to me. "Oh, yes, Debbie, I remember it well." That night she had talked hopelessly of a failed Christian life. She said she didn't respond to the invitation to consecrate her life to the Lord because she was sick and tired of doing it over and over. After a recommitment she said life typically went well for a few days and then she was back to the same lifestyle of defeat.

"Debbie, who's in the driver's seat of your life?" I asked.

"Jesus is . . . ." She paused, then added, "Most of the time."

"It doesn't work that way. You don't let Him drive down the road to the first intersection and then grab the wheel. I think this is what you're saying." On a piece of paper I wrote two words: *No* and *Lord*.

"Well, yes, sometimes I do say that."

"But you can't," I insisted. "What does *Lord* mean?"

"Savior?" she asked.

"The Savior is Lord, but what does the word *Lord* mean?" I asked. After a few more guesses she gave up. "Well," I tried again, "How about *king*? What does *king* mean?"

"That's easy. A king is the big boss."

"Would you say no to the king?"

"It wouldn't be healthy."

"Right," I said. "And Jesus is King of all kings, Lord of all lords. You can't say no to Him! It's either 'Yes, Lord' or 'No, Jesus.' *No* cancels out the meaning of *Lord*." I tore the paper in half, with *No* on one piece and *Lord* on the other. "Which will it be?" I asked. "*No* or *Lord*?"

She dropped her head and her long hair covered her face as she wrestled with the choice. Minutes passed. Finally she threw her head back, tears streaming down her face. She reached for the paper with *Lord* written on it, but I pulled it away. "How long do you want Him to be Lord, Debbie?" I asked.

"I want Him to be Lord forever!" she said. At that moment Debbie experienced something the Bible describes as being filled with the Spirit. Now, a year later, I was hearing the result of Debbie's commitment. Her entire campus had been impacted by her decision.

[Unit Memory Verses]

Do not get drunk on wine, which leads to debauchery. Instead, be filled with the Spirit.

—*Ephesians 5:18*

The fruit of the Spirit is love, joy, peace, patience, kindness, goodness, faithfulness, gentleness and self-control.

—*Galatians 5:22-23*

[DAY 1] ·············· INTERNAL RELATIONSHIP: WHO'S IN CONTROL?

Do you sometimes wish the Bible would just tell you straight out what it means? Like *full*—what does it look like to be "filled with the Spirit"? What actually happens? What does it feel like? The Bible never defines it for us. It just points out people who are said to be filled full of the Spirit: John the Baptist even as a baby *(Luke 1:15)*, Stephen in the face of death *(Acts 7:55)*, and Zachariah when he sang *(Luke 1:67)*. We may not be able to describe full precisely, but it's a wonderful picture word. There's excitement in it, a completeness, a satisfaction. And a mystery.

In the margin describe what you think it means to be filled with the Spirit.

DEFINITIONS: 3 TYPES OF FULL
We use the word *full* in many different ways.

- Bob is full of whiskey.
- That kid is full of mischief.
- Judas was full of the devil.
- John is full of Betsy.

- The Book of Philippians is full of joy.
- He opened the jet full throttle.
- We've got a full tank of gas.
- The people were full of fear.

From the list of uses of the word *full*, write below any that might be similar to what it means to be full of the Spirit?

Type 1: Full can mean a relationship between two persons where one allows the other to dominate. *Luke 22:3* says Satan entered Judas. The chief idea seems to be that he was under the devil's control. Although the devil "entered in" to Judas and the Spirit "indwells" our bodies, the idea of being filled is not physical like a tank of gas. Full control is the first meaning of being filled with the Holy Spirit.

Type 2: Full also means showing evidence of the Spirit's presence. When a child is said to be full of mischief or John to be full of Betsy we mean they have characteristics that are highly visible. Everyone is aware of the mischief or the infatuation. Most of the Scripture references to being full of the Spirit indicate some evidence, some outcome of that filling: teaching, acting courageously, preaching, singing, meeting a crisis. To be filled with the Spirit is to have so much of His wisdom or power that things happen and everyone can tell.

Type 3: Being filled also includes a mystery that defies analysis. The mystery has something to do with an inner surge of emotion. For example, joy is a feeling often associated with being filled with the Spirit.

WHAT CAN I CLAIM?
Notice something about these three aspects of being filled with the Spirit. I am the only one who knows for sure who is in control. You cannot possibly tell whether or not I'm fully yielded to the Spirit. The same is true of any feelings resulting from that relationship. While only I can know about two of these aspects, only others can evaluate the outward evidence, the result of the Spirit's full control.

If you ask me if I'm filled with the Spirit, I can say, "Yes, God is in charge here." But if you're asking whether I seem to be a God-intoxicated person in my quality of life and service, it wouldn't be right for me to claim that kind of "fullness." Making such a claim would seem to disqualify me for the condition! Those who watch me

Then Satan entered Judas, called Iscariot, one of the Twelve.
—Luke 22:3

are the ones who can verify my fullness. People in the Bible didn't claim to be filled with the Spirit—it was a condition the Bible author said was true of them.

AN OVERVIEW OF FULLNESS

The first option on the list I gave, "Bob is full of whiskey," is a good example of fullness as obedience. In our memory passage Paul makes a contrast between being filled with alcohol and being filled with the Spirit.

What happens when a person drinks alcohol? The change of control is clear. The drug takes charge. We refer to it as "under the influence." Being filled with the Spirit also parallels being full of alcohol in another way. Because alcohol is an anesthetic to the brain, it hides a person's awareness of inadequacy and fear. The Spirit also resolves our problems of inadequacy and fear, but it doesn't merely cover them up. The Spirit teaches and empowers us so that we may overcome. The Spirit affects our emotions and attitudes because we begin to solve problems and live effectively.

To summarize the meaning of being filled with the Spirit we say: (1) You are under the controlling influence of another; (2) that influence is very evident, it's the dominant characteristic, something everyone is aware of; and (3) it affects your emotions.

CONTROLLING INFLUENCE

Since this first meaning of *full* refers to a relationship between two persons, it's quite possible for the relationship to change, as we saw with Debbie. When she refused to let God have the steering wheel of her life, she felt the anguish of a failed relationship. If we can turn control over to Him, we can take it back! The Bible uses another word to describe that, another picture word that contrasts with *full*: We can quench the Spirit—we can put out the fire. The Spirit of God won't force His way on you. So any kind of no will quench the Spirit, put out the fire of passion, stop the flow of power. Whenever I take back control of my life I'm shutting off His free flow of life.

PUTTING OUT THE FIRE

How can you tell when you are quenching the Spirit? He seems more distant, close companionship seems to have slipped away, service for God lacks power, temptations win out, you begin to spiral down. Here are some ways to "quench" the Spirit:

- neglect my daily quiet time of prayer and Bible study;
- watch TV shows with anti-Christian values;
- make excuses for some failure instead of acknowledging it;
- refuse to forgive someone who hurt me;
- flip through a magazine with sexually stimulating pictures;
- say yes to too many people and get overloaded;
- nurse my bruised ego and lapse into self-pity;
- let my mind dwell on envy;
- listen to a song that promotes worldly values.

 Put a check by any of the above Spirit-quenchers that have caused the fire of the Spirit to dwindle in your life. Then list in the margin any other activities or attitudes that have been a problem for you. Refusing to do something you know He wants you to do kills the fire instantly.

MAKING GOD SAD

The Bible uses another expression to describe our relationship to the Spirit. The Holy Spirit is a person with feelings—we can make Him sad. Paul says, "Don't do that!" Earlier in Ephesians Paul gave a detailed list of ways in which we can grieve the Spirit, quench His fire in us, or drain off the "filled" relationship.

Do not get drunk on wine, which leads to debauchery. Instead, be filled with the Spirit.
—Ephesians 5:18

> **The first meaning of being filled with the Spirit, is to yield full control to Him. Are you a Spirit-filled Christian in that sense?**
> ❏ **Yes** ❏ **No** ❏ **Unsure**

You should be able to answer with a resounding yes if, as far as you know your own heart, He is in charge. Let's be sure our unconditional yes to the Spirit is up-to-the-minute current. A suggested prayer is in the margin.

[DAY 2] .... EXTERNAL EVIDENCE: WHAT DO PEOPLE SEE?

SPIRITUAL FRUIT

When I was 12, I was filled with the Spirit in the sense we studied yesterday: As far as I knew my heart, I yielded my life to God. But the results weren't all that visible. I wasn't filled in the sense of being a showcase for Jesus' characteristics. I displayed some fruit—the result and evidence of God's indwelling presence—but it wasn't so great that people said, "That young man is so Christlike!" I worked for the Lord, too, but no one said, "The only way to explain what happens through that boy is that God's Spirit is at work!" Today we'll study about the evidence of Spirit-control.

To be filled with the Spirit, means more than turning over control of our lives to Him. It includes bearing fruit. There's another picture word! What does *fruit* mean?

> **In the margin write what you think of when you hear of spiritual fruit.**

SEEING THE EVIDENCE: JESUS' DESCRIPTION OF FRUIT

Fruit—the product of a plant or tree—is also the evidence of what kind of plant or tree it is. A peach tree produces peaches. If you see a peach, you know what kind of tree it came from. So it is in your life. If you've become a "Jesus plant," you'll produce Jesus fruit. Everyone is a fruit inspector; they can tell what's on the inside by what comes out. *"By their fruit you will recognize them,"* said Jesus *(Matt. 7:20)*. Jesus never intended us to have a few little shriveled fruits, just enough to prove what kind of tree we are. He promises a bumper crop—lots of Jesus characteristics. You might call it a *(full)* crop. He told us about it Himself.

> **Read *John 15:1-17* (Jesus' description of fruit) and list in the margin everything that looks like every characteristic that only the Holy Spirit can produce.**

You discovered lots of love-fruit, right? *(vv. 9-10, 12-13, 17)*. And joy! *(v. 11)*. There's that word *full* again—He's teaching us about fruit-bearing for the specific purpose that our joy will fill to the brim. Did you find "obedience"? He speaks in many different ways of obeying His commandments—all of them! (See *vv. 10, 14*.) The passage points to all possible fruit. Jesus says we must allow His words to take up residence inside us *(v. 7)*. Do you get the image of a vine or tree so heavily loaded that the fruit is not just a visible evidence, but the major characteristic? Everyone can tell, except possibly the person himself or herself. The person yields so much Jesus fruit that people are drawn to Jesus, either to embrace Him or to crucify Him.

—Galatians 5:22-23

SEEING THE EVIDENCE: PAUL'S DESCRIPTION OF FRUIT

> **Another way to inspect fruit is to use our memory verse as a checklist. In the margin write out *Galatians 5:22-23* (Paul's description of fruit).**

These characteristics are the product of the Spirit's activity. They can't be explained by the influence of a person's early environment or present circumstances. The kind of love, joy, or peace that can be explained by genetics and conditioning—though desirable and beautiful—is natural, not supernatural.

 Write about someone you know or know about who is an example of one of these qualities when there was no human reason to have it. Choose three characteristics to illustrate. I'll do the first "fruit" as an example.

love: _Rev. Kim asked the judge to pardon the man who killed his sons._

joy: _____

peace: _____

patience: _____

kindness: _____

goodness: _____

faithfulness: _____

gentleness: _____

self-control: _____

SEEING THE EVIDENCE: TITLES OF THE SPIRIT

Another way to identify the evidence of the Spirit's activity is to examine the titles given Him. He is called the Spirit of Truth *(John 14:17; 16:13)*. He is also called the Spirit of Grace *(Zech. 12:10)* because He is the dispenser of all God's free gifts. A marvelous passage in Isaiah describes many characteristics of the Spirit that He will produce in the coming Messiah: *The Spirit of the Lord will rest on him—the Spirit of wisdom and of understanding, the Spirit of counsel and of power, the Spirit of knowledge and of the fear of the Lord (Isa. 11:2).*

 How many characteristics of the Spirit in the paragraph above do you find?

Number of characteristics _____. His title throughout Scripture is _____ Spirit.

I found nine, but the most important one I left out! He is holy, apart from moral pollution, pure. His objective is to make holy people. Notice that the picture word, fruit, in the sense of Jesus-like attitudes and behavior is what we've been thinking about most of the time as we've studied life in the Spirit. Paul describes what we become in *Romans 6:22*. He connects the two key words *fruit* and *holiness*. The ultimate fruit of the Holy Spirit is to make us like Himself—a holy people *(1 Pet. 1:15; 2:9)*.

 Put a check by any of the nine characteristics above that you feel God is developing in your life. His job is to conform us to the image of Christ *(Rom. 8:29)*. Star the characteristics you sense that God wants to cultivate in your life.

SEEING THE EVIDENCE: A FRIEND'S EVALUATION

One sure-fire way exists to know what your crop looks like. Do you have an accountability partner? Remember, Christlikeness is the one meaning of *full* only others know for sure. You need a fruit inspector! Show someone you can trust to be honest about it, the work you have done in this unit. Ask the person for an evaluation—"Is my life obviously full of any of these characteristics? Are there others you have to search for to find?" Write down their answers in your journal.

But now having been set free from sin, and having become slaves of God, you have your fruit to holiness, and the end, everlasting life.
—Romans 6:22

[DAY 3] ···················· POWER-FILLED MINISTRY

There are different kinds of gifts, but the same Spirit....Now to each one the manifestation [visible evidence] of the Spirit is given for the common good....All these are the work of one and the same Spirit, and he gives them to each one.
—1 Corinthians 12:4,7,11).

Another evidence of being filled with the Spirit is results in our work for God that we can't account for by human explanation. Every believer has at least one God-given ability to serve Him (See *1 Cor. 12:4,7,11*).

MINIMUM EVIDENCE

The Bible doesn't tell us how to distinguish spiritual gifts from natural gifts. One key distinguishing mark is the fruit the gift produces. Is the outcome supernatural? The Corinthians said Paul was an unpolished speaker, in fact a sorry communicator. He didn't dispute their judgment, but when Paul taught the Bible, lives were transformed. There's the touch of the Spirit! The Bible leaves us in the dark on how natural abilities and Spirit-giftedness relate. Maybe we should look at the tasks that need to be done and trust God to give us the right combination of natural and supernatural ability to fulfill the tasks He calls us to do.

 What is your current role in the church or in other service to God?

How can you tell if you have the touch of the Spirit to accomplish the task or ministry involved?

 Here are some abilities the Holy Spirit gives. After each describe what a supernatural outcome that indicates the touch of God might look like.

To teach the Bible _____

To preach _____

To "practice hospitality" _____

To evangelize _____

To do pioneer missionary work _____

To counsel hurting people _____

To lead in the church _____

To help the poor _____

To encourage _____

Other? _____

The possible answers are almost limitless. Here are some examples that would show the power of the Spirit at work:

- teaching: in response, someone yields her life to God
- preaching: after the sermon, someone trusts God to change his life
- hospitality: people are drawn to the church and then to Christ because you served them and made them feel welcome
- evangelizing: someone is saved
- missionizing: new churches come into being
- counseling: someone begins to become more like Jesus
- leading: the church begins to move together toward biblical goals
- helping the poor: someone is drawn toward Christ through the assistance received
- encouraging: someone begins to draw strength from God.

MAXIMUM IMPACT

The apostles were filled with the Spirit at Pentecost and 3,000 people were converted (*Acts 2:41*), I'd call 3,000 responses *really* full. Yet a few weeks later their leaders had been arrested and threatened. So they called a prayer meeting and prayed for courage to witness in the face of persecution.

Once again they were filled with the Spirit *(Acts 4:31)* and as a result proclaimed the word with boldness. Amazing! Spirit-filled men were filled! The same pattern is common throughout Acts—Spirit-filled people are said to be filled again. How can that be? Remember, it's a picture word. I get the picture of a great schooner plowing through the ocean with sails full of wind when suddenly a gust of wind sweeps down and the schooner surges ahead under really full sail. So it is with the wind of the Spirit. (In both the Hebrew and Greek the word *spirit* means "breath" or "wind.")

 Have you experienced the "breath of the Spirit" at a critical time in your life? Check any of the following experiences you can relate to.
- ❑ Someone at school wants you to lie, threatens you if you don't; you ask God for help and suddenly have a surge of courage to do right.
- ❑ A friend makes fun of the church. You don't know where the ideas came from but scriptural truth just flowed as you spoke and the attack failed.
- ❑ You haven't been able to give a clear explanation of the gospel to your classmate, you plead with God for help, and you're astounded to hear yourself share your testimony and present the plan of salvation so clearly and easily.
- ❑ Your friends were mad at each other, no solution could be found, so you suggested a time-out for prayer. The Spirit moved, brought unity and a clear vision of what to do.

When we practice surrendered, obedient, faith, we will experience the movement of the Spirit. The Spirit moves in with wisdom, courage, and words that just weren't naturally there. You know God is at work and others can tell, too.

My responsibility is to preach and write. Before I preach I always ask the Spirit to move with power. If I rely on myself I can explain Scripture and tell stories. People will listen and say nice things, but nothing of eternal value will happen if the Spirit doesn't act. When the Spirit works, I watch in wonder as God transforms lives.

When I write, I'm always grateful to note any small amount of "fruit" God gives. But once in a while the words flow almost uninvited out of my computer like they're on fire. When published, the work seems to take on a life of its own. When I read it later I say, "Where'd that come from? Did I write that?" The Spirit had been working that day, and the result wasn't just my work.

> *But now having been set free from sin, and having become slaves of God, you have your fruit to holiness, and the end, everlasting life.*
> *—Romans 6:22*

 Do you have some gift working at a minimal level? Can you tell God is at work through you, but it's not full-throttle so that other people can tell? Ask Him to fill you. Open your heart to the wind of the Spirit and trust Him to empower and use you. Begin the habit of asking Him, at the time of special opportunity or challenge, to empower you so that He may get the glory.

THOSE ELUSIVE FEELINGS ························· [DAY 4]

The picture word *full* seems to have three different emphases. A person is full when in his or her relationship with the Spirit the Spirit is in full control and there is plenty of evidence, "fruit" or "gifts," showing the Spirit at work.

A MYSTERY, LIKE A GOOD MARRIAGE

How do you analyze a *full* personal relationship? Like a good marriage, the outward evidence, such as a home and children, may be obvious, but the feelings are more mysterious. A relationship includes moments of shared happiness and shared sadness, a deep and constant sense of well-being and surges of passionate love. So it is living in a deep relationship with the Spirit.

If I'm filled with the Spirit I'll have joy, for example, or confidence or peace when there's no earthly reason to have any peace at all. My affection for God will be filled with passion—an excited sense of anticipation when I pause to worship Him, a rush of pleasure when I think about His love for me. I may not sustain an emotional high, but there are moments of uninhibited happiness, especially in those devotional times alone with Him. But also, unexpectedly in the midst of a busy day the wind of the Spirit may blow in gale strength. I can't explain it, but I can feel it.

 Have you had such a surge of affection or some other emotional response to God's presence? In the margin briefly describe your experience.

If your relationship with God is ordinary and you're thirsty for a full surge of awareness of God's presence, right now tell Him. Tell Him how much you love Him, how grateful you are for Him, for His constant companionship and for all the blessings in your life. Ask Him to fill you up with Himself.

 Write in your journal either the description of your experience of fullness, the prayer for fullness, or both.

DOWNERS AND UPPERS

 In the margin, write your memory verse from Galatians. Now in the verse circle all the fruits that are emotional words to you.

You may have circled some or all. For example, to love is to act lovingly no matter how you feel. Maybe that's why God seems to expect us to have these qualities constantly in our lives—all the fruit, all the time. Their presence shows the Spirit at work. But the emotions that accompany them may not be surging all the time.

Perhaps God intends the fruit to be constant and the surges of feelings to be special outpourings?

- Jesus was a man of sorrows and acquainted with grief. He agonized in the garden of Gethsemane, but there were also times of surging joy—*At that time, Luke tells us, Jesus, full of joy through the Holy Spirit (10:21).*
- David, the joy-filled singer, experienced dry times. When God seemed distant, David cried out in alarm, *Do not…take your Holy Spirit from me (Ps. 51:11).*
- Paul had times of fear and called on friends to pray for the Spirit-gift of boldness *(2 Cor. 7:5; Eph. 6:19-20).*

These Bible characters didn't constantly have the inner sense of fullness. In my own life I can count on having a truly exalted experience of God when I go away for my annual time of fasting and prayer. So much so, I can remember most of those occasions, even years later. But only occasionally do I have that rushing sense of God's presence in my daily quiet time; even less often do I have it unexpectedly in the midst of a busy day. How I long to have those experiences daily, but I don't.

I'd say, "It's OK. No one does." But I'm not so sure. Christian's through the ages give testimony of such a walk with God. My son, Kent, is an example. He lives among the slum dwellers of Calcutta, surely the nearest place to hell on earth. Kent keeps so in step with the Spirit that those highs seem to come daily, right in the midst of agonizing suffering. He is so pained when he doesn't experience God on a daily basis,

For myself, I'll keep praising God for the times when I do experience Him on a higher plane—and I'll keep seeking the fullness however God defines that for me.

Fullness, in the sense of an inner feeling is not subject to analysis, but it can be a glorious experience. The Holy Spirit gives it to those who love and stay close to Him.

MEASURING THREE KINDS OF FULLNESS

 If full feelings are hard to explain or define, the other meanings of full are not. By each of the following examples of being full of the Spirit, mark an O by those which emphasize Obedience to the Spirit's control; S for evidence of Spirit empowered service; and, F for a Feeling or subjective sense of fullness. Mark more than one if several meanings seem present.

_____ 1. Billy Graham preaches and thousands respond to Christ.

_____ 2. Paul was not gifted as a public speaker, but when he taught lives were transformed.

_____ 3. Hubert said, "If I know it's wrong, I never deliberately choose to do it."

_____ 4. Only I know for sure if I'm "full."

_____ 5. Many in that church are spiritually gifted.

_____ 6. Widow Smith is dying of cancer, but she's always so joyful.

_____ 7. I could feel God's presence in church Sunday.

_____ 8. Debbie chose to say "Lord" rather than "no."

My answers would be 1: S; 2: S; 3: O; 4: O; 5: S; 6: F; 7: F; 8: O.

The following are most of the examples in the New Testament where the context indicates the meaning of being filled with the Spirit.

❑ _All ...were filled with the Holy Spirit and began to speak in other tongues (Acts 2:4)._

❑ _The disciples were filled with joy and with the Holy Spirit (Acts 13:52)._

❑ _Then Peter, filled with the Holy Spirit, said to them, "...Enable your servants to speak your word with great boldness."...And they were all filled with the Holy Spirit and spoke the word of God boldly (Acts 4:8,29,31)._

❑ _"Choose seven men ...known to be full of the Spirit and wisdom" (Acts 6:3)._

❑ _He was a good man, full of the Holy Spirit and faith, and a great number of people were brought to the Lord (Acts 11:24)._

❑ _Then...Paul, filled with the Holy Spirit, looked straight at Elymas ...(Acts 13:9)._

 Check each example above where the evidence of the Spirit's fullness seems to be subjective awareness or feeling. Don't mark those that emphasize yieldedness to the Spirit, miracle behavior, or powerful ministry as evidence of the Spirit's fullness.

Most of the examples have to do with power in ministry, but some subjective evidences appear. I found joy, boldness, and faith. However, both the boldness and faith are related directly to ministry! So, in the biblical examples, the subjective element of feelings, which we so emphasize today, is not prominent.

My obedience to the Spirit is clear to me. My fruits and gifts are clear to others, but the inner sense of fullness may not be so obvious. God promises, in filling us with Himself, to give us love that is beyond comprehension _(Eph. 3:19)._ Yet, we can't even fathom the kind of peace that guards our hearts and minds. However, Paul says we can experience it _(Phil. 4:7)._ How exciting to feel the surge of the Spirit!

_EPHESIANS 5:18—_STEADY-STATE FULLNESS

One of our memory verses ties together the three different aspects of being filled with the Spirit. The verb _be filled_ is unusual in that it is a command—something I must do—but it's in the passive form, something the Spirit does to me. "Be being

When we came into Macedonia, this body of ours had no rest, but we were harassed at every turn—conflicts on the outside, fears within.
—2 Corinthians 7:5

Pray also for me, that whenever I open my mouth, words may be given me so that I will fearlessly make known the mystery of the gospel, for which I am an ambassador in chains. Pray that I may declare it fearlessly, as I should.
—Ephesians 6:19-20

filled" would be an awkward translation, but gets at the meaning. So how do I obey if He is the one who does it? I take the initiative and deliberately yield control. Then I keep on praying and expecting Him to produce the fruit of godliness and power for ministry. If He surges through with a flood of some special emotion, how blessed!

The command be *filled* is also a continuous action verb: "Keep on being filled with the Spirit." Being filled is a constant in that sense, an abiding relationship. Steady-state filled, you might call it. If the Holy Spirit has control of my life, He'll continuously fill me with power to live and serve.

In *Ephesians 5:18-20* Paul names examples of each kind of fullness. He talks about singing, praise, and prayer. Paul says, let the Spirit fill you always as a way of life. Then, from time to time, out of His grace, He'll blow into your life with gale force and fan the embers into an all-consuming fire of His Spirit's own making. When that happens simultaneously to a lot of people, we call the result revival.

In the margin, explain the Scripture memory verse in your own words. Now write the verse from memory.

[DAY 5] •••••••••••••••••••••••••••• REVIVAL

We are a part of a larger community of believers. Can you imagine the power unleashed when a group of Christians simultaneously surrender to the Spirit? What would a worship service be like with such a group? How would their prayer meetings be? What kind of impact would they make on unbelievers? Do you ever long to be part of such a Holy Spirit outpouring? We call it revival.

Since the Bible doesn't use the term *revival* why have Christian people always used the term? The Bible repeatedly describes great movings of the Spirit and the church has experienced such movings periodically through its history. We've called those times revival—*re* means "again" and *vival* means "life." So when I speak of revival I mean a renewal of life that once was or ought to have been. Even with the examples from the Bible and church history coupled with the plain meaning of the term itself, however, revival doesn't seem to mean the same thing to everyone.

 Check each of the stories below which you think could be a Spirit-sent revival.

❏ In the midst of the speaker's message students began to stand all across the college chapel and confess their sins, often with tears. The meeting went on till midnight, and the movement continued for days in the dorms and across the campus. The results included changed lives and spontaneous eruptions of joyful singing.

❏ At the revival meetings at Bent Creek Church last week an alcoholic, a business man and his wife, three teens, and an adult were saved.

❏ The "Second Great Awakening," powerfully advanced by John Wesley, transformed the entire British social structure. It led directly to the abolition of slavery and revitalized the Christian community so that the modern Protestant missionary movement was launched.

❏ When the invitation was given, the leading deacon in the church came to the front of the church and tearfully confessed that his opposition to the pastor had caused grief in the church. He asked for the pastor and the church to forgive him. Then a stream of people came forward or went to others in the congregation, asking forgiveness, embracing, weeping, and laughing. Healing of old wounds began.

❑ Jan studied about life in the Spirit, sensed that something in her life was lacking and turned her life over unconditionally to the Spirit's control. She experienced such a surge of His life-force that she found herself spiraling up toward greater likeness to Christ. She began to see spiritual results from her work for God and sensed God's own loving companionship. She was puzzled that not everyone in the church seemed interested in her discovery.

Did you check all of them? I did. But they are so different! Instead of helping us understand the term, the exercise may confuse us. So let's try a few definitions I've taken from various sources.

 Check the ones you think best define the term *revival*.

❑ 1. Revival is a powerful activity of the Spirit in large numbers of people at the same time.

❑ 2. Revival is a quickening of believers to extraordinary levels of praise and prayer, of powerful witness, of loving concern for others.

❑ 3. Revival is a renewal of God's people in which lives are reclaimed and the dying embers of spiritual life are fanned back into a flame. It's a visitation of life where there had been signs of death.

❑ 4. Revival is an evangelistic campaign.

❑ 5. Revival is an outpouring of miraculous signs and extraordinary emotional up-heaval.

❑ 6. Revival is a time when spiritual concern becomes the pressing and absorbing concern of many.

❑ 7. Revival is a time Christians are restored to their first love for Christ. Shame and hypocrisy are exposed; bitterness and strife in the body of Christ are revealed and repented of with the result that sinners are brought to Christ in great numbers.

❑ 8. Revival is a sovereign act of God that cannot be anticipated or brought about by human effort.

Among these "definitions" I like #7 best, though each touches on some aspect of what has been called "revival." Since the Bible doesn't use the term, but does report movements of spiritual renewal of various kinds, perhaps we are safest not to prescribe the details of what must happen to qualify as true revival. We can, however, discern some common features among these examples and definitions:

1. Revival is the work of the Holy Spirit.

2. He revitalizes or renews those He has already given life.

3. This renewed spiritual vitality is visible to others and leads to change in them also, seen both in a spreading revival among believers and a turning to Christ among unbelievers.

This last characteristic would seem to rule out the idea of a "personal revival," which some use to describe a fresh encounter with God. Anyone can experience this renewal at any time he or she is prepared to acknowledge a need, yield to God's control, and trust Him to give renewed life. Personal renewal may best be referred to by terms like the theme of this unit—being filled with the Spirit. I can experience the fullness of God's blessing whether or not others participate.

 Does your church need revival? Choose from the examples and definitions in the two lists above the ones you'd most like to see in your church. Perhaps you sense other needs or things you would like to happen in widespread spiritual renewal. List them in the margin.

Here are some signs of revival. Check the ones that sound like your church.

❑ We express excitement in our times of worship, both for young and old.

❑ People often find Christ through our youth group and church; baptisms of new believers are common.

❑ There is a feeling of family closeness among our people, a loving spirit of care for one another.

❑ The people in our community who don't join us, still know something is going on and have to admit we're alive.

❑ When one member of our youth group fails, the others reach out in love and restore the person; repentance, confession, reconciliation are common.

❑ Prayer meetings are vital, God is answering prayer and changing lives, and people are spontaneously clustering with others to pray.

❑ Our church wants to reach the whole world for Christ. Concern for missions is a powerful factor in our praying, giving, and preparing for local and world mission service.

Did you easily identify spiritual needs in your church or youth group? Were evidences of spiritual vitality hard to find? Are you satisfied with the way things are, or do you hope for revival in your youth group and church? If you are experiencing a spiritual drought in your youth group or church, you can do two things(1) Be sure that you personally are experiencing the fullness of the Spirit as a continuing pattern of life; and (2) Pray for revival, recruiting others to join you in prayer.

"We cannot legislate spiritual awakening, but we can set our sails to catch the wind," said G. Campbell Morgan. My son Bob and I were trying to cross a large lake on the boundary between the United States and Canada, but the wind kept driving us toward the shore long before we reached the end of the lake. We paddled our canoe with all the energy we could muster, like the poor remnant in a church that stays faithful and tries to move things forward. Also, like that remnant, we wore out, went with the wind and beached our canoe. After a rest we started out again, but made little progress. Then Bob, the veteran canoer, told me to tie his poncho between two paddles, sit in the prow and hoist my "sail" to the wind while he relaxed in the stern and navigated. Amazing! We began to skim across the lake under full sail, much to the astonishment of other canoeists struggling vainly to make progress. So it is when the mighty Wind of God blows through His people with renewing power.

So let us set our sails, covenant to pray and keep on praying till revival comes. In the meantime, until God chooses to unleash a widespread renewal, you can make very sure that you personally are eligible for revival and thus no barrier to what God would do. That's the first meaning of being filled with the Spirit—unconditional yieldedness to His will, making sure each day that He is in charge.

By keeping a close connection with the Spirit we can be sure of a full harvest of godly characteristics and powerful service, and at least a periodic inner sense of God-intoxication. We can do what Paul says in *Ephesians 5:18* and keep on being filled with the Spirit! As He "pours in," we will be truly filled full, or we could say fulfilled.

On top of that—as if that were not exciting enough—by daily obeying the command to keep on being filled, we open the door for the Holy Spirit to do His work. We do our part to set up the whole church for joining in that filling. We pray that the entire church will experience a "chain revival," leaping on from one degree of glory to another.

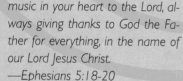

Do not get drunk on wine, which leads to debauchery. Instead, be filled with the Spirit. Speak to one another with psalms, hymns and spiritual songs. Sing and make music in your heart to the Lord, always giving thanks to God the Father for everything, in the name of our Lord Jesus Christ.
—Ephesians 5:18-20

 Stop now and tell God how you feel about all this good news of Spirit fullness. And begin your own revival prayer watch, too, committing to keep at it till God's Spirit renews His church.

BATTLE PLAN

In this unit you will develop a personal battle plan for partnering with the Spirit in winning the victory over temptations that assault you daily. Your memory verse provides an outline for the unit.

Diane had been a Christian for two years, spiraling upward, open and eager for all the Spirit was teaching. Then she made a discovery. She took a class I taught on the Christian life. The assignment was to write a paper on developing a battle plan for overcoming temptation. The paper wasn't just about how to overcome temptation. The assignment was very personal: "A Strategy for Overcoming My Own Strongest Temptation." Diane should have known about temptation—even Jesus had to slug it out with the devil! But in the exuberance of her new found faith, she missed the issue of dealing with temptation. She added a note to her paper:

> As a "toddler" Christian, I have had very little knowledge about Satan and his tactics. Because I lacked knowledge and understanding, I never felt plagued by temptation. Consequently I did not feel a need to devise a plan to overcome temptation.

> After researching this paper, life isn't as comfortable. I now realize the devil is working in my life, and I see the temptations that beset me. This discovery is both terrible and wonderful. I've already defeated Satan in one way because I'm no longer ignorant of and oblivious to his attacks in my life.

Students really got into the project, some writing almost book-length papers, many telling how the project was life-transforming. "My life has been radically changed. For the first time I'm beginning to see progress toward victory." Once in a while I get a letter from a former student, "Remember the assignment on developing a strategy to overcome temptation? That was the turning point in my Christian experience." Each of these students discovered that being filled with the Spirit doesn't lift one beyond temptation. In fact, the battle will escalate! Unfortunately, this battle catches too many sincere, growing Christians off guard, faltering before they know what hit them. Others know they are being tempted, but they don't know how to defend themselves, so they go down in defeat.

[Unit Memory Verse]

Therefore, I urge you, brothers, in view of God's mercy, to offer your bodies as living sacrifices, holy and pleasing to God—this is your spiritual act of worship. Do not conform any longer to the pattern of this world, but be transformed by the renewing of your mind. Then you will be able to test and approve what God's will is—his good, pleasing and perfect will.
—Romans 12:1-2

[DAY 1] ·· PREPARATION FOR BATTLE

This unit's memory verse, *Romans 12:1-2*, is so familiar, we're tempted to let the words run through our minds without engaging their powerful meaning.

> **In the margin, rewrite *Romans 12:1-2* in your own words. Briefly explain the meaning as you understand it.**

Each student's paper offered a different approach to overcoming temptation. However, the temptations were similar. The guys most often wrote of sexual temptation such as lustful eyes and thoughts. The girls spoke of emotional struggles such as feeling smug when someone else wasn't as well-dressed, attractive, or intelligent. Even weak Christians were fair game for the condescension.

REST OR WRESTLE?

Everyone needs a workable battle strategy to conquer temptations. Apparently some seek to deal with temptation in a different way. Once or twice in every batch of papers I found a "paper" that was one sentence long: "I have no strategy; the Holy Spirit lives in me and that's all the strategy I need." Which will it be? Do I get out of the way and let God manage my life for me, or do I personally slug it out with the enemy? We may be tempted to go to one extreme or the other—to opt for a spectator role and leave it up to God, or develop a do-it-yourself mind-set.

> **Put a check where you find yourself in your present attitude toward your main temptation(s).**

God does it all—   It's up to me—
rest in Him   wrestle it out

The Bible teaches both a faith that rests and a faith that wrestles. We trust the Spirit to do the work of remaking us. But we must also use the weapons He provides to fight the evil in our lives. If we concentrate solely on what He does, we may slip into complacency and get ambushed by the enemy. If we concentrate just on our responsibility to fight, we may become battle weary and give up the battle. We've got to develop a spiritual war mentality. Here are some specific steps to take. We must approach spiritual battles as seriously as a commander planning a military campaign.

STEP 1—SURRENDER

The spiritual war differs from all other battles. In this battle, surrender is victory. The first step in winning spiritual war is surrendering to the Lord. When faced with temptation, the only way to win is to give up! Not to the enemy or to the temptation, we must surrender to the Victor. "I plead with you," says Paul, "surrender yourself, your rights, even your very life. That's where victory begins" [my paraphrase]. Sacrifice can be painful. Sometimes you must give up:

- a friend who keeps you from God's highest and best
- the ambition that is really an ego trip
- that fun thing that eats up the time you should spend on God's business
- a purchase so that the hungry of the world may eat.

Those sacrifices can hurt. God wants all of you—a living sacrifice. That's where victory begins. That alone starts you on the way to holiness and is acceptable to God, but this living sacrifice is only reasonable.

STEP 2—IDENTIFY THE SOURCE OF TEMPTATION

The next step is to identify the source of temptation. Be clear about the battle you're fighting. In our memory verse, Paul states that the pressure of "the world"—other people, things, and circumstances can cause us to stumble *(Matt. 18:6-7)*. The world presents us with occasions to become angry. It makes sin look attractive. Circumstances like poverty or riches *(Prov. 30:8,9)* can also put pressure on us.

Paul also identifies minds that need renovation—our inner desires and impulses. Ultimately our source of temptation isn't the people or circumstances, it's our response to them. We've given ground already in our minds—*Each one is tempted when, by his own evil desire, he is dragged away and enticed (Jas. 1:14).*

Satan is the original source of all temptation; and he's on the prowl, ready to pounce on us *(1 Pet. 5:8)*. We should always be on guard *(Eph. 6:11)*, never give up *(Eph. 4:27)*, fight back *(Jas. 4:7)*, and stay alert to his tricks and deceptions *(2 Cor. 2:11)*.

 What are your greatest temptations? On the line beside the source, write your most frequent temptations. Number them in order of their strength.

Source	Example
___ Satan	_____
___ inner desires, impulses	_____
___ other people	_____
___ things, circumstances	_____
___ God	_____

All the sources of temptation in the last activity can be sources of temptation except one—God. *James 1:13* clearly states that God tempts no one. How then does the Bible sometimes credit the same tempting circumstances as coming from both Satan and God? *(See 2 Sam. 24:1 and 1 Chron. 21:1)*. The motive is the key. Satan uses people or circumstances to bring us down. God uses those same circumstances to test or prove our allegiance, or to make us stronger.

STEP THREE: RECOGNIZE THE ROOT SIN

Temptation looks good; otherwise it wouldn't tempt. God purposely gave us the ability to experience desire. Enticement to sin is the temptation to abuse a God-given desire. God created us to enjoy our bodies, acquire possessions, and accomplish worthwhile goals. But when we try to fulfill those desires in the wrong way, we sin.

The next step in our plan is to see the difference between God-given drives and our destructive responses to those desires. God's given us the ability to enjoy many things, but we easily twist the ability to enjoy into sinful responses that become destructive life patterns. When we recognize the legitimate desires, we can identify the root sin behind our temptations. The following chart shows examples of the God-given desire, the sinful response, and the end result of a lifestyle of sinful response:

God-given Desire	Sinful Response	End Result
• to enjoy food sex, rest	lust	self-indulgence
• to own things	covetousness	materialism
• to be somebody have significance	pride	selfishness

Some people believe that all sin can be placed under one of these categories—

- lust (abuse of our desire to enjoy food, sex, rest)
- covetousness (desire to own something not mine or not in God's will for me)
- pride (taking credit for something God has achieved).

If I give in to any impulse long enough, I will become that type of person. Lust

Steps to winning over temptation
1. Surrender
2. Identify the source

When tempted, no one should say, "God is tempting me." For God cannot be tempted by evil, nor does he tempt anyone; but each one is tempted when, by his own evil desire, he is dragged away and enticed.
—James 1:13-14

Steps to winning over temptation
1. Surrender
2. Identify the source
3. Recognize the root sin

yielded to creates a self-indulgent person. Covetousness too often given in to ends in a materialistic outlook. Pride may so often prevail that I'm more interested in what the world thinks of me rather than what God thinks of me. To win the battle against temptation, we need to recognize the root sin, not just the outward result. We especially need this understanding when a sinful attitude becomes a character trait.

For example, outbursts of anger may actually be rooted in some unresolved bitterness. From where did the bitterness come? What caused it? To root out the basic problem, we must identify both the problem and the source.

STEP FOUR: ACKNOWLEDGE THE TAPROOT

Let's picture temptation as a tree with three roots: lust, pride, and covetousness. However, some scholars point to an underlying taproot—unbelief. Some say unbelief is the source of the other three! Eve fell before temptations to lust, covet, and act arrogantly because she doubted God's word. The taproot is the single root that grows deepest into the ground.

Other scholars say the fundamental flaw in human nature is self-love. A problem exists with that idea. Self-love is more like the innocent drives God built into us—the desires to enjoy, possess, and be significant. However, concern about one's own interests can run out of control. When I act in my self-interest at the expense of God or someone else, I've sinned. Perhaps I've committed the most fundamental sin of all, since the first and great commandment is to love God supremely. If self-love is the source of my sin, I'm not going to win the battle till I obey God's first commandment.

We must identify the roots of our temptations. Unbelief and love skewed toward self-interest seem almost always to be present, but they're so general it may be more helpful in our battle plan to look at the root sins: lust, covetousness, and pride.

➤ **In the margin answer the following three questions: What current temptation are you facing to be enjoyed in the wrong way (lust)? What, specifically, are you tempted to covet? What are you tempted to be proud about?**

Temptation wears a mask—it looks appealing and promises good. That's why it's a temptation. If it wore its own face, it would be so ugly we'd run! The first task, then, is to unmask the temptation—identify it for exactly what it is: lust, covetousness, pride, unbelief, or just plain self-love. These enemies take away the power or filling of the Holy Spirit in our lives, and they grieve Him. Our sins of unbelief and self-love reveal themselves in the temptations of lust, covetousness, and pride.

To start development of your battle plan against temptation, begin with:
- an unconditional surrender to the will of God (it puts you out of a dangerous no-man's land solidly on God's side).
- identify the enemy (the source of the temptation may not be that easy to spot. Temptation fights dirty and wears a mask, but you can spot any disguised temptation by focusing Scripture on your situation).
- make your choice (choose right and grow stronger, choose wrong and grow weaker).

Steps to winning over temptation
1. Surrender
2. Identify the source
3. Recognize the root sin
4. Acknowledge the Taproot

1.

2.

3.

[DAY 2] · · · · · · · · · · · · · · · DEFENSIVE STRATEGY

Every battle plan needs defensive and offensive strategies. Today we'll study ways to defend, to ward off temptation even before it strikes.

LEGITIMATE DESIRE OR SINFUL DESIRE?

Sometimes it's hard to tell if something is a legitimate desire or a sinful desire. Is this new CD player a real need or coveting what God doesn't intend? Is my reaction to this guy righteous anger or sinful anger? Is the pain I feel justifiable, or am I so unhappy because my ego took a heavy hit?

 How do you most often decide between real need and temptation to sin?
- ❏ I trust the Holy Spirit to show me what's right.
- ❏ I recall Bible teaching on the subject.
- ❏ I quote a Bible command I've memorized.
- ❏ I listen to my conscience.

All of those answers do help us know right from wrong, but the first and last are tricky. None of them works without the first one. But we must not assume that the Spirit within is all we need. He provided other means of knowing His will, so we are sure to go down in defeat if we neglect any of them. The Spirit's no substitute for the others; He's their energizer.

What about depending on our conscience? Natural conscience is an unreliable guide since it's no more than our judgment of right versus wrong. Judgment is programmed by home, school, and society, not to mention our sinful nature. We seem to have the ability to con ourselves into believing what we want to believe. For conscience to be a reliable guide we must constantly be transformed into a new creation by the Spirit; use Scripture as a guide for the decision-making process; keep in tune with the Spirit; and, develop judgment by consistent, obedient practice.

FOUR ESSENTIALS FOR A TRUE CONSCIENCE
- __ *Transformed into new creation by Holy Spirit*
- __ *Use Scripture as a guide*
- __ *Keep in tune with the Spirit*
- __ *Develop judgment by practice*

 In the margin, number the four essentials needed to have a "true" conscience in the order of the priority you place on each.

CONFORMED OR TRANSFORMED?

In Japan, we rarely watched TV, which was very tame by American standards. I visited American friends and was shocked to hear them laughing over sexual innuendos of the characters in a popular TV program. "They put that garbage on TV?" I asked.

Twenty years passed. I hadn't watched TV much, but enough to get a feel for the programming. Suddenly I woke up to an astonishing change in me. For a year or more I enjoyed watching reruns of the same program that I had criticized previously. What had happened? I had been molded by my world into its way of thinking. And Paul says, "Stop!" Our second memory verse might be literally translated: "Resist the conforming influences of your environment and keep on resisting." Popular media is hell-bent (literally) on cultivating lust, covetousness, and pride. And I was letting it happen to me. In fact, I recently made a covenant with myself to stop some TV watching; when I was honest with myself and God, I had to admit what I was actually looking for—and it wasn't purity, contentment, and humility!

 Have you ever come to a similar realization? Have you found yourself watching, doing, or buying something that you previously considered destructive or off limits? ❏ Yes ❏ No. If so, describe your experience in the margin.

Sometimes I watched just to relax and unwind after a difficult day, but doing so ate up priceless time. It was subtly molding me into a different kind of person. Paul says to resist and keep resisting—eternal vigilance is the price of spiritual freedom.

To resist and keep resisting we must do four things (1) realize it is a constant battle, (2) decide firmly on whose side we belong, (3) identify our major enemies, and

(4) take hold of or use our weapons. In the fight for our spiritual freedom the Bible, prayer, and the church are our front-line weapons. The Spirit uses them in combination to create an effective defensive strategy. Let's look at each of these weapons.

THE BIBLE: STOCKPILING YOUR AMMUNITION

Scan the war stories in *Genesis 3:1-6* and *Matthew 4:1-11*. Here we have deadly battles. First between Satan and Eve, then between Satan and Jesus—the welfare of billions depended on the outcome of each battle. Eve met Satan with a perfect heredity and a perfect environment while Jesus' heritage on His mother's side was a fallen humanity and His environment was a sinful world. But Eve lost, Jesus won.

Circle the names of those in the previous paragraph who quoted God's Word. Read *Psalm 119:9-11*. In the margin, briefly explain how if Eve had heeded these words she could have won her battle with Satan.

Eve quoted God's Word, but she wasn't all that committed to its authority. She quickly abandoned her only defense and accepted the enemy's word over God's. Satan used Scripture to push his ungodly ends. Only Jesus used the Word of God as His weapon. And He won! You will, too. But you must stockpile your ammunition or you won't have it available at the time of testing. Jesus knew His Bible.

We can stockpile ammunition by regularly reading the Bible and selectively studying it. For example, I may be blind to the discontent in my life that is choking out the growth of joy and peace. As I read the Word daily, I see how great God is and how greatly He cares about me. Then I realize how sinful my discontent really is, how foolish it is in the light of His greatness. The Word has spotlighted a temptation I didn't even know existed. God's Word alerted me to a hidden enemy. Selective study, is to search out all the Bible teaches about a specific issue. As I deal with a particular temptation, I study all the Scripture has to say about that temptation. The verses I find can then be used as a weapon against temptation. This knowledge will help me when I face this temptation the next time it strikes.

List again your major temptations that you listed in day 1. Write a Scripture reference that refers to each sin. Memorize and use these verses as ammunition when you are tempted.

1. _____
2. _____
3. _____

Do a more thorough study later of what the Bible says about your special enemies. Begin to stockpile your ammunition.

PRAYER: STRATEGIC BOMBARDMENT

Remember the story of how I put in my prayer notebook "T & T"? Every day I pinpointed the enemies of an out of control tongue and an explosive temper. I didn't wait until the enemy was on the horizon and started his attack of temptations. I started every day asking the Holy Spirit to send in His troops and knock out the enemy in my life. He knew in advance what I'd face that day. I asked Him to prepare me, to give me strength to win, to alert me to ambushes I wouldn't even see. I didn't pray: "Lord help me be good today." I prayed about the sins that were winning in my life. I targeted my big enemies, and I prayed daily for victory over them.

From your list of personal temptations choose the one that brings you down most and write in the margin a model prayer you might use on a daily basis until God gives you victory over that temptation.

How can a young man keep his way pure?
By living according to your word.
I seek you with all my heart;
do not let me stray from your commands.
I have hidden your word in my heart that I might not sin against you.
—Psalm 119:9-11

"Watch and pray so that you will not fall into temptation."
—Matthew 26:41

"Lead us not into temptation, but deliver us from the evil one."
—Matthew 6:13

THE CHURCH: BUILDING A DEFENSIVE TEAM

The defensive use of the church body is primarily to build a support network of people who grow strong together in studying the Word, uniting in prayer, encouraging one another, and setting the example for one another. Together we build—in a way we never could on our own—spiritual muscle in preparation for the battle.

An accountability partner is someone you can share with openly about your temptations, your victories, and your defeats. A word of caution, though: to share with a partner who is vulnerable to the same temptation you are fighting is usually unwise. A drowning man doesn't need another drowning man to come to the rescue! But one of the greatest defenses against temptation is a buddy in the battle, an accountability partner to pray with you about your temptation.

 If you have an accountability partner and haven't shared your struggle with temptation, do so this week. Ask God to help you find an accountability partner. It could be an older person too. When you have someone in mind, write their name here: _____.

"Reject and keep on resisting the conforming influences of your environment," says Paul. Our defensive strategy works when we use use the Word, prayer, and our fellow soldiers.

All of you stand shoulder to shoulder, becoming one in heart…put together your strength and fight..
–Philippians 1:27-28, translated from the Japanese

OFFENSIVE STRATEGY ·························· [DAY 3]

We use the same weapons at the time of enemy encounter that we used in building up our defenses: the Bible, prayer, and the church. But we use them differently.

 Let's start with our memory verse. In the margin write *Romans 12:2*.

The mind is the battleground where spiritual battles are won or lost. I use the term *mind* to include all of you, what you think, how you feel, what you choose. You need all the activities of your mind renewed. The word for *renew* in Greek is *metamorphosis*. Consider how we use that term: The little earth-bound fuzzy worm metamorphosed into a gorgeous creature of the skies! That's what Paul says we're to work at—"be totally changed in our entire outlook and response." We must have a decisive turning point, then we must keep working at changing.

The mind is the battlefield of a deadly war. You either win or lose the battle in your mind. The first step in the battle is to have your entire mind-set transformed. To transform your mind-set use the Bible, prayer, and the church not only to build up a defense in advance, but as offensive weapons at the time of confrontation.

No temptation has seized you except what is common to man. And God is faithful; he will not let you be tempted beyond what you can bear. But when you are tempted, he will also provide a way out so that you can stand up under it.
—1 Corinthians 10:13

THE BIBLE: OFFENSIVE WEAPON

About 4:00 a.m. my telephone rang. The voice said, "Is this Mr. McQuilkin?"

"Yes," I responded. A dread settled in as I recognized the officer on the phone.

Oh, no, not again, I thought. Three months ago my car had been stolen from my backyard. I looked out the back window and, sure enough, my car was gone again. Once again, the police found it, torn up as before.

I was angry. *I'd like to put a booby trap on that car. Guess what would happen to the next person who touches it!* I thought to myself. And I was afraid. *Was it the same people? Will our house be next? Maybe we should move out of this inner-city neighborhood we deliberately chose to live in…*

> **Here are some of the emotions and thoughts I had this morning. Check those you think are unacceptable to God.**
> ❑ 1. *I'm angry*   ❑ 2. *I'll booby trap that car*
> ❑ 3. *I'm afraid of what will happen.*   ❑ 4. *I'm outta here, forget this place*
> ❑ 5. *Why did God let this happen? I asked Him only last night to protect my car, since the police certainly couldn't.*

A couple of those are clearly bad. The booby-trap strategy is vengeful, and I would be disobedient if I left my calling to live for God in this neighborhood. Anger and fear are not necessarily sinful (#1 & 3); it depends on what I do in response to the emotions. The last item could become sinful depending on how I respond to the emotions. I lapse into unbelief if I conclude God won't care for me (#5).

No use to go back to bed—I was too agitated. So I turned to Scripture for an earlier-than-usual devotional time. I was in *Hebrews 10*, but I couldn't concentrate. This chapter seemed irrelevant to my crisis, so I decided to quit halfway through. I'll pick it up here tomorrow, I told myself. Then, listlessly, I decided to read on. The next words hit me like a bolt from heaven: *You…joyfully accepted the plundering of your goods, knowing that you have a better and an enduring possession for yourselves in heaven (Heb. 10:34, NKJV).*

The Word of God was a sword to annihilate those evil temptations that had been winning out in my mind. Joyful? Hardly. Better and more lasting? Definitely. A couple of chapters later the Spirit gave me more reassurance about my situation: Be content with what you have, because God has said, *"Never will I leave you; never will I forsake you." So we say with confidence, "The Lord is my helper; I will not be afraid. What can man do to me?" (Heb. 13:5-6).* God is my better and lasting possession!

The Bible is not only our defensive weapon as we stockpile its truth against the hour of temptation, it's our offensive weapon at the moment of temptation. My agitated mind settled down in a miraculous calm, and cheerfulness actually began to bubble up as I focused on the positive things God is doing in my life.

- Though it was all the transportation I had, it wasn't much.
- They broke into my car, not my house.
- They took my car, not my life.
- They were the thieves, not I.
- They can take my possessions, but they can't take my God.

I was tempted, but the Spirit delivered me—through the Word. Hallelujah!

> **Put yourself in each of the following situations, then match the Scripture verse that could help you fight the temptation described.**

__ 1. Since you didn't get a raise you're tempted not to work as hard as you used to.

__ 2. You just heard an unbelievable story about your pastor; you reach for the phone to call your best friend about it.

__ 3. Jerome didn't speak to you in church Sunday. "He must be mad at me," you concluded. "Wouldn't be surprised, he's such a moody person."

__ 4. You have your rights, so you decide not to follow what you think is a stupid rule.

__ 5. Some friends are going to the lake Sunday so maybe you'll just skip church this time.

A. *"Remember the Sabbath day by keeping it holy" (EX. 20:8).*

B. *Be kind and compassionate to one another, forgiving each other, just as in Christ God forgave you (Eph. 4:32).*

C. *"Do not judge, or you too will be judged" (Matt. 7:1).*

D. *Do not entertain an accusation against an elder (1 Tim. 5:19).*

E. *Submit to one another out of reverence for Christ (Eph. 5:21).*

What mighty firepower we have right in our hands! I would have answered 1-B; 2-D; 3-C; 4-E; 5-A.

PRAYER: OFFENSIVE WEAPON

Not only do we pray about our attacking temptation as the day begins in preparation for the battle, but we also use prayer as a mighty weapon at the time of temptation. Many guys have talked with me about their sexual temptations with movies, magazines, TV, girlfriend, classmate, or coworker. I always ask, "Do you ask God to help at the moment of temptation?" If they called on God for help, they won the battle. Those who did not call on God were never victorious in overcoming the temptation. Men tell me: "At that point, I didn't want deliverance,"—they are telling me something about their spiritual state. Do they really want the will of God? It's not enough to love the good, we must hate evil. We will hate it if we think about what it will do to us in the end, and what it does to Jesus at the time. Only when I hate evil will I cry out for help in the moment of temptation.

 Review the temptations you noted in day 1. Check below whether or not you prayed at the moment of the temptation and then check the outcome.

My Attacking Temptation	Most recent encounter: Did I pray?		Outcome Success/Failure	
	Yes	No		
_____	☐	☐	☐	☐
_____	☐	☐	☐	☐
_____	☐	☐	☐	☐

Another key to victory through prayer is to confess sin immediately. That is a great test of where my heart is. If I'm yielded and truly want only God's will in my life, the moment I realize I've failed I'll eagerly repent. I'll tell Him how sorry I am and ask for deliverance and strength. When I feel the enemy overpowering me, if I'll only admit it's sin and ask God for help, the Spirit intervenes and delivers.

 Do you have any unconfessed sin? Tell Jesus! Don't continue this lesson until you have told Jesus, because that sin breaks contact with the Spirit.

THE CHURCH: OFFENSIVE WEAPON

When my brother-in-law died, the church stood by us. And they stand by us still. At a time of testing God's people come to the rescue. In the longer dying of my beloved—18 years now due to Alzheimer's—what would I do without God's people? The temptations they deliver me from include: discouragement, self-pity, worry, loneliness, and fear. Don't hesitate to call on your brothers and sisters for help in the time of need! That's what they're there for! A brother is born for adversity (Prov. 17:17).

Before we were married I wrote Muriel about how we wanted to be one in every sense. "Let's not have any secrets," I wrote. She became my accountability partner. When the enemy launched a rocket, she warned me! A spiritual buddy will help us win in the hour of attack.

We've examined two overlapping weapons: the church in general and an accountability partner in particular. Many times Muriel served both functions. She was an expression of the body of Christ and she was a partner to help me be accountable to Him. That's part of "church," a powerful weapon when facing temptation.

We've studied a defensive strategy of preparation for battle and an offensive strategy for the moment of attack. We need both. To build up your defenses against the hour of temptation, use the Bible and prayer every day, the church at least every

God handed the Hagrites and all their allies over to them, because they cried out to him during the battle. He answered their prayers, because they trusted in him.
—1 Chronicles 5:20

Call upon me in the day of trouble; I will deliver you.
—Psalm 50:15

If we confess our sins, he is faithful and just and will forgive us our sins and purify us from all unrighteousness.
—1 John 1:9

week. Then, when the enemy strikes, reach for those same weapons to fend him off. You'll win the victory!

▸ **Review your memory verses from all of the units you have studied so far. Use each memory verse as the basis for prayer.**

[DAY 4] ···················· VICTORY CELEBRATION

God's purpose for us is to be like Him. No wonder Paul calls His will good, pleasing and perfect *(Rom.12:2)*. What does he mean by approving it? As we "approve" His will, we will experience a distinct result of obedience to God's will. Just as His will is *good, pleasing and perfect*, we will grow to more closely resemble those aspects of His will.

The following seven steps describe the process from temptation to character development. When we resist the conforming influences of the world and work with the Spirit in the renovation of our thinking, we will increasingly prove by our experience those excellent qualities of God's will. We will become a showcase for all to see, conclusive evidence that God's will really is good, pleasing, and perfect. When we ignore the Spirit and surrender to temptation, we become a showcase for defeat, sin, and hypocrisy. Here is my description of the seven-step process:

Step 1. Temptation comes, either from without or within. Remember that temptation itself is no sin, it just pulls you into sin.

Step 2. We have an emotional response: like or dislike, love or hate.

Step 3. We make a decision: give in to temptation or reject temptation.

Step 4. If we consent, sin follows; if we reject temptation, we experience a victory.

Step 5. Our responses give birth to a pattern. Failure leads to weakness and susceptibility to further failure, success strengthens to win future battles.

Step 6. Habit is formed; we develop a pattern of failure or a pattern of success.

Step 7. Character is formed; we spiral down or up.

▸ **In the margin describe your responses this week to the temptations you listed earlier. This is a practical beginning for developing your battle plan.**

▸ **Using separate paper, or in your journal, write the seven steps for each of the temptations you identified earlier.**

When in battle you make godly choices, you put on display, or prove, for all to see how good, pleasing, and perfect the will of God is by exhibiting God's character. Look at the words Paul uses to describe what you'll look like: good, pleasing, perfect.

GOOD

▸ **In week 6, day 4 we learned that the two purposes God always has for allowing suffering in our lives. Those two purposes are—**

_____ and _____.

The purpose of suffering is always growth and glory: our growth, God's glory. Would He have those same purposes for allowing temptation to assault us? Yes and no. Yes, both suffering and temptation are tests (often intertwined) and His purpose in allowing either kind of test is always our growth and His glory. But there is a big

---

Therefore, I urge you, brothers, in view of God's mercy, to offer your bodies as living sacrifices, holy and pleasing to God—this is your spiritual act of worship. Do not conform any longer to the pattern of this world, but be transformed by the renewing of your mind. Then you will be able to test and approve what God's will is—his good, pleasing and perfect will.
—Romans 12:1-2

Step 1. My temptation

Step 2. My emotional response

Step 3. My decision at the time

Step 4. The short-term result

Step 5. The pattern in my life

Step 6. The habit I am forming

Step 7. The character result

difference between suffering and temptation. Sometimes we are to accept suffering as God's will for us, but we can never accept temptation—we fight it! God's good will is to overcome temptation. If we don't, we neither bring credit to Him nor growth to ourselves.

 When a leading Christian falls to sexual temptation, what bad things happen to God's reputation?
When you give in to temptation and throw a "pity party," what happens to you?

When we yield, we grow weaker, less like Jesus, and that's not God's good will. We demonstrate God's good will when we do His will. Victory is His good will, defeat is bad and certainly not His will. God's good will is to nail our evil desires to the cross, not excuse them.

PLEASING

Another word Paul uses to describe God's will is *pleasing*, or as in some translations, *acceptable*. Success in overcoming temptation is pleasing, all right, but to whom?

 Who do you think Paul had in mind as being pleased?
❑ God ❑ Yourself ❑ Others

Bible scholars may debate which of those Paul had in mind, but I would say, all the above! To overcome temptation brings joy. It's a victory celebration! To fail and not do the good will of God is pleasing only to unholy men and unholy spirits. To you, God, and all good people, surrender to temptation is distressing.

PERFECT

 In the margin are some meanings of *perfect* in Scripture. Check the one(s) you think best fits Paul's meaning describing God's will worked out in your life.

❑ *flawless, without defect*
❑ *mature, adult, full-grown*
❑ *loyal, sincere, whole-hearted obedience to the known will of God*
❑ *ability and readiness to meet all demands, outfitted*
❑ *having reached appropriate or appointed end, goal, purpose*

I checked all but the first and last. Those are indeed our ultimate goals, that we will one day be flawless, just like Jesus. The other three are more appropriate to describe what we can fulfill in this life—His will is that we demonstrate maturity and obedience.

MY PERSONAL BATTLE PLAN ⋯⋯⋯⋯⋯⋯ [DAY 5]

Every battle plan needs to be custom designed for the individual. It may change for each stage of life. Where are you today in your spiral up toward likeness to Jesus? It's time now for the big assignment: write out your own battle plan for overcoming the failure that most grieves the Holy Spirit and embarrasses you. This is for real, not just an assignment to be fulfilled. Create your own plan to battle temptation.

 Ask the Holy Spirit for wisdom. Ask Him to enlighten your mind and to bring to mind both Scriptures and principles you have been studying.
1. For what temptation do you need to develop a battle plan? _____
2. Do you really want victory over this temptation? ❑ Yes ❑ No
   Are you yielded unconditionally to the Spirit about it?
   ❑ Yes ❑ No ❑ Not sure

Then he said to them, "Suppose one of you has a friend, and he goes to him at midnight and says, 'Friend, lend me three loaves of bread, because a friend of mine on a journey has come to me, and I have nothing to set before him.'
"Then the one inside answers, 'Don't bother me. The door is already locked, and my children are with me in bed. I can't get up and give you anything.' I tell you, though he will not get up and give him the bread because he is his friend, yet because of the man's boldness he will get up and give him as much as he needs.
"So I say to you: Ask and it will be given to you; seek and you will find; knock and the door will be opened to you. For everyone who asks receives; he who seeks finds; and to him who knocks, the door will be opened" (Luke 11:5-10).

When you can say yes from your heart, Holy Spirit power is released and you're on your way to victory. Go ahead with your plan! But if you couldn't answer yes to that question, no need to proceed. First you must become willing to obey. How do you become willing to obey? Read the words from *Luke 11* in the margin. Jesus was speaking specifically about persisting in prayer.

Ask God to make you willing to obey. Ask Him to give you a desire to overcome. Don't just ask and give up. Keep asking, knocking, and seeking until God gives you the desire to obey Him and overcome temptation.

3. Skim through days 1-3 and put an asterisk in the margin by any of the points in my strategy that you think may work for you.
4. Using those points you've chosen, plus others you may have heard about, discovered in Scripture, or learned through experience, make a broad outline of your own personal strategy for overcoming temptation. The following is an outline of how you might proceed:

1. Who or what most often causes this temptation? _____
2. What are the masks this enemy uses—how do I tend to rationalize the attitude or behavior? _____
3. Among lust, covetousness, pride, and unbelief, which is most likely the root cause(s) of my temptation? _____
4. What is my defensive strategy—how do I plan to use the Bible, prayer, and the church to build up in advance strength to face this particular temptation when it comes? _____
5. What is my offensive strategy—how do I intend to use the Bible, prayer, and the church at the time of temptation? _____

How did it go? Are you pleased with the outcome? Time and space may not have permitted you to finish your plan to your own satisfaction. Your strategy will need revision as you put it into action. Let it be a developing plan. No matter how satisfied you are with your strategy, remember that success in the Christian life, including consistent success in overcoming temptation, does not ultimately depend on a technique, a strategy, or your own activity.

Ultimately, the Holy Spirit within is the overcomer. The indwelling powerful One does not displace your personality with His. Rather, He is a personal companion, living in you to—

- strengthen you when you stumble
- remind you of truth from His Word when your focus is blurred
- point out the enemy when you're under attack
- comfort you
- lift you up when you fall
- forgive you when you fail
- guide you when you're confused
- sensitize your moral judgment
- strengthen your will when you waver.

Glorious as those activities of the Spirit are, it's not all He does. He prays for us when we don't know how to pray *(Rom. 8:26-27)*; and as we rely on Him, He enables us to pray effectively. God the Spirit gave us His Word and enables us to understand and use that Word in the face of testing. He helps us to live in the kind of relationship with other Christians that will make us overcomers together.

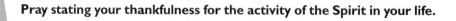

Pray stating your thankfulness for the activity of the Spirit in your life.

the SPIRIT'S GIFTS

In this unit we will focus on the basic, clear teaching on which we all can agree about spiritual gifts. The Holy Spirit empowers us so we can accomplish the tasks that He gives us to do.

I asked a group of high school students, "Are all occupations of equal importance?" They unanimously agreed that all are equal.

"That's an interesting concept," I said, and told them the story of my flight to Norfolk. "On the way here I sat by a man who wanted to sell me stock in his company. He said it was the fastest growing industry in the country."

"What's the industry?" I asked him.

"Cosmetics," he answered.

"In your industry is there some segment that is growing faster than others?"

"Oh, yes. Male cosmetics."

"Like—what? Deodorant? After-shave lotion?"

"Oh, no," he said. "Last year we sold a quarter million dollars worth of false eyelashes for men."

"There's an occupation," I told the students, "selling false eyelashes for men. Here's another one. My nephew is a surgeon who could make a bundle of money in the United States. Instead, he chose to care for a forgotten people in the heart of Africa. He barely escaped one country as the communist leaders swept to power. Now, in Kenya, he tells me he does more surgery in a week than he used to do in a year at a famous hospital in Pennsylvania. Then he adds with a wry smile, 'and none of it is cosmetic!' "

"There you have it," I said, "selling false eyelashes for men or healing the bodies and souls of thousands for whom you're the only hope? Let's vote again: Are all vocations of equal importance?"

That split the crowd and about half wavered. On the front row sat a 12-year-old who didn't vote either way.

"Not going to vote?" I asked her.

"No. It's a bad question."

"What's bad about it?"

"You didn't say important for what."

She caught me! Which is more important: a knife, a fork, or a spoon? The answer might depend on whether you had a bowl of soup or a steak. Vocations need to be considered likewise—important to whom? for what?

Unit Memory Verses

To each one the manifestation of the Spirit is given for the common good.
—1 Corinthians 12:7

Eagerly desire the greater gifts.

—1 Corinthians 12:31

[DAY 1] ············· DEFINITIONS: WHAT THE GIFT IS NOT

A spiritual gift is a Spirit-given ability to serve God. So much confusion exists in the church over the subject of spiritual gifts that many give up and avoid the whole subject. But the only way the church will be effective, and the only way we'll spiral up into likeness to Jesus, is by each believer using the abilities the Spirit gives. Unless the Holy Spirit empowers us we can never accomplish the tasks He gives us to do. Let's look at three things the Spirit's gifts are not. They are not fruits, talents, or offices.

GIFTS AND FRUIT

You may have wondered, *Why no chapter on the fruit of the Spirit?* The reason is because so far in our study we have concentrated on the fruit of the Spirit throughout all these units. Our focus has been on how the Holy Spirit produces Christlike characteristics in us, and that is the nature of the fruit. Now we need to ask another question: "How do the fruits and gifts relate?"

First Corinthians 12–14, fruit is said to be more important than gifts. Right in the middle of Paul's discussion of gifts, immediately following our memory verse, he says, "Now I'm going to describe something far more important than all these gifts combined" (my paraphrase). Then he gives the magnificent "love chapter," *1 Corinthians 13.* Love is a fruit. In fact, some say it is the summation of all the fruit of the Spirit.

 In the following mixed list of gifts and fruit circle the ones you think all Christians should have:

love	pastoring	evangelism	patience
goodness	teaching	helping	administration	peace
joy	missionizing	preaching	humility

God intends for all His children to be like Him—to bear all the fruit of the Spirit, but *1 Corinthians 12–14* demonstrates clearly that the Spirit does not give all the gifts to any one person. In the list of gifts and fruit, love, patience, goodness, peace, joy, and humility are fruit. I hope you circled all the fruit and none of the gifts.

God wants everyone to be completely like Him in character, but not like Him in His abilities. He never intended anyone have infinite wisdom or power. However, He does want His church to have wisdom and power, so He distributed abilities among the members to enable the church to accomplish His purposes. No one member can be godlike in power lest he or she be tempted to use the gifts in gathering personal authority and influence. In summary, fruit is for everyone, always; gifts are spread around. The exciting fact is that every member is given at least one ability to serve God. That includes you!

How the gifts and fruit relate is a mystery. The Bible does not spell it out for us. We see a person mightily used of God who may be egotistical or quick-tempered; and we see another who is very godly in character but is not gifted to serve in any obvious way. How can that be?

 Of the possible reasons listed in the margin, circle those you believe help explain the puzzle of why God sometimes gifts those who lack character and gives inconspicuous gifts to those who are godly.

I would have checked all but c. A person may have great natural ability to lead, sing, preach, teach, or manage money (e), so great that most of us would be unable

---

To one there is given through the Spirit....to another....to another....and to still another....Are all apostles? Are all prophets? Are all teachers?
—1 Corinthians 12:8-11,29

a. God doesn't necessarily evaluate giftedness as we do.

b. "Fruit" is a more certain measure of spirituality than giftedness.

c. Rewards will be based on how great a gift you had and how prominently you used it.

d. Rewards will be based on faithfulness, a fruit of the Spirit, not on the kind or effectiveness of one's gift.

e. Some giftedness can be natural rather than spiritual.

to tell whether the Spirit is at work. God is the judge (a). He will judge us on the basis of faithfulness, not giftedness (d). Faithfulness will include our use of the gifts the Spirit gives, to be sure, but faithfulness implies our Christlike choices (b).

GIFTS AND TALENTS

The first thing to note about a natural ability and a spiritual ability is that both are gifts from God. God gave us whatever ability we have; and we must use both natural and supernatural gifts for His glory. To use either natural or spiritual gifts for our own glory is sin. We are responsible to use all that we are to glorify Him. The second thing to note is that the Bible doesn't explain the relationship between the two.

 In the margin is a list of church activities. Circle those that people might be successful at without Spirit-enabling, provided they had great natural ability.

singing witnessing ushering preaching teaching counseling leading a group hospitality managing finances

No two people would have exactly the same answers, but I circled all except witnessing. Even witnessing can be faked if the person has enough personal charisma; but we're talking here of those who truly lead people to Christ. If my opinion is anywhere near correct, the conclusion is scary! Most of the work of the church could be carried on by gifted people without the Spirit of God doing anything.

Some people refer to ministry as either "in the flesh" or "in the Spirit." A difference does exist, but the difference may not be between spiritual gifts and natural abilities. The difference is between depending on self or depending on the Spirit. Evidence of a supernatural touch indicates that a ministry is accomplished in the Spirit.

For example, Paul wasn't a world class public speaker—he agreed with the Corinthians in that judgment *(1 Cor. 2:1)*. But when he taught the Bible, lives were transformed. A Spirit-gift will have the Spirit's miracle touch.

 Below the verse in the margin, write in your own words what 1 Corinthians 12:4-7 means. Give special attention to the term *manifestation*.

There are different kinds of gifts, but the same Spirit. There are different kinds of service, but the same Lord. There are different kinds of working, but the same God works all of them in all men.

Now to each one the manifestation of the Spirit is given for the common good.

—1 Corinthians 12:4-7

Though the word *manifestation* in our memory verse means "visible evidence" and that is the ultimate proof, we need to exercise two cautions.

- some may have "visible evidence" resulting from strong natural ability, not really the work of the Spirit. For example, the magicians in Pharaoh's court managed to duplicate some of the signs Moses performed *(Ex. 7:11)*, but they certainly did not do them through the power of the Spirit.

- a person may have been given a gift and still experience a lack of evidence because of tough circumstances. For example, Ezekiel was God's own prophet, but the people were rebels and wouldn't listen *(Ezek. 3)*. Paul was no doubt the greatest of evangelists, but in Lystra they stoned him out of town *(Acts 14)*.

If no evidence shows the Spirit at work, or the ministry makes no spiritual impact, we need to ask if the ministry is God's. When I fail to see evidence in my own ministry, I ask myself several diagnostic questions.

1. Am I Harboring Unconfessed Sin? When I've preached my heart out and lives aren't changed, I examine myself to see if something in me blocked the flow of the Spirit—an unconfessed sin, a wrong motivation, unbelief, or lack of prayer. I don't immediately conclude that I don't have the gift or that He hasn't called me after all.

2. Do I Need to Be Persistent? When I felt called to do missionary work, I kept asking God for the gift of evangelism. People came to Christ through my ministry only sporadically, and I longed for the ability to consistently win people to Christ. The principle is to keep asking until you see one of two things: "visible evidence"

Then Paul and Barnabas answered them boldly: "We had to speak the word of God to you first. Since you reject it and do not consider yourselves worthy of eternal life, we now turn to the Gentiles."
—Acts 13:46

Vindicating Himself--
God intends gifted persons to stand firm while allowing evil to be in control and the consequences of sin to happen around them; we must take personal responsibility for our sins; however, even in hard times God doesn't forsake us.

Now the overseer must be above reproach, the husband of but one wife, temperate, self-controlled, respectable, hospitable, able to teach, not given to drunkenness, not violent but gentle, not quarrelsome, not a lover of money. He must manage his own family well and see that his children obey him with proper respect. (If anyone does not know how to manage his own family, how can he take care of God's church?) He must not be a recent convert, or he may become conceited and fall under the same judgment as the devil. He must also have a good reputation with outsiders, so that he will not fall into disgrace and into the devil's trap.
Deacons, likewise, are to be men worthy of respect, sincere, not indulging in much wine, and not pursuing dishonest gain. They must keep hold of the deep truths of the faith with a clear conscience. They must first be tested; and then if there is nothing against them, let them serve as deacons.
—1 Timothy 3:2-10

of the gift you long for or the assurance that God doesn't intend that gift for you. Stop asking only when God shows you that the gift is not for you.

3. Am I in the Right Place? In Japan, we discovered that we were ministering in a very unresponsive area. We asked God if there should be a change of location to a place or people who would respond. Paul did this more than once. (See *Acts 13:46*.)

4. Is God Vindicating Himself? Perhaps, on the other hand, God intends a gifted person to stand firm when there is no "fruit" or outward result, as His vindication among an unresponsive people (as in Ezekiel's case).

A gift may be without "visible evidence," but in general we distinguish between natural ability and supernatural ability by the outcome of the ministry.

GIFTS AND OFFICES

Just because a person is appointed or elected to an office is no guarantee he or she has the Spirit-given abilities needed for that office.

> **Read the lists of qualifications for office in *1 Timothy 3:2-10* that appears in the margin. Underline those qualifications that seem to be fruits of the Spirit and circle those which seem to require gifts of the Spirit.**

You probably only circled one for sure on gifts required to serve, the ability to teach the Bible with faithfulness. A couple of others might require a spiritual gift: hospitality and ruling well. The focus seems to be more on character than giftedness. Perhaps encouraging others with the truth and refuting those who oppose it could be more than teaching, hinting at other related abilities.

> **The exciting thing about the gifts of the Spirit is that He's given some ability to serve God to every Christian. List the gift(s) you have or you believe you may have. If you aren't sure, then list any job(s) you do reasonably well.**

> **Fill in the blanks of Scripture memory verse below. Practice saying the verse until you can say it from memory.**

To each one the _____ of the _____ is given

for the _____ _____.

—1 Corinthians 12:7

DEFINITIONS: WHAT IS A GIFT?

The New Testament contains several lists of gifts or abilities given by the Spirit to do some work for God in the church or in the world. In the margin is *Romans 12:3-8, 1*

Corinthians 12, Ephesians 4, and 1 Peter 4:10-11 along with a listing of the gifts and abilities mentioned in those verses. Read the lists carefully.

Some gifts clearly reveal themselves by the results of their use. The name explains the meaning. Others are not that clear, so it's hard to decide whether or not you have that gift.

 In the gift-lists you just read, check the words you think represent gifts that are easily recognized.

DEFINING THE GIFTS

The following gifts seem to have clear outcomes:

1. Teaching—a person explains the Bible/spiritual truth so that lives are changed.
2. Healing—people are consistently healed through the prayers of a particular person.
3. Evangelism—people routinely come to Christ through a person's witness.

These three are the only gifts I feel have clear outcomes: teaching, healing, and evangelism. You may have put others, such as tongues or interpretation. Since many differ on what tongues and interpretation refer to .I listed only those gifts in which the meaning is evident by the word used to identify the gift.

You may have included prophecy. A prophet was a Spirit-ordained spokesperson for God. Sometimes they foretold future events, but that wasn't the defining activity.

In the Old Testament, musicians, even instrumentalists, were in the order of the prophets *(1 Chron. 25:1-3)*. How could that be? No prediction there, not even words! But if they officially represented God in leading His people in worship, that was considered prophecy. The Scripture does not clearly define what is and what is not included in the gift of prophecy.

IMPORTANCE OF EACH GIFT

Are all the gifts of equal importance, or are some more important than others? Remember how the young lady asked, "Important for what?"

1. First consider how the gifts are important for you.

 Circle those gifts listed at the beginning of day 2 that are most important to you personally?

You circled those you have or those you would like to have, right? For you personally, the most important gift is the one God has for you; and the most important thing for you is to find that gift or pattern of gifts and develop them to the maximum.

2. The gifts are also important for the church.

 Which of the gifts from the lists are the most important for your church?

You may have given a number of good answers. You could even have answered *all the above!* Paul seems to be saying the Spirit puts into each church all the gifts (gifted people) needed to accomplish His purposes in and through that church. Members should function in the way He designs. The Spirit's will for the church is for every member to function as designed, because every member is needed to accomplish His purposes. Members can function effectively only when they are fully using their gifts.

3. The gifts are important to God.

The central purpose of *1 Corinthians 12–14* is to get the church to understand that gifts are not all of equal importance for accomplishing God's will. Some gifts are

Romans 12:3-8
prophesy
service
teaching
encouraging
giving
leading
showing mercy

1 Corinthians 12
wisdom
knowledge
faith
healing
miracles
prophecy
discernment of spirits
tongues
interpretation of tongues
apostleship
teaching
helping others
administration

Ephesians 4
apostleship
prophecy
evangelism
pastoring
teaching

1 Peter 4:10-11
various unnamed
speaking
serving

David, together with the commanders of the army, set apart some of the sons of Asaph, Heman and Jeduthun for the ministry of prophesying, accompanied by harps, lyres and cymbals.
—*1 Chronicles 25:1*

less important. The church at Corinth was focusing on one of those (speaking in tongues).

Furthermore, the church at Corinth should have focused on some very important gifts, but they didn't—gifts like apostle, prophet, teacher. Paul even numbered them 1, 2, and 3 *(1 Cor. 12:28)* so they wouldn't miss the point. He doesn't continue his numbering system beyond those three, so they may just be representative. But these three give a hint as to what Paul considers more important—roles which seem to have the greatest impact for God's purposes in the church and in the world.

If you read *1 Corinthians 12–14* in a hurry, you may conclude that Paul is contrasting lower gifts with the highest gift, love. If you draw that conclusion, you will miss the point. Paul is teaching the people at Corinth about spiritual gifts, and having urged them to seek the higher ones, he pauses for a midcourse correction. "Don't get me wrong," he says. "These gifts, even the more important ones, aren't the most important. Love is most important." Love isn't a "gift" in the sense Paul is talking about; he calls it a "way." "I'll show you an even better way"—better than the best gift (see *1 Cor. 12:31* in the margin).

Elsewhere Paul describes love as the fruit of the Spirit. So let's not confuse fruit with gift. Gifts are Spirit-given abilities; fruit represents Spirit-given character. Paul's command in *verse 31* is to desire Spirit-given abilities to serve God, but his teaching in all of *chapter 13* is that love is more important than any gift.

The importance of a gift does not imply that one gift is more spiritual than another. Spiritual has to do with fruits of the Spirit, likeness to Jesus, as Paul concludes in *1 Corinthians 13*. Also, importance does not equal greater reward. Reward is based on faithfulness, not outward results.

To accomplish God's mission on earth however, some gifts are of greater importance than others. For 12 years I was a pioneer missionary evangelist. My job was starting churches, a very high calling according to Paul. Today I'm primarily a homemaker, which calls more for fruit than for gifts. My Spirit-given gifts have a limited outlet through some writing and speaking. But I'm not arrogant, claiming that my role in life is as important as anyone else's. My calling can't compare with that of others in terms of eternal impact. God wants us to be faithful to our own calling. Then the whole body functions smoothly, we have personal fulfillment, and God is pleased.

> *Eagerly desire the greater gifts. And now I will show you the most excellent way.*
> *—1 Corinthians 12:31*

Gifts = Spirit-given abilities
Fruit = Spirit-given character

[DAY 3] ·················· FINDING MY ROLE IN THE CHURCH

We had just finished a faculty workshop on helping students identify their gifts when the former editor of *Christianity Today* came to the microphone. "I've never known what my gift is," he said, to our astonishment. "All my life I've seen a need, been asked to fill it, and trusted the Holy Spirit to enable me to do it."

Maybe this former editor is on to something. I finally understood that the Scripture did not define all the gifts for a reason. I recognized that I should focus on the tasks that needed to be done. We should ask God for the abilities necessary to accomplish what He has clearly told us are His purposes for the church. Leave the combination of abilities, natural and supernatural, to the Holy Spirit to decide—*just as he determines (1 Cor. 12:11)*. We can tell when that custom-designed pattern of gifts is from Him: the outcome demonstrates the supernatural power of God.

TASK-RELATED GIFT DEFINITIONS

Each of the biblical lists of gifts are quite different. No one particular gift appears in all of them. Teaching and prophecy appear in three, apostle shows up in two, and the others occur only once. None of the lists is intended to be exhaustive; they're just representative or suggestive.

Perhaps other gifts are not listed. Tasks may need to be done in your church which Paul didn't include in any of his lists. Can you think of any?

You may have listed music, drama, youth ministry and other major ministries of your church. Perhaps you listed these because you don't want your efforts to be purely human talent but have eternal outcomes produced by the Spirit. Some other activities don't clearly fit under any of Paul's categories, or can either be listed as separate gifts or be combined as forms of "teaching" or "prophetic proclamation." Writing, for example, might fit under one of those.

Maybe you listed counseling. I listed "pastor," which means "shepherd." Today we use it to describe the chief church leader. But the original idea was more like what today we call discipling, counseling, or nurturing. *Encouragement* in the Romans list of gifts might fit here, too.

Many Christians are like Barnabas, good at helping others through the tough times. Professional counselors who see supernatural results in the counseling process are also an example. Tasks today can be linked with biblical gifts. Leading, administration, wisdom, discernment, or helps, for example, are capable of wide application. Be sure not to claim that your understanding of a gift is the only meaning it could have. Always identify the touch of the Spirit by spiritual outcomes.

DEFINING GIFT BY PURPOSE OF THE CHURCH

Remember the purposes of the church—worship, fellowship, discipleship, ministry, and evangelism. How do these five purposes of the church relate to the opportunities and responsibilities that belong to every disciple?

The Holy Spirit gives gifts or abilities so that the purposes of the church may be fulfilled. Think about how the spiritual gifts empower the church to fulfill its purposes. Rather than using the extensive lists as they appear in the Bible, let me combine and describe some of the key gifts Scripture points toward—abilities clearly needed to fulfill the purposes of the church.

My description of eight key spiritual gifts includes the abilities to:

1. teach the Bible in such a way that lives are changed
2. lead people to Christ
3. help the physical and social needs of the community and draw people to God
4. understand a person's spiritual need and help him grow spiritually
5. lead people to worship in spirit and in truth
6. preach God's truth with life-changing authority
7. understand God's direction for the church and get people to go that direction
8. practical help like running errands, mowing lawns, seeing and meeting needs

 On the following chart, write the number of the Spirit-given ability that could help fulfill each of the purposes of the church after the appropriate purpose. You may use a gift (Spirit-given ability) in more than one place on the chart.

Purposes of the Church	Gifts That Contribute to the Purpose
Worship (united praise, adoration, thanksgiving)	_____
Fellowship (caring for one another, family solidarity)	_____
Discipleship (teaching, accountability/discipline)	_____
Ministry (to a hurting community outside the church)	_____
Evangelism (bringing people to a conversion decision)	_____

Not everyone will connect the same gifts with the same purpose of the church, but here are my choices. I put the gifts of preaching, leadership, and administration (6,7,8) by all the purposes since those are gifts needed to accomplish the over-all purposes of the church. The worship purpose of the church obviously fits gifts number 5—this could include all the music ministry of the church, for example.

I left fellowship off the list. Though some people seem to be more gifted at caring than others, the whole family shares the responsibility to care lovingly for the emotional, physical, material, and spiritual needs of the other members. Fellowship seems to be fulfilled more by people bearing the fruit of the Spirit than by any special giftedness.

I included teaching (1) and counseling (biblical pastoring) (4) as gifts that especially advance personal discipleship. Ministry in the way we use it here refers to those who are called to minister to the needs of the surrounding community (3). Though all participate in evangelism through faithful witness, some are effective in consistently winning others to faith (2).

> **Look back at the five purposes of the church again. Which of the purposes are most strongly fulfilled in your church?_____**
> **Which purposes would be better fulfilled with your involvement?_____**

Paul says to "earnestly desire" the higher gifts. That's a command! So if you don't feel strongly about something you'd like to accomplish for God, now is the time to pause and ask God to give you such a holy desire. If you already want a particular gift, pause now and ask God for it! Write out your request in your journal.

> **In the margin, write how the Scripture memory verses help or encourage you to use your particular gift to accomplish the job God wants you to do. Recite the memory verses from memory to a friend or family member.**

[DAY 4] ⋯⋯⋯⋯⋯⋯⋯⋯⋯⋯⋯⋯⋯⋯ DEVELOPING MY GIFT

Using the ability God gives you has a dual purpose: to prove what the gift is and then to develop it. Though most of today's lesson is devoted to developing your gift, we look first at getting to work—the way you confirm your gift.

KNOWING YOUR GIFT BY INVOLVEMENT

The churches we started in Japan were composed of people who didn't know the Gospel and nothing of what a church is supposed to be. We assumed that these new-born Christians would be given abilities to serve God, just as the Spirit promised.

We gave everyone a job. We even gave unconverted regular attenders a job—like cleaning up before and after services or serving tea and rice crackers. From the beginning they felt part of us. They assumed that to be a Christian meant to participate in God's work. At first the assignments were housekeeping, nothing that would test one's spiritual giftedness, but would test one's availability and heart for serving the rest of the family.

We trained and coached each believer until he or she seemed ready for the next assignment, stopping when one wanted to stop or the leaders in the church felt one was not yet gifted for the next assignment.

There are two reasons for this approach. First, how do you know whether you have a gift or would be given a gift till you try it out? Second, giftedness should be confirmed by the church.

Does your church have a plan for helping people discover their gifts?
❑ Yes ❑ No Is every member expected to serve in some way? ❑ Yes ❑ No
Are people encouraged to try out new roles? ❑ Yes ❑ No
If the answer to any of these questions is no, what changes need to be made?

Not only must the gift be confirmed by the church, it ought to be sought in the context of the church to begin with. And if God doesn't intend for me to have the gift I aim for, it is the church leadership that should help me reach that conclusion.

Once I've identified the gift I have or I'd like to have, or once I've identified the job I'd like to do, I must get to work. I must develop the abilities necessary to do that job effectively. The church's role is to help me identify the role I should pursue, free me to do it, and help me grow in it.

DEVELOPING MY GIFT

Paul told Timothy, *Do not neglect your gift…Be diligent in these matters; give yourself wholly to them, so that everyone may see your progress (1 Tim. 4:14-15).* In our churches in Tsuchiura, Japan, we used all the training methods we'll study in this lesson and the result was that we started five churches in five years. We could never have done that if we had to do all the important functions of the church. Because the people were freed up to use their Spirit-distributed abilities, I concentrated my energies on equipping them for their ministries *(Eph. 4:11-12).* We could move forward at the same time in every outlying community. Here's the plan we used—

1. Practice. We've seen how getting to work on a job is the way to confirm as well as develop your gift. If pupils throw spitwads the first day you help in children's Vacation Bible School, don't conclude you're not called to help teach! Work at it. The beauty of getting involved is that working in a job not only helps identify a gift, it's the only way to develop that gift. We need someone who has gone on before and knows how the job should be done to come alongside and help us grow.

2. Apprentice/mentor. Dan had just been called to his first assignment after graduation— associate pastor of a fine old church. He was excited because the senior pastor was a remarkably successful leader, and Dan intended to learn all he could. Dan requested this senior pastor to help him discover and develop his gifts. The pastor—a self-starting, can-do man who never asked anyone for help—said, "Who do you think I am? The Holy Spirit?" Crushed, Dan eventually dropped out of church work. I've often wondered; *If Dan had encountered a true mentor, would he have been building the church all these years?*

If your church has a structure where everyone has a mentor, or if someone has reached out to help you grow in your ministry, how blessed you are! But if not, you can do the reaching out. Ask for a mentor program.

Is there someone you would like to mentor you? Write their name below. Why not talk over the possibilities with him or her?

You can take the initiative and recruit your own mentor, but the best way is for the church to provide mentors to apprentice everyone who begins a new ministry.

You are not alone in needing a mentor. Is there someone you could help in developing his or her gift? Pause now and pray for wisdom as to the best way to know how to be a mentor to another person. Pray that God will help you develop a trusted apprentice/mentor relationship.

Perhaps God would use you in an even larger role. Write in the margin the steps you could take to get the church into a mentoring mode.

Apprentice = one who learns by practical experience under a skilled mentor's guidance

Mentor = trusted guide, tutor, teacher that helps the apprentice to discover and develop his or her gifts

The Youth Section of the Sunday School Board has produced a booklet, Youth Apprenticeship Guide, *to develop youth apprenticeship in a church. This resource helps a church provide youth an opportunity in shared experiences with church leaders. Through apprenticeship, a youth can have an indepth leadership training experience.*

For developing an apprenticeship/mentoring program order the booklet, Youth Apprenticeship Guide, *from the Youth Section MSN 152, 127 Ninth Ave. North, Nashville, TN 37234-0152. The cost of the booklet is $2.00.*

3. Literature and media. In our churches in Japan we gave everyone, along with the job, a page of simple instructions on how to do that job. Today churches are rich in resources: teachers' manuals, how-to books, videos, and cassette tapes on just about every job in the church. Check with your church for these resources.

4. Special training. In Japan we opened a miniBible college on Tuesday nights to train people who were serving or wanted to serve in spiritual ministry. We taught believers teaching methods, preaching, principles of Bible interpretation, Bible survey, church history, theology, various Bible book studies, principles of Christian ministry, and evangelism. Your church could also provide similar training for your members. The booklet, *Youth Apprenticeship Guide,* could be used at this time to help a church provide youth an opportunity in shared experiences with church leaders.

> **Circle any of the courses above that would be helpful in your church. Are there others you think are needed?** _____

5. Interchurch seminars. Our miniBible college was an interchurch project and people came from a distance to attend. Today one of the most popular means of learning is through special training events. In many areas churches or groups of churches sponsor seminars on Christian education, counseling, witnessing, doctrine, family life, political action, preaching, prayer, missions—you name it.

6. Formal training. Formal training at Bible colleges and seminaries is available for those who have grown beyond what the local church offers.

> **It's time to develop a personal plan for developing your gift. Would you like to try any of the strategies I've suggested? Or maybe you know of other methods? In the list below, write out an action plan for any you choose:**

Method to develop my gift	Action plan
1. Practice: try a new job	_____
2. Apprentice-mentor	_____
3. Literature/media	_____
4. Training classes	_____
5. Interchurch seminars	_____
6. Formal training	_____
7. Other: _____	_____

> **Thank God that the Spirit has a calling custom designed just for you. Commit yourself to Him for action, ask for wisdom and strength in carrying out that plan.**

[DAY 5] ·························· DESIRING THE BEST

> **Write out your memory verses in the margin. Underline the words that encourage you to seek a gift you may not now have.**

First Corinthians 12:31 says, *Eagerly desire the greater gifts.* Today we'll examine three important things about this crucial command. It is an active command, a continuous action command, and a command for the whole church.

1. AN ACTIVE VERB

The command to "eagerly desire" is not a description of the feeling you have when you see a luscious slice of pizza on a television commercial. The word Paul used carries the concept of action. We would say "get with it!" If you pick up the phone and order that pizza, then you've "eagerly desired."

I had yielded my life to God, but it was a passive yielding. I wasn't excited about it. "God, you shove and I'll move," was my mode. But I was involved. Mother saw to that. Mom arranged for me to go with college students to help in their ministry to housing developments. I even helped start a little country church—I hauled wood for the stove in that one-room schoolhouse. Mother was my secret mentor, helping me discover my spiritual gifts! But I still wasn't desiring anything.

When I was 18, the desire began to stir. I desired most eagerly that my life should count to the maximum for whatever God designed me for. That meant getting involved. I joined other youth in preaching on the street corner. Folks didn't stop much, so we preached in jails. No one walked away! I obeyed the command to "get with it."

 You may not have eagerly desired the "jobs" you've held in church. You may have been drafted, in fact, like my mother drafted me. But whether you volunteered or were drafted, list in the margin every job you've held in the church or in ministry outside the church. Or maybe you are still waiting for the shove before you step into a "job." If that's the case, list any job you would like to hold in the church or in ministry outside the church.

 Now go back and circle any jobs that have really excited you. Does your effectiveness or excitement about any of those point to the possibility of your being used in a larger way, maybe even some other more important role? If so, name the larger ministry you would like to do.

2. SEEK AND KEEP ON SEEKING

The command to seek eagerly is not only an active verb. It also describes a continuous action. It means, "seek and keep on seeking."

 Think about your church and list in the margin some purpose of the church that's not being strongly fulfilled. Is something lacking that burdens you greatly?

Paul says, eagerly desire those gifts for your church and for yourself. Are you obeying the command? Are you and the church praying for those needs to be met? Is the church pleading with God for the gift of evangelism, Spirit-anointed teachers, and leaders? Continue in persistent prayer until God gives the answer!

 Is your church growing, at least five percent a year in baptisms of adult converts? Is there spiritual growth in your church? Are the members spiraling up? Is the church harassed with gossip, squabbles, or in danger of splitting? Is it stuck in the rut of some worn out tradition? If so, what gifts does the church need?

3. UNITED PRAYER

To obey the command to "eagerly desire" we must commit ourselves to prayer for the gifts needed to meet the needs of our church. But solo praying won't do. The church as a whole must obey the command. The verb Paul uses is in the plural—"you all eagerly desire." If you can't inspire the church as a whole, or a smaller group to focus on this kind of praying, you and your prayer partner could begin to focus on

Ministry jobs I have held:

Larger Ministry:

asking for the gifts the Spirit wants to give. Don't criticize or dwell on the negative parts of the church. The prayer must be an eager desire for God's highest and best.

What is your action plan to involve others in desiring earnestly the needed gifts?

Group	Action plan
The church as a whole	_____
A small group within the church	_____
You and a prayer partner	_____

HEART TROUBLE

Instead of saying eagerly desire, your Bible may use different words such as *covet earnestly, set your hearts, try your best,* or *earnestly desire.* This emotional desire for a gift to serve embodies a deep longing that moves us to action.

Notice that Paul doesn't say, "wait around till the desire hits you." Paul gives a command: set your heart on that gift that is so desperately needed by your church or by a dying world. Take the initiative! Go for it! The place to begin may be with your desire. Instead of asking for a particular ability, as I have often suggested in this unit, perhaps the request should be for the Spirit to ignite a great flame of desire in your heart. Ask Him to give you a passion for Him and a passion for people to know Him.

Tell God your heart's desire. If you lack a passion to know Him and to serve Him, commit to keep on asking daily until He lights the fire or gives the gift.

How exciting! The Spirit plans to use you in God's service more than you ever dreamed possible. And what a treasure hunt—to discover the gifts He has for you! What a privilege, too. Do you ever feel the wonder of God's amazing plan—to accomplish His purposes in the world through mere mortals like you and me? And what about the excitement of cooperating with the Spirit in developing and using your gifts to the maximum? Isn't it time to tell God how much you appreciate Him?

Giftedness is great, but never forget something greater—fruit. How do the two relate? Both are the work of the Spirit. Both represent a part of His intentions for every believer. But a difference between fruit and gifts exists; the Spirit longs to give all the fruit to all believers in maximum measure, while the gifts He distributes among believers. Some receive greater gifts, some lesser. Great fruit without great gifts can bring great glory to God, but great gifts without great fruit, clouds, perhaps even eclipses, His glory. When a godly person is also gifted, however, what glory to God!

Conclude this week's study with prayer. You may want to spend more time than usual in prayer. One way to pray about what we've been studying is to divide your prayer time into short segments.

1. Tell God how thrilled you are with the plan He has to use you to accomplish His purposes.
2. Thank Him for the abilities the Spirit has given you and offer it back to Him for His glory.
3. Make your desire for use of your gift a matter of regular prayer until God answers yes or no.
4. If you don't feel any burning desire to do something important for His kingdom, ask Him to start a fire in your spirit.
5. Ask God to protect you from taking credit for what He accomplishes through you.
6. Pray for your church, appealing to God especially for gifted people to meet the specific needs you sense.

POWER to CHANGE the WORLD

UNIT 11

Is missions at the top of the list, lost on the list, or not on the list of important purposes of the church? Some churches are committed to world evangelism. Are they misguided, or are they obedient to the Lord of the church? Finding an answer to that critical question is the goal of this unit.

The students at a leading evangelical seminary staged a debate to examine the question: What is the place of world evangelism in the life of a Christian and in the life of a church? They wanted to know what the Bible says about the issue. They invited the most influential man in world missions at that time, Donald McGavran.

One time I heard McGavran say, "Missions is a most important purpose of the church." After the meeting I approached him, "Dr. McGavran, the last time I heard you speak you said it was the most important task of the church. Which is it, 'a' or 'the'?"

"Well," he said, "if it's 'the' purpose, that includes 'a'; and some audiences aren't ready to call it the purpose of the church." He obviously ranked world evangelism near the top of his agenda of what the church is about.

On the other side of the debate was a leading evangelical theologian. The task of a theologian is to organize biblical truth in logical order. Most theologians consider missions part of the church history department or the practical theology division along with subjects like Christian education. They usually do not consider missions a proper subject for theology.

Before the debate began, the theologian said, "Dr. McGavran, before we begin I just want you to know that I believe in missions. It's even in my theological system. It's point number D-12 in my theology." By the designation D-12 he meant that missions was a part of the outline but not a central part. It was simply lost in the list.

The theologian's statement set the stage, because missions was clearly A-1 in McGavran's theology. After the debate the theologian said, "Dr. McGavran, you're very persuasive and I admire you and your work. But I want you to know that missions is still point number D-12 in my theological system."

For most evangelical churches in America, world missions is point D-12 in the church program or off their agenda altogether. When the Holy Spirit was given, nothing was said of all the glorious truths we've been studying about. The initial emphasis in Scripture was not how He enables us to spiral up into likeness to Christ. The focus was not about teaching us to be free and fulfilled. The arrival of the Holy Spirit stressed reaching a lost world.

[Unit Memory Verse]

"You will receive power when the Holy Spirit comes on you; and you will be my witnesses in Jerusalem, and in all Judea and Samaria, and to the ends of the earth."

—Acts 1:8

[DAY 1] .... SEEING IT GOD'S WAY

More important than our stand in a debate on the importance of world evangelism is to discover where God stands! When we study Scripture, we find that—

- God's character makes world evangelism inevitable.
- God's activity proves His heart wants the world to know Him.
- God's promises assure a successful conclusion to His plan.
- God's command means we must think as He thinks and act as He acts.

In this lesson we want to get the big picture, reviewing Scripture from beginning to end to see what God considers most important.

GOD'S CHARACTER

 What characteristic of God do you like best?_____

John says that to God love is so central to His nature that you could even say He is that attribute *(1 John 4:8)*. John repeated the same words a few verses later: God is love, *(1 John 4:16)*. God didn't create love to give His creatures something to aim at. He is love by nature. As a result the Spirit created humans in the image of God, so that He could love them and be loved by them.

Creating humans with the power to choose was a risky proposition. We might not return His love. People might choose to walk away from a loving relationship. They might defy that love—which is what Adam and Eve did, and everyone since. But that didn't change God's character. He so loved the world that He gave His own Son to buy us back *(John 3:16)*. That's the purpose for His invasion of our humanity—to seek and to save the lost *(Matt. 18:11)*.

If love was the the reason for Jesus' first coming, love is also the reason He hasn't come again. People keep resisting God's loving advances to them, keep perishing, and it breaks His heart. The broken-hearted God delays His coming because He doesn't want anyone to perish *(2 Pet. 3:9)*. Consider the tension in the loving heart of God: longing to return to embrace His bride, the church, but at the same time, distressed over the many who are lost.

The Lord is not slow in keeping his promise, as some understand slowness. He is patient with you, not wanting anyone to perish, but everyone to come to repentance.
—2 Peter 3:9

 How many people need Jesus today? World population is approaching six billion at the end of the twentieth century. What is your guess as to the number of lost people?   ❑ **4 billion**   ❑ **5 billion** ❑ **more than 5 billion**

Although almost 2 billion people are called Christians, the vast majority are Christian in name only. The most generous estimates are that evangelical or born again believers number no more than 600 million. This means that more than 5 billion people today are lost. It's difficult to grasp such numbers and even harder to love those faceless multitudes. But God does love each one—they aren't faceless to Him.

The situation is more difficult than numbers alone can tell. Half those lost people are out of reach of any witnessing church. That must break God's heart. Because God is love, world evangelism is central in His thinking. Is it central in yours?

If what is central in God's thinking is barely in mine, I have heart trouble. But God doesn't. God is love, so much so that He gave His Son that no one might perish.

GOD'S ACTIVITY

God's activity demonstrates His love for the entire world. He does not care only for "His" people.

Several major acts of God in history appear below. Evaluate each example. If the act clearly is a part of God's love for the whole world, underline it. If the act is an expression love for Israel only, scratch it out. If you're not sure, leave it.

1. The call of Abraham
2. The exodus when the people of Israel escaped slavery in Egypt
3. The captivity when Jews were taken from Palestine into Babylon
4. The incarnation
5. Pentecost when the Spirit was given to a small group of Jewish disciples

1. Abraham wasn't called by God to shower all His loving attention on his descendants and let the rest of the world be doomed. He favored Abraham in order to bless the world though him *(Gen. 12:1-2)*. God created a people isolated from the moral pollution of the nations, so God could reveal Himself without distortion to them.

2. The exodus seems to be just for Israel—it meant the destruction of Egypt's military power and the capture of the people of Palestine. But God had a larger purpose. He was reestablishing His missionary task force.

3. God's missionary task force itself became corrupted, running after other gods. So God disciplined Israel, sending them into captivity to purify them. It worked! Never again did Israel worship idols.

4. The next major event was the greatest missionary act in all history. God's only Son became one of us in order to save us *(Matt. 18:11; John 1:14)*.

5. The Spirit came at Pentecost for the sole purpose of establishing a new method to carry out His saving purpose for the whole world: the church *(Acts 1:8)*.

So in the activity I underlined every example. Some of them seem at first glance to be for Israel only, but God was always at work to save the entire world.

GOD'S PROMISES

God shows His commitment to reaching the entire world through more than just His actions, His promises assure a successful end to His plan of world evangelization.

In the Scriptures in the margin *(Gen. 12:2-3; Ps. 67:1-2,7)*, underline the reason God blessed Abraham, the reason He blesses us today.

Remarkable! Abraham's blessings and ours are for the same purpose: that God's salvation may reach all people. God promises both Abraham and us that His purpose will be accomplished.

Read in the margin *(Ps. 2:8; Isa. 49:6)* promises of a coming Messiah. The Israelites in Jesus' day, including His disciples, expected Messiah to deliver them from bondage and set up a Jewish state. In these two promises of a coming Messiah underline the part that shows their expectation was too narrow:

The Old Testament prophesies repeatedly predicted the coming of the Messiah, but He was not for Israel only. He was coming for all. What does the New Testament predict about Christ's second coming? Jesus Himself said: "This gospel of the kingdom will be preached in the whole world as a testimony to all nations, and then the end will come" *(Matt. 24:14)*.

Finally, John pulls the curtain on the last act of earth's drama: After this I looked and there before me was a great multitude that no one could count, from every nation, tribe, people and language, standing before the throne and in front of the Lamb (Rev. 7:9).

Margin text:

Margin scriptures:

The Lord had said to Abram, "Leave your country, your people and your father's household and go to the land I will show you. I will make you into a great nation and I will bless you; I will make your name great, and you will be a blessing." —Genesis 12:1-2

"You will receive power when the Holy Spirit comes on you; and you will be my witnesses in Jerusalem, and in all Judea and Samaria, and to the ends of the earth." —Acts 1:8

"I will make you into a great nation and I will bless you; I will make your name great, and you will be a blessing…and all peoples on earth will be blessed through you" (Gen. 12:2-3).

May God be gracious to us and bless us and make his face shine upon us, that your ways may be known on earth, your salvation among all nations…God will bless us, and all the ends of the earth will fear him (Ps. 67:1-2,7).

The Father promises the Son: *"Ask of me, and I will make the nations your inheritance, the ends of the earth your possession"* (Ps. 2:8).

The Father promises the Son: *"It is too small a thing for you to be my servant to restore the tribes of Jacob…I will also make you a light for the Gentiles, that you may bring my salvation to the ends of the earth"* (Isa. 49:6).

From Genesis to Revelation, the Bible is full of promises about God's plan of world evangelization. The Spirit has a global plan. I told you the downside of the population explosion—more people are lost today than ever before. Now let me tell you the positive side. God is bringing in a harvest greater than any since the world began. In fact, more people have been born into God's family in the last quarter of the twentieth century than in all the centuries of church history from the apostles day until 1975! God's promises assure us His salvation purpose will be accomplished.

CHRIST'S COMMAND

Christ's command to preach the gospel in all the world is the Great Commission.

> **How many different times after the resurrection do you think Christ gave what is called the Great Commission?** ❏ 1 ❏ 2 ❏ 5 ❏ 8 ❏ 10

1. On the night of the resurrection, Christ appeared among the disciples in the upper room and said, *"As the Father has sent me, I am sending you"* (John 20:21). The same heart of love that sent Jesus must send us also.

2. Next, in Galilee, Jesus announced, *"All authority in heaven and on earth has been given to me. Therefore go and make disciples of all nations"* (Matt. 28:18,19).

3. Then, back in Jerusalem in the upper room, Jesus explained to them about His plan of world evangelism. He showed them from the Old Testament how *"Repentance and forgiveness of sins will be preached in his name to all nations, beginning at Jerusalem. You are witnesses of these things"* (Luke 24:47-48).

4. From there, He led them out toward Mount Olivet where He was to leave them, He said they should wait in Jerusalem till the Holy Spirit came on them. When that happens, He said, *"You will receive power…and you will be my witnesses in Jerusalem, and in all Judea and Samaria, and to the ends of the earth"* (Acts 1:8).

5. A comprehensive Great Commission is found in *Mark 16:15,* but the writer doesn't give us enough context to know if it was on one of the other four occasions or on yet a fifth: *"Go into all the world and preach the good news to all creation."*

Jesus gave the command four or five times! Can there be any doubt about the priority Jesus would have for my life? If God's program of world evangelism seems pretty far down the list of important things in your life, why not ask Him to move you toward likeness to Him in His passion for the lost.

> **Take time to copy *Acts 1:8*, this week's Scripture verse, onto a card. Practice memorizing it. Review your previous Scripture memory verses.**

[DAY 2] ·················· BEGINNING AT JERUSALEM

When God directed the church to reach the world, He told them to start at home—in Jerusalem. He's concerned about the lost people in your world: where you live, go to school, work, and play. If God's plan is the salvation of people and His method for reaching them is other people, surely the Spirit-given ability to win people to Christ is very important. But what does the gift of evangelism look like?

My ambition was to be a church-starting missionary among those who had never heard the gospel, but I was a school teacher. So I prayed earnestly for the gift of evangelism. And I went to work, preaching on weekends and during vacation. Sometimes many would come to Christ, sometimes no one would respond. I begged God to give me the gift of evangelism. After all, the Spirit had told me through Paul to do that: Eagerly desire the greater gifts *(1 Cor. 12:31)*. I thought of "evangelism" as a public meeting in which the gospel is proclaimed, an invitation given, and people respond. That is one type of evangelism, but it isn't the only form. I wasn't clearly distinguishing between witnessing and evangelism.

WITNESS OR EVANGELIST?

 To distinguish between an evangelistic gift and a witnessing responsibility, mark each of the statements in the margin *T* if you think the statement is biblical, *F* if you think it's not:

A witness is someone who has a personal experience and talks about it. Think of the term witness as used in a court of law. If I've only heard about the crime but haven't seen it, I'm no witness. If I've seen it, but won't talk, I'm no witness. In the last of the great commissions *(Acts 1:8)* all disciples are commissioned as witnesses. Disciples have experienced God and are to tell others the good news. So number 2 is true, number 4, false. But not all are given the gift of evangelism *(1 Cor. 12:29-30)*, 1 and 3 are false.

All believers are part of a "team" that brings people to faith. In that way the church grows. And God does expect His church to grow—"*I will build my church*," said Jesus *(Matt. 16:18)*. The Book of Acts records how He did it: the Spirit won large numbers to Christ and started local congregations all over the Roman Empire through many witnessing Christians and a handful of pioneer evangelists. Number 5 is true—every church should be baptizing new believers.

When I agonized over not having the gift of evangelism, my definition of "evangelism" was too limited. Perhaps God heard my prayer, was giving me the gift, and I just wasn't smart enough to recognize it. When we got to Japan, we found we could live in a community and love people in Jesus' name and many would come to faith. In a land where the average church has 25 members, even after decades of existence, we were baptizing 20 new converts a year. God had answered my prayer for the gift!

Or had He? I rarely prayed with someone to receive Christ, and we never gave a public invitation. Then how did they come? I call it body-life reproduction. We discovered that the Spirit-filled church as a body brings new believers to God's family. If church members are living authentic, Spirit-filled lives people come to faith.

BODY-LIFE REPRODUCTION

Every church should be baptizing new believers. Church-growth experts say that in the typical American community a church should be growing at five percent a year. New converts should account for a five percent increase. If a church isn't reaching new believers, something is wrong. Here are some possible reasons:

- The church may be spiritually ill and in need of revival. The passion for lost people may have died out, or united prayer for the lost may be weak.
- Too few members are faithful witnesses.
- Too few members have the gift of evangelism. Analysts say that most growing churches, through new believers coming to faith, about 10 percent of the members have the gift of evangelism.
- In some cases the people to be evangelized may be especially unresponsive. For example, a missionary working among Muslims in New York City would not likely get this kind of growth. Sometimes we use unresponsive people as an excuse. Wherever I am, if people are not being saved, I'm tempted to say it's "hard soil." Unusual hardness in a given community can be a cause of little fruit.

_ 1. Every true Christian will win people to faith in Christ.
_ 2. Every true Christian will tell others about Christ.
_ 3. Every Spirit-filled Christian has the gift of evangelism.
_ 4. Some show, others tell. It's OK just to witness by living a godly life since I'm shy and don't like to talk about religion.
_ 5. Every church should be baptizing new believers.

How is your church doing? Do you reach out to the lost in your community? If you see needs in your church, plan together on how to become more effective in doing what Christ commissioned us to do—reach our own "Jerusalem."

GETTING PERSONAL

Are you a faithful witness? List the names of three people you want to talk to about Jesus in the next month. Note what might be a good approach:

Name of person   *Possible approach*

_____   _____

_____   _____

_____   _____

Pray for each person and for yourself that God will give you (1) opportunity, (2) wisdom, (3) boldness, (4) sensitivity, and (5) Holy Spirit power. Do you have a growing desire to be a faithful witness, to have the gift of evangelism? Ask the Spirit for that gift. Keep on praying until He gives an answer, one way or another.

Fill in the blanks of your memory verse *Acts 1:8* located in the margin.

"You will receive _____ when the _____ _____ comes on you; and you will be my _____ in _____, and in all _____ and _____, and to the _____ of the _____."
—Acts 1:8

[DAY 3] ·········· TO THE ENDS OF THE EARTH

In the church God has appointed first of all apostles, second prophets, third teachers, then workers of miracles, also those having gifts of healing, those able to help others, those with gifts of administration, and those speaking in different kinds of tongues.
—1 Corinthians 12:28

Acts 1:8 contains a "snapshot" version of God's plan to evangelize the world. The Holy Spirit empowers all Christians to be witnesses. He gifts some as evangelists to reach their home community, their "Jerusalem." The church also has a responsibility for the surrounding area, its "Judea."

Not all can travel to begin a new work, so a few are chosen by the Spirit to reach out to places without a witness to start congregations. That kind of evangelist in Scripture is called apostle meaning, "one who is sent." We would probably call them home missionaries if they are in evangelistic church starting. Paul ranks apostle number 1 in God's plan to evangelize the world (*1 Cor. 12:28*). He isn't talking about the 12 apostles, but the gift of pioneer missionary evangelist. The growth of the Kingdom depends on such gifted people.

If the apostolic missionary crosses cultural barriers into another ethnic group, we might call that our church's "Samaria." Samaritans lived near the early Christians, but they were a different cultural and ethnic group. Ethnically or culturally different people near us are our responsibility. Finally, *Acts 1:8* mentions the "uttermost parts" or those peoples who live out of reach of present gospel witness.

TALE OF TWO CHURCHES

I spoke in two churches in the same state, the same month. The churches were similar. Both were known for their missions interest; in fact, one was the anchor church for the eastern end of the state, the other for the west. Both were large, vibrant, growing churches. Both had large budgets for missions. "East" had 1,800 members and supported 180 missionaries. "West" was half the size and supported about 75 missionaries. There the similarities ended. "East" was only 30 years old, but 180 missionaries had come from this church. They were their own sons and daughters.

"West" was 150 years old, but only one of their own had ever gone to the mission field. "West" paid for the children of others to go.

 Mark the spot with an *X* where your church fits on a scale between "West" and "East" so far as sending your own members into missionary service.

West
(0 % of members who
are missionaries)

East
(10% of members
who are missionaries)

├───────┴───────┴───────┴───────┴───────┴───────┴───────┴───────┤

"BUT THE NEED AT HOME IS SO GREAT"

Whenever we begin to talk about the needs of the world, someone always chimes in with: "But the need at home is so great." The need at home is great. Our first responsibility is for those nearby. The question is not either/or but both/and. Jesus' command was Jerusalem, Judea, Samaria, and the ends of the earth.

In America 1 out of 5 people you come into contact with will be Bible-believing Christians, in Calcutta, India 1 of 10,000. How many Bibles are in your home state? A million? Calcutta may have a few hundred Bibles; while many of the languages in that great city none at all. I use Calcutta as an example of the spiritually dark half of the world where people don't have access to the gospel. If someone doesn't go in from the outside—if an apostolic missionary doesn't come—they cannot even hear the gospel. Yes, our first responsibility is for "Jerusalem," but God loves the world.

GOD'S SCOUT

A large church contributed financial support toward 75 missionaries, including us. In fact, it was the second largest missions donor church in the nation, of any denomination. One day I walked down the long hallway in which photographs of the missionaries were displayed, studying the biographies of each. To my astonishment, not one of their missionaries was from that church! They gave lots of money to support other people's children. Frank, a young businessman, noticed the same thing and decided to do something about it. Calling himself "God's Scout," he volunteered to teach the college-and-career Sunday School class. Within 5 years 11 members of that church were on the mission field—all from that class! God hadn't called him to go as a missionary, but Frank heard the call to send.

 Do you know anyone that would make a great missionary? They are spiritually alive, gifted, and active in service to God. Write their names in the margin.

"HERE AM I, SEND ME"

Youth who haven't yet launched into some vocation are potential candidates for missionary service. Perhaps God would give you the high privilege of being His ambassador to a people who have had no chance to hear the gospel. Why not begin today to ask the Holy Spirit to give you that gift?

My wife and I had many obstacles but we kept on obeying the command to "desire earnestly"; we kept asking God to send us and use us. I'm so glad we did. Surely no joy is quite like living among people who have never heard the gospel and watching the Holy Spirit work in giving hope to the hopeless, healing broken lives, and forming a church where there was no witness before.

Write out in your journal how you feel about the idea of being an apostle. Or how you feel about being a sender. Then talk to Him about it.

[DAY 4] ·························· THE MOST IMPORTANT TASK

A magnificent southern thunderstorm was entertaining me one evening. From my porch, I watched the display of cosmic fireworks when all of a sudden there was a mighty explosion right in our backyard, an extravaganza of sight and sound. Lightning had struck the transformer. In a moment, we lost all light and power—for days we were without power. Just a half mile away giant electrical towers trooped through the fields, bearing unlimited supplies of light and power. The situation reminded me of how many Christians live. Power flows all around them, but they aren't connected.

HOW THE POWER FLOWS

Holy Spirit power flows through prayer. Prayer forms the human conduit for divine energy. Since the Spirit acts in response to the believing prayer of an obedient people, prayer is the most important part of evangelism. As E. M. Bounds said, "much prayer, much power, little prayer, little power, no prayer, no power."

 In his letter to the Colossians, Paul gives straight-forward instruction on prayer for missions. Underline the statement(s) in Paul's text that best match the conclusion about prayer I've given in the right column. Then draw a connecting line between the verse and the conclusion that best goes with it.

I want you to know how much I am struggling for you and for those at Laodicea, and for all who have not met me personally (Col. 2:1).	Prayer is not to be a sleepy routine but is spiritual warfare.
	Prayer is not to be sporadic or occasional but regular and persistent.
Continue earnestly in prayer, being vigilant in it with thanksgiving; meanwhile praying also for us, that God would open to us a door for the word, to speak the mystery of Christ, for which I am also in chains, that I may make it manifest, as I ought to speak (Col. 4:2-4, NKJV).	Prayer is not only regular but also on "battle alert," on the lookout to pray for special needs as the Spirit alerts us.
	Prayer should be so filled with faith that we can give thanks even before we see the answer.
	Prayer is not only for those we are with but for those we may never have seen.
Epaphras,…always laboring fervently for you in prayers, that you may stand perfect and complete in all the will of God (Col. 4:12, NKJV).	Pray for godliness of life.
	Pray for the Holy Spirit to work in the ministry of the missionary.

If we pray for our missionaries at all, it may be a routine reading over some brief request. But the kind of prayer Paul describes is very different. In these verses he calls such prayer "struggling." He describes it with the words *earnestly, always laboring fervently.* It sounds like a spiritual battle in prayer against unseen enemies that fight to hold captive those we aim to release.

Our prayer isn't to be occasional but continuing, regular—daily, at least. Also, our prayer should not only be the regular set times for prayer but in-between times. We are to be sensitive to the Spirit's leading us into times of special prayer. One more thing, when Paul says "with thanksgiving," he doesn't mean merely saying thank you when God answers, important as that is. We are to thank God for the answer even as we ask. In other words, faith-filled prayer.

Paul tells us to pray about: (1) the missionary's ministry and (2) the missionary's life. The Holy Spirit must empower both or nothing of eternal significance will be done. He said to pray that doors of opportunity would open up and that the missionary team would be able to make the gospel understandable to the lost. That's Spirit-energized ministry.

Paul saw the need for the fruit of the Spirit, so he instructs believers to: *Be wise in the way you act toward outsiders; make the most of every opportunity. Let your conversation be always full of grace, seasoned with salt, so that you may know how to answer everyone (Col. 4:5-6).* Paul also tells the Ephesians *(Eph. 6:19-20)* to plead with God so that he might have courage. If the missionary's life doesn't demonstrate the beauty, strength, and good news of Christ, his words will not be as effective. So we must pray for both the ministry and the life, the gifts of the Spirit and the fruit of the Spirit.

Choose some missionary you know about and write in the margin a prayer for that missionary. In addition to whatever you know to be the missionary's need, be sure to include all the ideas Paul gave the Colossians on what to pray for the missionary and the missionary team.

Did you have trouble with that assignment because you don't know any missionaries that well? If so, plan to get involved by praying for a specific missionary or missionary need. Here are some ideas.

- Ask your pastor or your youth leader to introduce you to a missionary who works in an area in which you have an interest.
- Most missionaries send out regular reports with prayer requests. Ask the missionary (s) you choose to put you on their mailing list.
- When missionaries visit your church, invite them to your home if you can. Ask about their work and learn their prayer needs. Then pray!

If you don't have a missionary you can call "my missionary," make a telephone call to the church office or write a letter right now. Get started!

Pray also for me, that whenever I open my mouth, words may be given me so that I will fearlessly make known the mystery of the gospel, for which I am an ambassador in chains. Pray that I may declare it fearlessly, as I should.
—Ephesians 6:19-20

MEASURING MATURITY ·························· [DAY 5]

The Holy Spirit has given, is giving, or will give you some wonderful gift, an ability to do an important job for Him *(1 Cor. 12)*. He then wraps that gift in the package called you and gives you as His gift to the church *(Eph. 4)*.

One of the greatest blockades on the road to victory for Jesus is something very practical, quite earthy. That thing is money, or should I say the lack of it, for the missionary enterprise. We seem to have plenty for our own needs. We provide to one degree or another for the needs of the local church, but when it comes to sending out missionaries, money dries up. Thousands of young adults are fully prepared and ready to go, but the money isn't there. What's the problem?

Jesus said spiritual immaturity in God's family is the root problem. He talked more about money than about heaven and hell combined. In fact, He taught far more about our relationships to possessions than He did about prayer! Apparently, He considered our bank statement an accurate measure of our spiritual maturity. In the following six stories and teachings, Jesus illustrates six attitudes about money. They are not necessarily in order of maturity.

LEGALISTIC GIVING

Jesus had problems with the Pharisees and their giving, but it wasn't with their legalistic measuring out one out of every 10 grains of "bird seed" for God. It's what they left undone—justice and mercy *(Luke 11:42)*. God expects His children to tithe! Yet very few church members tithe. At a large church with a four million dollar budget the business manager told me they had done a demographic study of their membership. "If every member quit his job, went on unemployment and started to tithe," he said, "we could double our budget!" Studies show that most churches are like that.

NONGIVING

The wealthy farmer in *Luke 12:16-21* was a self-centered nongiver. He spent it all on food and fun. Christ called him a fool, a dead man. Yet studies consistently show that most church members give very, very little.

FAITH GIVING

"O you of little faith!" Jesus said to his worry-wart disciples *(Luke 12:28)*. Living by faith is the only way to live and faith giving is one of the clearest evidences of God-focused living. Without faith it's impossible to please God at all *(Heb. 11:6)*. Giving in the confidence that God will take care of the outcome is the validation for every level of giving. For example, the widow living on Social Security must have faith that God will care for her on 90 percent of her income when she gives her tithe. But there seems also to be a special gift of faith *(Rom. 12:3)*. George Mueller cared for thousands of orphans on God's daily miracle provision. In fact, his faith stretched beyond caring for the orphans as he was able to give millions to foreign missionary work around the world. That's faith giving!

HONEST MANAGEMENT

Luke 16:1-13 is a tough passage to understand until you look for the one point Jesus is trying to make in His story about the cheating manager. That fellow was sharp—he used present resources to prepare for his future. And God's people aren't very smart, Jesus said, because they use their money to live well now and don't send it on ahead, investing in the Bank of Heaven at incredible interest rates. Besides, Jesus says, it's not your money to begin with. I'm the owner and you're just an interim manager *(16:12)*. The only question is, will you be an honest one? Or will you be a cheating manager, using the Owner's possessions for your own benefit?

As a young man, I gave God His 10 percent off the top. Then I had a traumatic encounter with Jesus in the Book of Luke. I saw I wasn't an owner at all. I didn't want to accept this teaching about managership—it would clip my wings, cage me in. But when I finally gave up and accepted God's view of my possessions, the very opposite of what I feared took place. It was like the cage door swung open and I was free. My intensity about making money was gone, my grief over losses and happiness over gains, my fear about the future went away. That's what happens when we get honest about who the owner is *(12:31)!*

IMPULSE GIVING

In the next story we meet an IRS agent up a tree! *(Luke 19:1-9)*. When Zacchaeus met Jesus he was changed into a new man and impulsively gave away half his estate

---

"Will a man rob God? Yet you rob me. But you ask, 'How do we rob you?' In tithes and offerings. You are under a curse—the whole nation of you—because you are robbing me."
—Malachi 3:8-9

The angels from their home on high
Look down on us with wondering eye
That where we are but passing guests
We build such strong and solid nests,
And where we hope to live for aye,
We scarce take thought one stone to lay.
—Anonymous

Sell your possessions and give to the poor. Provide purses for yourselves that will not wear out, a treasure in heaven that will not be exhausted, where no thief comes near and no moth destroys. For where your treasure is, there your heart will be also.
—Luke 12:33-34

(v. 8). One of the first signs of spiritual life is the desire to give. A person begins to get his kicks out of giving instead of finding his greatest pleasure in getting stuff, accumulating money, and spending it on himself. Impulse givers may not give systematically, but they can be very generous when presented with a great need. Most Christians most of the time give at the impulse level.

SACRIFICIAL LOVE GIVING

Jesus watched the offering plate and noted how much each one put in (Luke 21:1-4). No doubt He does so today as well. There He discovered a very beautiful woman. Thin, with hunger-pinched features, no doubt, and shabby in appearance, but how beautiful she was! Out of a heart of love she gave everything she had.

The young talk-show host was interviewing Mother Theresa. Her eyes sparkled as she heard Mother Theresa brag about the generosity of Americans. Then Theresa added, "But you give out of your muchness, no? You don't give till it hurts."

The young woman blurted out in astonishment, "Must it hurt?"

"Love," said Theresa, "will hurt." She had discovered the basic spiritual truth that love can only be measured by the sacrifice it makes.

Every level of giving must be proved by faith and motivated by love. But these sets of goals are clear enough for me to evaluate my life. I know the painful—then freeing—move I made from tithing to managing. And I know very well, as I see the poverty of the world, that I don't live a sacrificial lifestyle. I may evidence spurts of sacrifice, but I fall far from Jesus' model of giving.

 Honesty about your money may be the hardest honesty of all. How have you spent your money this past year? Review your giving for the past year. Are you pleased with that level? ❏ Yes   ❏ No   Is God pleased?   ❏ Yes   ❏ No   Explain your answers in the margin.

Remember God's style of giving. He created me so I am His property. But I stole His creation and took possession of me. So, in the most astounding outpouring of love, He purchased me at terrible personal cost. Thank God for His incredible gift! (2 Cor. 9:15). Next He guarantees my livelihood (Luke 12:31) and rewards me a hundred times over for any little thing I might give Him, as if I had done something grand (Luke 18:23-30). Then when I get to heaven He promises to reward me all over again!

In response to such love are you ready to move up one step? If you've never been a faithful tither, isn't it time to promise Him that 10 percent? Perhaps you've been a tither, but you did pretty much what you pleased with the other 90 percent. Isn't it time to become a manager? Whatever level of giving you've achieved in your walk with God, don't you want to step up? Lack of giving is a major obstacle to world evangelism. Spiritually mature Christians give sacrificially.

 Whatever your decision, tell Him about it and write it out now in your journal before finishing this lesson.

Our relationship to things is an objective way of measuring our spiritual maturity. Spiritual maturity is the theme of our whole study. Giving ties together the fruit of the Spirit (character) with evangelism (purpose). Because the key to our response about money is love, this study sets the stage for our final unit. Next we will examine the goal of life: loving oneness with God.

a MARRIAGE MADE in HEAVEN

UNIT 12

An intimate identity with God in love is truly a marriage made in heaven! This incredible revelation of what God intended from the start is the theme of our final unit of study.

Chapel seating was assigned, but I didn't mind. The girl I most wanted to be near was seated right in front of me every day! When she ran those lovely fingers, through her thick, beautiful hair, it drove me crazy. Finally, I got up enough courage to ask Muriel for a date. I was intoxicated with her infectious laughter, attractive face, delightful creativity, deep love for God, and her caring ways with people. And she was so much fun. Friendship soon blossomed into love and we talked of marriage. Would it be a marriage made in heaven?

By the time we were engaged, my mind was so consumed with Muriel I could think of nothing else. The wedding came, agonizingly slow. Could love ever be more intimate, more satisfying? We had a lot to learn. Children came and our love deepened with every shared pain, heightened with every shared joy. Our hearts got so intertwined they seemed like one.

Now at the end of the road, when Muriel's mind barely functions at the borders of consciousness, deep into Alzheimer's, the love still grows. I like to think it's been a marriage made in heaven.

There's one marriage, however, I know was made in heaven. Did you know that the chief image of human relationship to God in the Old Testament was of Israel as the wife of God? A chief image in the New Testament is of the church as the bride of Christ. There's a marriage made in heaven!

Which is the real marriage and which the reflection? Did the Holy Spirit take the human condition of marriage and draw an analogy with God's relationship to people so we could understand the unseen world better? Or was it the other way around? Was the plan for the relationship between God and His beloved so intimate that it required a temporary earthly model for us to understand the ultimate, eternal relationship? If so, God made humans on a dual model, man and wife, to show us what His grand plan of union with Him was to be. Either way, that intimate identity with God in love is truly a marriage made in heaven!

[Unit Memory Verses]

"My prayer is....that all of them may be one, Father, just as you are in me and I am in you. May they also be in us so that the world may believe that you have sent me....May they be brought to complete unity to let the world know that you sent me and have loved them even as you have loved me."
—John 17:20-21,23

If the Spirit of him who raised Jesus from the dead is living in you, he who raised Christ from the dead will also give life to your mortal bodies through his Spirit, who lives in you.

—Romans 8:11

WHERE ARE WE HEADED? ·······················[DAY 1]

This week is the last of our study of the activities of the Holy Spirit and our responses to Him. What will be the final outcome of this relationship? Why did God create you? Why did He recreate you? Bible scholars write volumes to answer those questions; and each of us, no doubt, have our own opinion.

 In the margin check the answer closest to your own idea of God's ultimate purpose in creating and saving you.

Let's examine each of these possible responses by category.

❏ *to become like Christ*
❏ *to be holy*
❏ *to glorify God*
❏ *to worship God*
❏ *to love God*
❏ *to experience loving oneness with God*

CHRISTLIKENESS
Since we've been studying spiraling up into ever greater likeness to Christ for 12 weeks, to become like Christ seems a likely choice.

 Go back now to the list of possible ultimate purposes; put an X beside any characteristic that does not describe Jesus.

That was an easy assignment! Jesus embodies all of them, so you could well choose "become like Christ" as the comprehensive goal of human creation and redemption. If we were like Christ in all the ways in the list, we would certainly fulfill everything God purposed in our creation and redemption. But in thinking of Christlikeness, we must be careful to include the relationship that Jesus had with the Father. We often limit the idea of "Christlikeness" to having attitudes and behavior like Christ. We use Christlike as something like a synonym for holiness.

HOLINESS
Holiness is important because without it no one will see God! *(Heb. 12:14)*. But it's a limited goal. We often use holiness to describe growing away from sinful attitudes and actions. That is a purpose God has for us, but not the ultimate goal. Holiness as a primary goal creates another problem. Striving for holiness can become self-centered and legalistic. Our ultimate purpose must be God-centered, not self-centered.

 Look back to the list and put an asterisk (*) by those goals in the list that focus exclusively on God.

GLORY OF GOD
Focusing on God is biblical and all we do should bring Him glory *(1 Cor. 10:31)*. The problem with making the glory of God our ultimate goal, is that, like Christlikeness it isn't very specific. So we must determine in detail how we can best glorify Him.

WORSHIP
Because glorifying God is quite general, worship makes a very specific goal for life. Worship is an exclusively God-centered choice. Our whole lives should be worship, demonstrating His worth.

Making either glorifying God or worshiping Him the ultimate goal presents a problem: Why would a God of love be so self-centered as to demand those responses as the whole purpose of making and saving us?

Five year old Kent was trying hard to get our guests to notice him and his talents. "Oh, Kent, quit showing off," I said.

He apparently devoted some deep thought to the subject, because the next day he had developed his response: "Daddy, why does God want us to brag on Him?"

 To understand why we worship, look at God's self-revelation in Scripture. What does He want above all else? In each of the sets below check the one you think better describes what God thinks or feels.

❑ (1a) God feels fulfilled when we worship and glorify Him.

❑ (1b) God knows we can be fulfilled only as we relate to Him as the glorious God He is.

❑ (2a) God knows we'll destroy ourselves if we break with reality and take credit for what He does.

❑ (2b) God likes to take all the credit.

❑ (3a) God is jealous—it angers Him for anyone else to be honored.

❑ (3b) God is jealous—it hurts Him when we love others more than Him.

Many Bible students believe God desires that we conform to the reality of who He is for our own good. To get out of alignment with reality is self-destructive, allowing self to take the honor that belongs to God alone. God expects us to recognize who He is and behave accordingly. I chose (1b), (2a), (3b).

Did you have trouble with the last set? The term *jealous* applied to God may jar us, but the Bible repeatedly tells us He's a jealous God. Perhaps we get a clue of what God is teaching us by considering the fundamental command to love God. When God came in person to reveal His heart purpose, He said, " 'Love the Lord your God with all your heart and with all your soul and with all your mind.' This is the first and greatest commandment" (Matt. 22:37-38). "First and greatest" makes clear what God is concerned about.

Jesus quoted this commandment from the foundational revelation of God's will in the Old Testament (Deut. 6:5). He then explained its importance. Everything else, He said—everything taught in the Bible, *"the Law and the Prophets hang on these commandments,"* along with the command to love one's neighbor (Matt. 22:40).

We'd be safe to make loving God our chief end, except for one thing. Genuine love must be mutual. It's not so much that we love Him, but that He loves us *(1 John 4:10)*. We must search for a more complete statement of God's purpose for us.

LOVING ONENESS WITH GOD

As we saw in unit 11, God's nature is love *(1 John 4:8,16)*. From all eternity the Father, Son, and Holy Spirit are bound together in bonds of eternal love. From the overflow of that love, He designed a us to love Him back.

God's purpose all along has been to have a loving, mutual relationship with us. That's why He calls His relationship to us a marriage! When a man "knew" a woman in Bible times it meant they became one in intimate identity. That's why we say the goal of life is knowing God—an identity so close it could be likened to marriage. Closer than that—it could be likened to the unity the Father and Son have with one another. Now we see how being like Christ fits into the ultimate goal! We are intended to be like Him not only in character but in relationship.

Our memory verse is taken from a prayer of Jesus that speaks of our unity with one another (part of being like Jesus) along with our unity with God. This also, we now see clearly, is part of our being like Jesus. Here's the whole passage, including both kinds of oneness—with God as a basis for unity with one another.

"My prayer is not for them alone. I pray also for those who will believe in me through their message, that all of them may be one, Father, just as you are in me and I am in you. May they also be in us so that the world may believe that you have sent me. I have given them the glory that you gave me, that they may be

one as we are one: I in them and you in me. May they be brought to complete unity to let the world know that you sent me and have loved them even as you have loved me.

Father, I want those you have given me to be with me where I am, and to see my glory, the glory you have given me because you loved me before the creation of the world.

Righteous Father, though the world does not know you, I know you, and they know that you have sent me. I have made you known to them, and will continue to make you known in order that the love you have for me may be in them and that I my- self may be in them" (John 17:20-26).

The love relationship He planned for us is so intimate, so permanent, that the only way to exhaust its meaning is to say it's like the Father's love for the Son and the Son's love for the Father! That's why the two of them made the greatest of all sacrifices—He died for us so that we, might live in union with Him *(1 Thess. 5:10)*.

Jesus' prayer in *John 17* speaks of two unities—among believers and with God.

(1) Unity among believers shows outsiders whose disciples we are. Such unity is often difficult to achieve. This unity is the mark of true discipleship.

(2) The basis for unity between believers is our oneness with the Father, the Son, and the Holy Spirit. This second unity is beyond comprehension. It's like trying to explain to a five-year-old the glories of married love.

A child doesn't have a clue. It's the same with us. If the unbeliever can't under- stand the glories of unity with Christ, no more can we understand ahead of time the joy of union with Christ in heaven following the marriage supper of the Lamb. We just don't have the capacity to grasp a whole new dimension of human-divine rela- tionship. We haven't matured yet. We've not undergone the final transformation into God-compatible beings. One day we will experience God in all His fullness. That's what He's showing us, teaching us all along.

At the beginning of this lesson we listed the purposes God had in mind for us. All are important, and we've looked at each of them briefly in an attempt to exam- ine the splendor of His plan for us. Let's have one more go at it.

 Here are the purposes God had in creating and re-creating us. They were listed at the beginning of this lesson to: become like Christ, glo- rify God, be holy, love God, worship God, and experience loving one- ness with God. On the building blocks below write each purpose in the order you think they build. Put the most foundational in the bottom block—without this one none of the others can happen. The purpose of this activity is not to get the "right" answer—I doubt one exists! The purpose is to see more clearly how all of God's purposes relate to you.

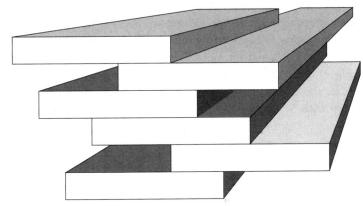

Whatever your order, isn't it exciting? Why, it's like a marriage made in heav- en! To reach that goal is the reason we've being studying the activities of the Spirit—*We know that we live in him and he in us, because he has given us of his Spirit (1 John 4:13).*

 Pause now and thank God for all the glorious purposes He has in mind for you.

[DAY 2] · · · · · · · · · · · · · · · · · ALL GLORY, WORSHIP, AND HONOR

Loving oneness with God has two sides: God's love for you and your love for Him. Focusing on God is the true evidence of love, but it's not just proof of where your heart is. Focusing your attention on God is also how you express your love for Him, and how you can grow in it, too. To glorify and worship God is evidence and expression of love, as well as a way to deepen love.

Have you ever considered the differences between glorifying and worshiping God? The two actions overlap, but each word has a slightly different emphasis. When we honor and glorify God the focus is on how we show Him off to others. When we worship we direct our attention completely to Him.

GLORIFYING GOD

 In the margin list ways you can put the spotlight on God—honor Him—causing others to see His majesty, wisdom, power, holiness, love, justice, and truth.

I listed (1) living a life that reflects His character, (2) praising Him to others in conversation and song, (3) winning others to faith so more will honor Him, (4) always giving Him credit for the good that happens, and (5) defending Him against false accusation. The list goes on, but those are some ways to put God's glories on display.

 Review the lists—both yours and mine—and asterisk any you want to emphasize more in your own life.

Glorifying God doesn't have to be a "major production." Muriel was often an example to me of spontaneously giving God credit. In everyday situations her heart full of love was forever bubbling over with expressions praising God.

WORSHIPING GOD

Many genuine Christians don't experience much worship in a "worship service"; they don't feel much warm devotion in their "devotional" time. Yet God longs for those who will worship Him in spirit and in truth *(John 4:23).* To get a running start on bringing to life your "worship service" next Sunday, let's worship Him now. We can do that in many ways—actually all of life should lift Him up. Telling Him how greatly we value Him, rejoicing in His person, that is worship.

• **Worship with Scripture**–Read a favorite Psalm of praise. If none come immediately to mind, try *Psalm 8* or *19.* To praise Him slowly read aloud the Psalm you chose, consciously speaking those words to God.

• **Worship in song**–Choose a chorus that really tells of your praise to God. Sing your heart out worshiping God!

• **Worship in your own words**–Now that others have inspired you with their expressions of worship, you're ready to worship Him in your own words. Follow the three easy steps of worship, praise, and thanksgiving, to write out in your journal a

1.

2.

3.

4.

5.

prayer of worship. Try putting it into verse—a hymn of worship! Write three stanzas:

1. First, tell God everything about His person you admire, His characteristics. (Many are listed above in the exercise on "Glorifying God"). That's worship.

2. Next, write about the major activities of God since the start of time, His works of creation and redemption, and praise Him for each of those activities you admire or are especially grateful. That's praise.

3. Finally, thank God for everything He has done for you personally. Be sure to include some of the ordinary earthly blessings as well as the spiritual. That's thanksgiving.

• **Worship Him forever**–If I asked you to name the hymnbook of the Bible I'm sure you'd name the Book of Psalms. You'd be right—it's the hymnbook of God's people of all the ages. But a close second is found in the New Testament.

 Do you have any idea which book it is? _____

John was overwhelmed with visions of future doom, but he constantly bursts into praise. In the last book of the Bible, Revelation, He records some of the worship that will one day be offered to God. As he lets us in on that heavenly worship, I think he's inviting us to join him in praise as a preview of the glorious worship in which we'll one day participate. To join him in worship now see the verses in the margin.

 If you know a contemporary song that sets music to the words in the margin, don't hesitate to sing it now! Look up these other verses in the Bible: *Revelation 7:12, Revelation 15:3-4,* and *Revelation 19:16*.

Perhaps your heart is just too heavy to sing joyfully. How could John be so joyful in his praise when throughout the book he continually tells about the judgment and doom that was coming? The secret is found at the beginning of his book:

On the Lord's Day I was in the Spirit, and I heard behind me a loud voice like a trumpet (Rev. 1:10).

After this I looked, and there before me was a door standing open in heaven. And the voice I had first heard speaking to me like a trumpet said, "Come up here, and I will show you what must take place after this." At once I was in the Spirit (Rev. 4:1-2).

John was *in the Spirit*. To be in the Spirit, no matter how threatening the circumstances, is to overflow with praise and worship to God. By the Spirit we can worship always. If we're filled with the Spirit, that's exactly what we'll do! Remember, a heavy heart lifts on the wings of praise. To love God is to worship and adore Him and to tell others about His greatness because He is worthy of all glory, honor, and praise!

BEST FRIENDS • [DAY 3]

I'm sure most of the disciples would have said, "Jesus is my best friend." They walked the village streets and dusty country roads together and they listened intently as He talked. But they didn't just listen—they talked, too. Such an intimate companionship! Do you ever wish you could have been there?

Jesus anticipated our loneliness so He sent another Comforter who would not just walk with us but who would actually be in us (*John 14:15-26; 16:5-10*). He was telling us, "I love you with an everlasting love. I won't leave you orphaned."

The God kind of love is more than my love for Him expressed in worship and praise. Much more. It's His love for me! As in marriage, love is the bridge that must reach out from both sides if ever there is to be a union.

*"Holy, holy, holy
is the Lord God Almighty
who was, and is, and is to come."
"You are worthy, our Lord and
God,
to receive glory and honor and
power,
for you created all things,
and by your will they were created
and have their being."*
—Revelation 4:8,11

*"Worthy is the Lamb, who was
slain,
to receive power and wealth and
wisdom and strength
and honor and glory and praise!
To him who sits on the throne and
to the Lamb
be praise and honor and glory
and power,
for ever and ever!"*
—Revelation 5:12-13

LEVELS OF INTIMACY

Consider the levels of intimacy in a human relationship:

___1. Muriel and I met and liked one another. We'd get together occasionally and talk about things of mutual interest.

___2. Then love began to fill the relationship, so each of us began to move out of our comfort zones. Muriel tried to figure out football, and I dragged myself to art museums. But still we didn't touch certain topics.

___3. Eventually we reached the stage of mutual trust and agreed that nothing is off-limits—we'll fully share our hearts, no secrets.

___4. Then we were married and intimacy was complete, or was it? We hadn't been together long enough to have pain. But we did enjoy one another's companionship and moments of delight.

___5. We hit the hard times and ran to embrace one another in shared agony.

___6. Finally, my life came to the place where fun wasn't all that fun if Muriel wasn't with me; heartache was almost unbearable if she didn't share it. It was as if the other was there even when they weren't; and when we were apart, the desire to be together became a gnawing hunger. There was freedom and comfort between us that outsiders couldn't disturb.

In the list above, put a check by the level of human relationship that is most similar to your present experience of God.

Actually, there's a seventh level, a closer intimacy than Muriel and I could ever experience, because we're humans. Such intimacy can only be experienced with God.

THREE LEVELS OF UNION WITH GOD

• **Basic Friendship**—Josh was furious about his Christmas gift. It wouldn't work right. Suddenly, he threw it across the room where it crashed through a valued lamp shade. In the following months, Josh tried, with varying degrees of success, to bridle his temper. Ours was an unlikely friendship. He was only three, and our conversations didn't rise to great heights. Josh taught me something about God and me—another unlikely friendship. I certainly can't converse on God's level. Sometimes I get angry with a gift God gives me. I sometimes say a bad thing, do a foolish thing, or enjoy a sinful thing.

Through it all God continues to love me. Against the backdrop of this lopsided love affair, Jesus calls us friends *(John 15:15)*. He doesn't call us slaves or even children, both of which we are, but friends!

Josh has been my friend now for several years. He's especially hard to resist when a smile breaks across that pixie face as he offers a gift of atonement (usually some well-loved toy), hugs me tight, and says, "Sorry, Pawpaw." Josh moved to a distant city and entered first grade. A few weeks later I received a letter, the first from my buddy: "I Luv Yoo Yoo Are The Bes Fred I everhad." It's so good to be best friends with God! But there's a level of intimacy above basic friendship.

• **Daily Companionship**—My youngest son Kent, has always had a prayer life I envied—from his high school days on. But I wasn't prepared for what I discovered when he recently came to stay with me for six weeks. I hadn't finished cleaning the guest room when he arrived, so when he went out for an errand, I finished. As I picked up a scrap of paper from the floor, I noticed a cryptic message: "get up at 3:00 a.m. every day and stay awake." Sure enough, every morning at 3:00 the light in the kitchen would go on and stay on. It was good for me to know what was happening; that way I wouldn't intrude on Kent's time with his beloved God.

Jesus is his beloved. In reporting to the students and faculty of Columbia International University on his work among the slum dwellers of Calcutta, Kent reminisced about his student days. He told of how he decided not to get married, on the advice of the apostle Paul *(1 Cor. 7)*, so he could serve God more fully. Then he said, "I was walking down the campus road toward the dining hall when I was met by several dating couples. They seemed so happy. Then the thought struck me, *They can't even imagine what a great time God and I are having.*"

Later I talked with him about his prayer life and how, in my judgment, he was jeopardizing his health with all his fasting and prayer. He seemed so God-intoxicated. "Dad," he said, "I think I have more fun with God than you do!" I'm afraid he does.

 Has your sense of God's companionship in that daily time...
❑ grown closer, more real
❑ stayed about the same
❑ grown more distant and formal

• **Constant Awareness of His Presence**—At age 20 I discovered the motto of Frederic Franson, the pioneer who founded Scandinavian mission agencies at the close of the nineteenth century. Franson's life theme was *CCCC*—Constant Conscious Communion with Christ. The moment I heard it, my heart leaped. "That's what I want, Lord!" I cried out. And God heard my prayer. For about two months that summer I was not only always conscious of the Lord's presence, I seemed to be constantly, consciously conversing with God. Then the feeling of closeness slipped away.

I begged for the return of that experience, but it never came back. I'm not sure why He gave me that foretaste of heaven nor why He withdrew it. Was it something like Paul's brief visit to "the third heaven," not intended to be permanent, not designed for daily human experience? Yet some people have testified of a life-pattern of constant conscious communion with Christ. Perhaps God would give you that high level of intimacy if you sought it. Don't let my experience discourage you.

In the meantime, until that day when we all have such a life-filling experience in His presence, I can promise something very special: a constant relationship of intimacy, an uninterrupted awareness of the Spirit's presence.

 Place a check below to indicate your level of intimacy with God today.
❑ basic friendship
❑ a special time of intimate companionship every day
❑ constant awareness of His presence

Don't settle for "a superficial relationship with a friendly stranger," as someone has described it. Don't be afraid of intimacy. He won't reject you because you don't measure up. No one measures up. He loves you and longs for your companionship. Run and embrace Him—He's waiting, eagerly.

ACCOMPLISHED · [DAY 4]

Romans 8:11—

The highest and best levels of intimacy lie ahead. All the Spirit's work in us is accomplished as we find ourselves "filled to all the fullness of God." That, too, will be the Spirit's work.

THE SPIRIT'S LAST GREAT ACTIVITY

 In the margin write Romans 8:11, one of this week's memory verses.

Then I heard what sounded like a great multitude, like the roar of rushing waters and like loud peals of thunder, shouting:

"Hallelujah!
For our Lord God Almighty reigns.
Let us rejoice and be glad and give him glory!
For the wedding of the Lamb has come,
and his bride has made herself ready.
Fine linen, bright and clean,
was given her to wear."
(Fine linen stands for the righteous acts of the saints.)

Then the angel said to me, "Write: 'Blessed are those who are invited to the wedding supper of the Lamb!'" And he added, "These are the true words of God" (Rev. 19:6-9).

Now it is God who has made us for this very purpose and has given us the Spirit as a deposit, guaranteeing what is to come.
—2 Corinthians 5:5

Having believed, you were marked in him with a seal, the promised Holy Spirit, who is a deposit guaranteeing our inheritance until the redemption of those who are God's possession—to the praise of his glory.
—Ephesians 1:13-14

Some understand this verse to refer to spiritual rather than physical resurrection. They take the verse to say Holy Spirit power energizes the spiritually dead to make them alive in Christ. The immediate context of the passage does speak of that regenerating work of the Spirit, but Paul addresses Christians here, not the spiritually dead. He assures them that the Spirit will yet give life to their physical bodies.

I believe that Paul is speaking here of the final resurrection. A clear parallel and a connection does exist with the already-accomplished spiritual resurrection. But the final resurrection is a major theme of the last half of Romans 8. I take it Paul is inserting a preview of that in our memory verse. Our physical resurrection is the completed work of the Spirit in us. It is the accomplishment of all He intended from the start: God's image fully restored, and union with God fully complete.

Read John's beautiful description of that occasion in the margin.

WHAT A DAY THAT WILL BE!

In a sense we're already married to God, united with Him forever. But in another sense, the completion of that marriage is yet to be. You might call our present relationship an engagement and the Holy Spirit our engagement ring. God *set his seal of ownership on us, and put his Spirit in our hearts as a deposit, guaranteeing what is to come* (2 Cor. 1:22; see also 5:5 and Eph. 1:14). Exciting as the engagement has been, our present experience of God will fade into the dim recesses of memory when the marriage is completed! The climax of all the Spirit's work is to usher us into the banquet hall to meet Jesus *face to face* (1 Cor. 13:12). The Spirit's work will be complete when *we shall be like him, for we shall see him as he is* (1 John 3:2).

Many of God's promises about eternity will be fulfilled when we die and are instantly with Him. Others will be fulfilled when the bride, the church, is completed and Jesus returns to take her to the final celebration. Since the Bible doesn't explain all the mystery of it, I'm not sure exactly what will happen when; no one knows. As I think about eternity, here are some of the things I look forward to:

- Jesus. Seeing Him, feeling His warm embrace, being united with Him in a union so intimate I don't have the capacity now to even imagine.
- The Father. Seeing Him smile and hearing Him say, "Well done." I want to tell Him how grateful I am for His love for me, so great He let His own Son go for me. In fact, for the first time I'll be able to worship Him as I've always longed to, but never seemed able.
- The Spirit. I want to tell Him in detail how I appreciate all He's done for me.
- Being reunited with my son, Bob, my parents, and other loved ones who got there before me, and, especially, my precious Muriel fully restored.
- All sorrow, pain, sickness, weakness, sin, and failure gone forever.
- Jesus' smile when I give Him my wedding present—my life investment for Him.
- Being transformed into the likeness of Jesus, the spiral complete.

Do you relate with any of those hopes? What do you most look forward to? Number my list in the order of your own priority, leaving out any you don't anticipate and adding in the margin any I haven't mentioned.

NOT EVERYONE WANTS TO DIE...

Not everyone looks forward to that day. One of my best friends, John, was dying of bone cancer. When I visited him in his home he said, "Robertson, you probably want to go to heaven, but I don't. I've got too many things planned to get done for God right here on earth." His health became worse, and soon I heard he had made his final trip to the hospital. I flew into town, rushed to the hospital, and found his room. No sooner had I entered the door when John said, "Robertson, I've got something to tell you about death. It takes too long." I reached his bedside and searched for words of comfort, but he continued: "I can't figure out the purpose of all this pain."

I responded, "I haven't got it all figured out either. But I do notice one thing it's done for you. A few weeks ago you didn't want to go to be with Jesus. Now you can hardly wait."

John grimaced. "You're right, pal." A few hours later he had his desire.

 As you think about death or, better, about that grand celebration at the end of time, how do you feel about it? Check the one that is nearest to how you feel.

❑ I'm with John. I look forward to that last great Day and glad I'll be there, but I'm in no hurry; I've got too much important and fun things to do right here.

❑ I'm with Paul. I'm so excited I can hardly wait to be with Jesus.

❑ I'm more than a little apprehensive about that Day; I'm afraid my wedding gift to Jesus won't amount to much.

❑ I dread the Day. What an embarrassment I'll be to Him and to myself.

❑ I wish it would go away; I'm not even sure I'll be there.

❑ Other: _____

If you think the Spirit would be pleased if you felt differently from what you marked, what's gone wrong? We began our walk with the Spirit in eternity where He designed us to be God-compatible. We've kept *in step with the Spirit (Gal. 5:25)* through His work of transforming us, a spiral up from one degree of Christ's glorious likeness to another. We're headed toward the grand finale when the Spirit will complete His work. But somewhere we must have gotten out of step, because we don't rejoice with the Bridegroom in anticipating that glorious heavenly wedding day. If that's your situation, don't you want to get back in step with the Spirit?

 To get back in step, turn to the table of contents of *Life In the Spirit* and see if you can identify the work of the Spirit you've missed out on. Circle the title of that unit or lesson and then reread it. Is the Spirit gently nudging you to do something about it in preparation for your heavenly wedding day? Do it now!

LIFE IN THE SPIRIT:SPIRALING UP ·····················[DAY 5]

We've come to the end of our study of *Life In the Spirit*. Perhaps for you it's not the end but a new beginning. It has been for me. As I walked through Scripture with you, I experienced many fresh encounters with the Spirit and with His truth.

LIFE IN THE SPIRIT: SUMMARY

We started in fellowship with God since the Spirit created us in God's very image. When we chose to abandon that love relationship and headed for hell, the Spirit gave us a great revelation of truth—of our true condition and of God's salvation, so hope was born. Next the Spirit stopped our downward spiral by doing two or three things at the same time. As we responded to His truth with repentance and faith, he regenerated us. He changed our very nature and came to live in us. On the course map I summarized those activities with the word *redeeming*. A part of the process of regeneration is indwelling; in some mysterious way He filled us with Himself. This began the great spiral up, the process of sanctification. Sanctification actually describes the

How many of the 10 activities of the Spirit can you recall?

1.
2.
3.
4.
5.
6.
7.
8.
9.
10.

Here are the 10 activities of the Spirit in a scrambled list. Number them in the order we studied them.

_____ *glorifying*

_____ *indwelling (regenerating)*

_____ *creating*

_____ *revealing (including both inspiration and illumination)*

_____ *filling*

_____ *redeeming*

_____ *teaching (sanctifying)*

_____ *gift-giving*

_____ *overcoming*

_____ *sending*

entire process of spiraling into likeness to Christ, so on the course map I used the word, *transforming*.

For most of us, however, the process of sanctification isn't an unbroken upward spiral. Through drift or rebellion we break fellowship. We grieve the Spirit. When we drift or rebel, we are no longer filled—He is no longer in full control, the dominant characteristic of our lives. Even in our rebellion God continues to offer grace and restoration; whenever we reenter the close relationship by yielding to His will and trusting Him, the process begins again.

As we trust and obey Him, the Spirit produces all kinds of Jesus fruit in us and custom designs a pattern of unique abilities so we can serve. We call that combination the fruit of the Spirit and the gifts of the Spirit. Isn't it marvelous? He provides everything to be what we were designed to be (fruit) and do what we were designed to do (gifts).

One of those gifts is the ability to win others to faith. Whether or not I have the gift of evangelism, though, the Spirit builds His church. He does it through that very church itself, body-life reproduction for world evangelization. Finally, He will one day raise our dead bodies just in time for the marriage celebration; unless we're still alive when the Bridegroom comes. But even then we'll not by-pass the work of the Spirit; for we shall all be changed, in a moment, in the blink of an eye!

On the spiral below write in order from bottom to top the following characteristics in the order you have experienced spiritual growth: conscious companionship with God, obey, trust, yield, love God, become like Jesus, know God, perfect oneness with God.

DON'T BE AFRAID!

When our children were small, I occasionally took speaking engagements away from our home base in Japan. The children developed a celebration response when I returned. One day when I came in the gate, our four-year-old Kent was playing in the backyard. He'd flooded it to make a gigantic mud pie and was thickly coated with sticky goo from head to toe. He sighted my entrance and sounded the alarm: "Daddy!" he shouted and ran to embrace me. Here I was, all dressed up in my one preacher-suit. What should I do? Oh, hug him good, of course.

His older brothers and sisters—all five of them—swarmed out to greet me. Then each dashed to prepare my welcome—one got a chair, another plugged in an electric fan. As if that weren't enough, another got a fistful of hand fans and began to fan the hot, humid air. Someone else took my mud-spattered jacket. Kent stood in the background and silently watched. Suddenly he disappeared. In the kitchen he pushed a chair over to the wall cabinet where the instant drink mix was stashed. He'd never done it before, but he poured an ample supply into a tall glass and, anchored it with two chubby, muddy fingers grasping the rim on the inside.

What do you suppose I did? No, I couldn't pitch it out into the garden, for the little guy was watching me like a hawk.

"Did you make this all by yourself?" I asked. Standing first on one foot, then the other, twisting his grimy T-shirt up till his whole dirty midriff stuck out, he nodded two silent, quick jerks. As he eagerly watched, I took a sip of the gritty, brown drink.

Kent waited a moment and then eagerly he asked, "Did you like it?" You think I lied, don't you? But I didn't. I told the truth.

"Kent, I loved it!" Oh, I didn't love the gritty, brown water, but it was his love-gift to me. I loved it!

When the Lord returns and we gather to celebrate, the gift offered by the best among us will have in it a muddy finger or two. But if it's the gift of our true love, He'll be well-pleased. "I love it!" He'll say, and our joy will be complete. Our next stop on the spiral up is the marriage made in heaven. Rejoice! Don't be afraid.

 Here's my journal entry for our final time together. Join me in prayer.

> Holy Spirit of God, what a wonder You are! From beginning to end You made it all happen. And You not only do for me, You love me and want to be with me. That I can't understand, but I love You, too, and want to be Your intimate companion always. Hold me close and when I start to drift away, draw me back. I want to become all that a mortal can be, so here I am, Yours to do with as You will.
>
> Father and Dear Son, how can I ever express my gratitude for Your great gift at Calvary and Your great gift at Pentecost? I cannot, so I offer You all of me with the hope that it will bring You some small joy.
>
> On the authority of Jesus' name I come. Amen.

CHRISTIAN GROWTH STUDY PLAN
Preparing Christians to Serve

In the **Christian Growth Study Plan (formerly Church Study Course),** this book Life in the Spirit, Youth Edition is a resource for course credit in the subject area "Personal Life" of the Christian Growth category of diploma plans. To receive credit, read the book, complete the learning activities, show your work to your pastor, a staff member or church leader, then complete the following information. This page may be duplicated. Send the completed page to:

**Christian Growth Study Plan
127 Ninth Avenue, North, MSN 117
Nashville, TN 37234-0117
FAX: (615)251-5067**

For information about the Christian Growth Study Plan, refer to the current Christian Growth Study Plan Catalog. Your church office may have a copy. If not, request a free copy from the Christian Growth Study Plan office (615/251-2525).

LIFE IN THE SPIRIT, YOUTH EDITION
CG-0379

PARTICIPANT INFORMATION

Social Security Number (USA ONLY) — —

Personal CGSP Number* — —

Date of Birth (MONTH, DAY, YEAR) — —

Name (First, Middle, Last)
☐ Mr.　☐ Miss
☐ Mrs.　☐

Home Phone — —

Address (Street, Route, or P.O. Box)

City, State, or Province

Zip/Postal Code

CHURCH INFORMATION

Church Name

Address (Street, Route, or P.O. Box)

City, State, or Province

Zip/Postal Code

CHANGE REQUEST ONLY

☐ Former Name

☐ Former Address　City, State, or Province　Zip/Postal Code

☐ Former Church　City, State, or Province　Zip/Postal Code

Signature of Pastor, Conference Leader, or Other Church Leader　Date

*New participants are requested but not required to give SS# and date of birth. Existing participants, please give CGSP# when using SS# for the first time. Thereafter, only one ID# is required. **Mail to:** Christian Growth Study Plan, 127 Ninth Ave., North, Nashville, TN 37234-0117. Fax: (615)251-5067